Praise for

"Sleath invites you to marry ritual magic, Goddess traditions, and bardic wisdom to the practice of lucid dreaming, which she calls 'the ultimate spiritual classroom.' She thrills with the suggestion that, fully charged, lucid dreaming may be the philosopher's stone. Read *Dream Sorcery* to step lightly between the worlds, fill your quiver with stories and symbols that will find their mark, and practice time folding, shape-shifting, and talking with the dead. Come ready to walk in faerie woods where tiny owls are on the wing, and to fly in your subtle body, call in elemental powers, and entertain the spirits."

— **ROBERT MOSS**, best-selling author of *Conscious Dreaming, Dreaming the Soul Back Home* and *The Dreamer's Book of the Dead*

"*Dream Sorcery* provides a fascinating look into lucid dreaming for magickal purposes. Anchored by a strong foundational knowledge of dreamwork and grounded in the framework of alchemy, author Nikki Wardwell Sleath provides hands-on, user-friendly activities and techniques to make dream sorcery accessible for her readers. I would highly recommend this book to anyone with an interest in dreams and/or a desire to enhance their magickal practice."

— **ROBIN CORAK**, author of *Dream Magick*

"In this much-needed 'missing manual' for lucid dreaming, Nikki Wardwell Sleath illuminates how alchemical dream practices are essential for the modern ritualist. Highly recommended for the discerning reader looking for a serious introduction to lucid magick."

— **RYAN HURD**, author of *Lucid Talisman: Forgotten Lore* and *Sleep Paralysis*

"A lucid dreaming guide created by the founder of the Society of Witchcraft and written especially for occultists with the aim of allowing practitioners to enhance their magickal power while they sleep."

— **CHARLIE MORLEY**, best-selling author of *Dreams of Awakening*

"In *Dream Sorcery*, you are given the methods to reliably pass through the gates of horn. There are many books on lucid dreaming, dream interpretation, and such, but this is the first book I've read that truly joins the work of a witch or sorcerer with the state of dreaming. *Dream Sorcery* does so in an orderly fashion with an abundance of exercises, rituals, and summations of key ideas and insights. One of the more unique aspects of this book is its introduction to working with spirits and casting spells while in the dream world. I strongly recommend this book for any practitioners who wish to bring their astral work and dreamwork into intentional harmony."

— **IVO DOMINGUEZ JR**, author of *Keys to Perception*

"From lucid dream basics to dream herbology and sigil work to advanced spellcasting and dream-crafting technique, Sleath has gifted us with a lucid dream compendium. Weaving together the practical, philosophical, magical, and mystical with her clear and creative prose, expertise, and guidance, not only is *Dream Sorcery* illuminating, instructive, and inspirational—it is devotional. Her love and reverence for the mystery that is dream is clear from page one, and it is wildly contagious. There is a deep well of magic here!"

— **MATTHEW ASH MCKERNAN**, LMFT, psychotherapist, bard, author of *Wyrdcraft: Healing Self and Nature Through the Mysteries of the Fates*

DreaM
sorcerY

© Allison Prince

About the Author

Nikki Wardwell Sleath has been practicing Witchcraft for thirty years and was formally trained as an initiate and priestess in the Religious Order of Witchcraft. She has since founded her own private order, the Society of Witchcraft and Old Magick. Nikki holds a master's degree in Integrative Health and Healing, is a Reiki Master/Teacher, and is a full-time professional occult teacher and practitioner. Nikki is trained through the highest level of shamanic dream teacher/facilitator trainings in Robert Moss's School of Active Dreaming. She has worked with clients for many years, focusing on dreamwork, shamanic-style healing sessions, tarot readings, addressing spirit issues, and more. Visit her at NikkiWardwellSleath.com and SocietyOfWitchcraft.com.

DreaM Sorcery

THE RITUAL & MAGICK OF
LUCID DreaMING

NIKKI WarDWELL SLeaTH

WOODBURY, MINNESOTA

FIRST EDITION
First Printing, 2025

Book design by Samantha Peterson
Cover design by Shannon McKuhen
Editing by Stephanie Finne
Interior illustrations:
    Illustrations on pages 80, 92, 93, 96, 97, 201, 202, 208, 209, 212, & 216–218, 305–313 by Llewellyn Art Department
    Illustrations on pages 202 & 203 by The sixth and seventh books of Moses by L.W. De Laurence, 1910. In the public domain and on file with Library of Congress.
    Illustrations on page 204 by Raphael's Ancient Manuscript of Talismanic Magic, 1916 by Raphael, with help from L. W. De Laurence. In the public domain and on file with The HathiTrust.
    Pentacles of the Moon on pages 205 & 206 by Emrys Abner
    Seal of Nightshade on page 207 by Jane Starr Weils from *Grimoire of the Thorn-Blooded Witch* © Raven Grimassi published by Weiser Books, an imprint of Red Wheel/Weiser LLC. Newburyport, MA www.redwheelweiser.com

Llewellyn Publications is a registered trademark of Llewellyn Worldwide Ltd.

Library of Congress Cataloging-in-Publication Data (Pending)
ISBN: 978-0-7387-7851-8

Llewellyn Worldwide Ltd. does not participate in, endorse, or have any authority or responsibility concerning private business transactions between our authors and the public.
    All mail addressed to the author is forwarded but the publisher cannot, unless specifically instructed by the author, give out an address or phone number.
    Any internet references contained in this work are current at publication time, but the publisher cannot guarantee that a specific location will continue to be maintained. Please refer to the publisher's website for links to authors' websites and other sources.

Llewellyn Publications
A Division of Llewellyn Worldwide Ltd.
2143 Wooddale Drive
Woodbury, MN 55125-2989
www.llewellyn.com

Printed in the United States of America

Other Books by Nikki Wardwell Sleath

*The Goddess Seals: Sacred Magickal Symbols
for Modern Magickal Practitioners*

You Might Be a Witch

I dedicate this work to my spirit guides of dreaming: Njorun, Caer Ibormeith, Ulcha, and the Lady of the Lake. May we continue to unite and adventure as earth awakeners for the highest and best good.

CONTENTS

Part Three
The Sulfur–Casting Lucid Dream Spells   163

THE ARCANA:
EXERCISES

DISCLAIMER

The publisher and the author assume no liability for any injuries caused to the reader that may result from the reader's use of content contained in this publication and recommend common sense when contemplating the practices described in the work.

ACKNOWLEDGMENTS

I wish to express deep gratitude for my husband, Duane, who is my unending supporter, intellectual partner, and best friend. I love you forever, whether or not it turns out that we share the same soul.

Special thanks to Stephanie Woodfield for being an inspiration and magickal coconspirator, for always giving great advice, and for contributing to this book.

Heather Greene, your skill level, poise, and adept communication are a huge boon to my whole process. I am continually an improving writer thanks to you. Thank you.

Lastly, thank you to the Society of Witchcraft and Old Magick. Your community support, togetherness, strength, and integrity inspire me every single day to be the best magician, priestess, and woman that I can be. I love you.

FOREWORD

Dreams are a universal magic that we all share. Our dreams carry us to fantastical places, expose our fears, inspire us, and hold boundless magic. Whether you are a Witch or not, we all dream. There is a reason why we call our hopes and aspirations *dreams*. Our dreams are a place where we can manifest and shape the reality around us in accordance with our will. Sounds a lot like the definition of magic, doesn't it? To the magical practitioner, the realm of dreams holds endless possibilities.

We have all experienced psychological dreams—the ones where we are in school in our pajamas and forgot to do our book report. Then there are the other kinds of dreams that make us question what realities we are connecting to as our bodies sleep. Through our dreams we can speak to the Gods, interact with other realms of existence, receive psychic information, and most importantly of all, do magic.

My own dreams have always held special significance in my magical practice. Many times, the information I received in my dreams were things I had no way of possibly knowing, and they were later confirmed in waking reality. Yet, even after almost thirty years of being a practicing Witch, it never occurred to me that there was more that I could do in the realm of dreams besides receive information. That changed when I met Nikki Wardwell Sleath.

I first met Nikki through our mutual devotion to the Morrigan. She attended a Morrigan event I was organizing, and I messaged her about a magical experiment that was proposed in one of the classes at the event. We messaged back and forth and that eventually led to her teaching at the event. Now, years later, she both runs the temple at the Morrigan's Call Retreat and has taken on the role as one of the lead organizers. In addition to all that, she leads her own magical order, the Society of Witchcraft and Old Magick.

If you have the pleasure of attending one of Nikki's classes, it will quickly become apparent that she is a true student of the occult with a vast depth of knowledge and a love of learning. What I love about Nikki's approach to teaching is both her enthusiasm for magical learning and her down-to-earth nature. She'll tell you how it is, but she will also outline a path to help you get to your magical goals. Nikki is also an innovator, taking magical techniques that are tried and true and creating new things with them. Innovation is exactly what she has achieved in *Dream Sorcery*.

Dream Sorcery doesn't just guide you through the basics of achieving lucid dreaming; it is a fully fleshed out system of dream magic. Nikki guides you through multiple techniques to empower your magic through dreamwork, from dream divination to spell craft. She offers her own dream experiences to help you on your own path of discovery, regardless of whether you are a beginner or an adept. *Dream Sorcery* offers readers magical seals and other workings you can use in waking to enhance your dreamwork and make it even more powerful. She doesn't just give you open-ended suggestions; she outlines in depth what has worked for her and provides the many different types of magic you can perform in your dreams.

While I have experienced lucidity in dreams, it was never intentional and often startled me back into a waking state. Nikki's enthusiasm for dream magic is infectious, and after hearing about Nikki's own magical lucid dreaming experiences, I began using her techniques to try to consciously achieve lucidity. I can't quite explain how life altering it can be to experience magical energy in your dreams.

Yes, you can do magic in your dream, but you can also explore the very nature of magic and connect more fully with the techniques, beings, and energies you are already calling upon in your magic. The experiences change you and how you perceive your magic. In doing a magical technique outside of normal reality, you can literally see the energy and how it interacts with the environment and yourself in a way that is not possible while awake. Then upon waking, you can connect to that energy in a deeper way and with a greater understanding of what you are casting. You return to waking with a kind of auric download.

In one of my own lucid dream experiences, I performed the Morrigan LBRP (an Irish version of the standard lesser banishing ritual). It is something that I do daily in my waking life and know well. Yet, in my dreamscape, I experienced the energy in a new way. It sounded like my own voice was amplified and reverberated with several other voices intertwined at once. The energy of the Morrigan flowed through me and out of me like an energetic freight train. It was invigorating and not at all what I had been expecting to happen. Now, while I am awake and performing this practice, the way I connect to that energy has changed. I feel those many voices resonating with me, and I feel the energy of the Morrigan flowing through me in an even more powerful way.

One of the most common things I hear in the Pagan community is that there are only 101 level or beginner level books out there. Where are all the 201 level, the advanced books? This, my friends, is that book you've been searching for. If you want to bring your magical practices to the next level, enhance your understanding of magic, and perform spellwork in an even more powerful way, this book is for you. I feel what Nikki has done with *Dream Sorcery* is open a whole new branch of Witchcraft. In doing so, she has created many new possibilities for the magical practitioner.

May your dreams be filled with magic and be lifted to new heights!

STEPHANIE WOODFIELD
Autumn Equinox 2024

INTRODUCTION

Lucid dreaming is the state of being completely aware that one is dreaming while still operating and existing within the dream. It is quite possibly true that this state of being fully awake within the dreamtime is the only state of being in which most physically embodied humans can really and truly *see*, in the deepest spiritual sense. This refers not to physiological seeing, of course, although vision can certainly be much crisper in lucid dreaming than in waking, but rather to the ability to see past the illusions of reality and into the deeper nature of conscious awareness itself.

The lucid dream state can be seen as the ultimate, naturally occurring alchemical laboratory for the exploration of conscious awareness. The ability to skillfully engage it could very well be the elusive philosopher's stone after which many an ancient mage adept has sought. Any occultist, or for that matter any person who aspires to make a priority of navigating the mysteries of energy and consciousness, would not deign to disagree with this statement once they had experienced the opportunity to do purposeful magick while lucid dreaming.

When the magician finds themselves completely consciously awake, or lucid, in a dream world, such that they understand and remember everything about ordinary reality while simultaneously realizing that they are experiencing themselves in a dream realm, infinite magickal scenarios and potentials open. In the dreamscape setting, there are fewer hindrances or limitations related to the body, there is a separation from the stressors of the mundane world, and there are fewer limitations based on the atmospheric and earthly laws of physics by which one lives in ordinary reality.

In the practice of lucid dreaming, not only does one encounter the ideal setting for the practicing of magickal and ceremonial skills, performing divinations, and communing with spirits but one also encounters a myriad of ways in which the magician can accumulate invaluable wisdom. In lucid dreaming, it is possible to have experiences that fuel precious evolution on a deep personal and spiritual level. In fact, within lucid dreams the occultist can explore the mysteries in ways that exceed those which are possible in every other medium.

My Goals for This Book

This book is not a basic, general lucid dreaming primer but is more of an intermediate-level book for magickal practitioners. It caters to folks who know something of magick and something of lucid dreaming and are looking to enrich a practice that weaves them together skillfully. There are lots of books out there on the topic of lucid dreaming, but I have not come across a decent and thorough lucid dreaming book that is specifically aimed at the audience of magicians and occultists. On the other hand, there are lots of magickal books on dreaming in general, but hardly any magickal works pertaining specifically to lucidity. I aim to highlight just how profound dream lucidity is for practitioners of magick and to provide you with both the motivations and the methods to help you reach your own lucid magick goals.

Within this book, I present an approach to lucid dreaming that suits the enchanted mindset of Witches, Pagans, and occultists. Such a mindset often includes beliefs about dreams, such as the presumption that real spirit interaction and real divination information is available through dreaming, to give a couple of examples. In addition to presenting lucid magick in light of these viewpoints, I will also teach about spell crafting specifically to help manifest lucid dreams. I will present incantations, symbols, and spirits that can be used in waking by the magician to help induce lucid dreams, as well as fine-tune some clear instruction and inspiration for how the lucid dream space itself can be utilized magickally.

The goals of this book are fourfold. The first goal is to ensure you have a solid understanding of the fundamentals of lucid dreaming as well as some basic practices in place to help you begin cultivating lucid dreams. The second goal is to demonstrate the broad scope of active magick that can be conducted directly within the lucid dream space and to highlight what the benefits of these magickal acts are to the practitioner. This will help you decide while lucid what magick you would like to conduct and help motivate you to continue to do the work of getting there.

The third goal is to provide actionable ideas for crafting spells that can be done while waking that will help predispose you, the magician, to becoming lucid, as well as help you meet specific lucid dream goals. This will involve considering all the components of a custom spell cast formally within a structured ritual and then understanding how to put all those components together effectively. You will be able to use the things you learn as a composite ritual or separately as smaller acts of spontaneous magick.

Lastly, this book aims to support the thesis previously suggested: Lucid dreaming can be understood as a metaphorical alchemy lab with the cultivated ability to become lucid intentionally standing as the elusive and sought-after philosopher's stone. More so than basic manifestation magick, the goal of the sorcerer adept is raising one's own vibration and evolving as much as possible spiritually in this life. This is the path of transforming the baser parts of the spirit to gold, and where the missing ingredient of the philosopher's stone is needed. It is likely that you will only be able to assess this statement after amassing lucid magick experiences for yourself, making the engagement of the work described in the book very important.

How My Passion for Lucid Magick Developed

I have always had clear dream recall as well as an interest in engaging actively with my dreams. In my late thirties, I had already been studying the occult for almost twenty years. Also at that time, I decided to do a master's degree program in Integrative Health and Healing. During this learning, I experienced a module on the topic of Active Dreaming led by a trained teacher from the Robert Moss School of Active Dreaming, which provides shamanic dreamwork facilitation. Having learned to perform waking journeys back into my dreams during these classes, I became more focused than ever upon exploring the interactive realities of my dreams.

I began thinking about it all the time and scrutinizing much more closely the very nature of not only dreaming but also waking reality. It was during this time of intensely increased focus upon dreaming that the following important lucid dream experience spontaneously ensued:

I am walking down a long hallway inside of a stone building that feels like a castle. I am moving slowly, feeling a bit aimless and with the vague yet intangible discomfort of not really feeling sure of just why I am here. At the end of the hall, I find myself entering a round sort of turret or tower room. There are built-in niches in the stones all around the curved walls that form the perimeter of the room, and in each hollow is a stone statue of a different mythical creature. I take note of gargoyles, griffins, and dragons, looking at them with casual interest. I am startled when I notice that they have started moving, coming to life.

A tingling flush of alertness washes through me, and all my senses heighten and intensify as I spontaneously become completely lucid. This means that I know full well, with a sudden and unmistakable revelation, that I am dreaming. While aware that my body is safely tucked into my bed, I continue to take in this magickal scene from the vantage point of a nonphysical although very real feeling version of my body. As I watch the movements of the creatures with all my awareness and memories from ordinary reality now intact, they regard me in turn. I have no fear because I know that I am dreaming. I realize that I can fly, access super strength, shoot fire from my hands, or simply wake myself up whenever I need to if it comes to that. Most importantly, I understand at a very deep but also conscious level that I cannot be physically injured here.

As I look at the creatures and they make eye contact with me, I begin to receive a very clear sort of telepathic download of knowledge from the scene. It is as if a deep truth about the nature of the universe has just been embedded in my mind, my energy field, my spirit. It's quite difficult to put into words in any way that someone could understand. The wisdom is internally very clear. I understand at a primal level that things such as that can be experienced in clear dreaming are just as, if not more, real than that which we experience in our physical reality.

I understand deeply that our physical reality is most certainly not the most important reality in which we engage and that consciousness is certainly not confined to be local only to the brain or the human body. As different levels of this realization sink in, I am so overwhelmed with awe, wonder, and incredulity that the intense sensation of my emotional state pulls me back into waking.

I awoke from this dream feeling permanently changed, as if something within myself had been rewired through the experience. While it was a relatively simple lucid dream scene without any purposeful action on my part, the feeling of internal downloading and revelation was earth-shattering. I knew I would be hooked on lucid dreaming for life and was resolved to the fact that from that time forth I would always make consistent efforts to keep my chances of attaining lucidity as strong as possible. I knew that it was to be the main key to my personal spiritual growth, and the primary route by which I would be able to explore the truths that underlie the magick of the mysteries.

While I inherently knew there was a trove of magick waiting to be discovered through lucid dreaming, I did not yet know the extent to which my lucid dreaming practice would so directly enhance my practice and understanding of magick. I had no idea how much magickal energy and wisdom I had yet to bring forth from the dreaming back through to ordinary reality. Lucid magick would eventually come to help me develop sorcery skill like no other approach could.

At the time of this inspiring lucid dream experience, I had already been keeping a dream journal consistently for about seven years. I had also already completed formal training into the priesthood of a private occult order called the Religious Order of Witchcraft. I was no stranger to the idea that there are limitless sources of magick to be learned and explored, and I had already taken a very studious and committed approach to my personal magickal practices.

After that dream, however, I had a period where I was quite driven to learn as much as possible about dream lucidity and to build the highest quality lucid dreaming practice that I could cultivate. I read every decent book on lucid dreaming that I could find, and took the meditations, practices, reality checks, and other suggestions very seriously. I diligently added more focused daily meditations, reality tests, and dream magick to my already established dream journaling habit.

Using my magickal skills, I also got into the practice of doing intermittent formal spellworkings to enhance my lucid dreaming skills. The combination of all these things paid off, and I began to find myself becoming lucid in dreams more regularly. I made sure to purposefully highlight all the dream journal entries that contained lucid dreaming experiences for two reasons. The first was that I wanted to be able to easily go back and compare happenings from one bout of lucidity to another to really learn and experiment with this medium as a form of magickal and philosophical development. The other was that I simply wanted to be able to keep track of my frequency and quality of lucid dreaming so that I could always be striving to improve upon it. The results and effects of many of my lucid experiments through the years to follow have had far-reaching magickal and spiritual implications, and some of them are, therefore, explained in this book.

How to Use This Book

Part 1 of this book, "The Salt," exemplifies the base set of practices and beliefs upon which your lucid magick practice will rest. In alchemy, salt stands for the body—the material and the solid. This section provides a solid foundation with which you should feel comfortable prior to diving into the deeper magick of lucidity.

Since this is a specialty book for magick users and is not meant to be a lucid dreaming primer, see how you feel about the initial review chapters before proceeding further. If it doesn't feel like a review, and you are hearing some of the ideas for the first time, then it would be wise to pause and consult the recommended reading section at the back of the book to help find supplementary works so you can augment your foundation of the basics.

Part 2, "The Mercury," will take you through some of the detailed magick you can execute within the actual space of lucid dreaming and outline the benefits of it to you as a magician. In alchemy, mercury stands for the spirit, or that which is changeable, ever evolving, and transcendent of the earthly plane. Part 2 aims to open your mind to the infinite potential for spiritual growth and magickal skill development that lies in the space of lucid dreaming so that you are more motivated than ever to reach for that gold by moving on to working the magick of part 3.

Part 3, "The Sulfur," is about magick you can do while you are awake and at the altar to help you become more predisposed to lucid dreaming and to help you manifest specific lucid magick goals. In alchemy, sulfur generally stands for the soul, or the unique circumstances of expansion and transformation that unite the material and the spiritual. This section of the book is geared toward setting you up to be able to execute personally customized formal magickal castings that happen in sacred space.

Part 3 purposefully comes after the Mercury section because you first have to know what you hope to achieve before you can formulate magick to support your goal. This is the waking magick that fuels your ability to become lucid. In alchemy, salt, mercury, and sulfur are intertwined and always part of an evolving whole. Such is the case with your foundational work, magickal practices, and actual dream sorcery when it comes to lucidity.

Throughout all three sections, you will find suggested magickal exercises, each labeled "Arcanum," aimed at helping you to set up a lucid magick practice and attune to the various concepts being introduced. This instructional arcana will be your dream sorcery skill builders and will vary from ways to hone mental focus and reality checks to planning dreamtime divinations, lucid magick, and dreaming spellwork. You should not feel pressured to carry out all the suggested or described magick in the book. As long as you are implementing the foundational practices described in part 1, you can then customize the supplementary magick according to your tastes and intuition.

You will also find the alchemical "Distillation" at the end of each chapter. This is a place to help you rehash and integrate what has just been presented and prepare you to move on to the following material.

The suggestions here are meant to help you choose and find the right combination of things that are powerful for you, personally, and applicable to where you are in your practice at the given moment. One of the nice things about having a list of lucid dream magick techniques and correspondences is that you can choose to add one in here and there on top of your basic lucidity cultivation skills at various intervals, or at any time in the future, whenever you intuitively feel that your practice needs a boost, or some fresh energy.

The contents of this book are meant to be absorbed with an attitude of humility and patience for oneself. As with much of the magick in this reality of dense physical existence, lucidity does not tend to happen miraculously. You will still need to perform all the necessary steps on the material plane that are needed for a goal to happen. In other words, if you perform magick for the goal of getting a great job, you still need to update your resume, get it out to as many potential employers as possible, prepare for interviews, and continue making new contacts. The magick you work for the process of manifesting the job can help speed the process, highlight your talents so they are received as well as possible, shine a greater light upon you than other competing applicants, and enhance your communication skills, thus catalyzing or smoothing your path to the goal.

The same parallels exist in the context of performing magick to vivify your lucid dreaming life. A spell to induce a lucid dream may help provide you with a little bit of a greater predisposition for it, but it isn't likely to outright produce one if you haven't established great recall, instituted routine reality checks, and given deep thought as to why you truly want to get lucid and what you plan to do with that precious time once it happens.

This book seeks to help you gain lucid dreaming skills as an asset to your magickal arsenal and to use your magickal arsenal to gain access to lucid dreaming. There is also the hope that you will develop a life of increasing appreciation for the magick of the dreaming in general, lucid or not.

Let's Go! Establishing Your Inner Alchemy Lab

So, what do you need to get started? Initially, a dedicated dream journal and handy writing implement are the only material requirements. It is nice to have a journal you really love and which has a special feel for you. This is, after all, a place where you are going to document the wanderings of your spirit and all the liminal adventures that are part of your sacred birthright. It will be important to develop an almost scientific diligence in your journaling habits as you hone your skill as dream alchemist and sorcerer.

As far as nonmaterial requirements are concerned, you need an alert mind that is open to the possibility of waking up while sleeping to engage the ultimate magickal training grounds. You also need an honest and humble commitment to yourself and the extent of practice you wish to develop.

Now it is time to dig into the development of your lucid magick practice. Get ready to be inspired and awakened by all the possible experiments you may conduct and adventures you may have. As you read on, allow excitement to build regarding the potential spiritual growth that you may experience through the cultivation of a lucid magickal practice. Envision yourself experiencing some of the lucid phenomena I describe and start assuming you will become lucid in your dreams tonight.

Part One

THE SALT–LUCID MAGICK FUNDAMENTALS

The first steps to developing your skill as a lucid dream sorcerer lie in the bones of your fundamental lucid practices. You need to ensure that the salt, which is composed of the structure of your approach and the understanding of lucid dream basics, is nicely established. Here we will review magickal philosophies and beliefs regarding lucid dreaming and ensure that you understand what you should be doing as a base practice prior to adding magickal goals and workings to it.

The raw building blocks that make up the alchemical salt of a lucid magickal practice are not only the foundations of lucid dreaming but also include some primary skills of a magician in general. Concepts such as divination hygiene, ethics, and magickal mindset are some examples of areas of needed development that will be discussed here in addition to our basics review. Prepare to dive in and lay the salt, setting the foundation of your growing lucid magickal practice.

WHAT IS LUCID DREAMING?

As previously mentioned, a lucid dream is one in which you are 100 percent aware that you are dreaming. This means that during the dream you retain all memories and orientations to your waking life and are also able to release any prior fear of harm in the dream scene due to the depth of the understanding that you are dreaming. It is a conscious waking up to a full awareness of the dream while the body still sleeps. When you become lucid in a dream, you know it without doubt, and the freedom of functioning as a supernatural spiritual being opens to you.

So, You Think You Are Lucid Dreaming?

I have had countless people describe a dream to me and want me to tell them whether it was a lucid dream. For the most part, whenever a person is unsure or must ask whether a dream was an example of a lucid dream, that means that it most likely was not. A lucid dream is quite unmistakable. It happens when you are dreaming, and you become *acutely* hyperaware of the fact that you are dreaming. It's not just vivid, and it's not lucid just because you were talking or thinking about dreaming within your dream—it's lucid because you are completely aware that you are in a dream body and that your physical body is safely asleep.

If you think you may have been lucid because you became aware that you were dreaming but then still had obvious fear of dream events, then you were likely not fully lucid. Alternatively, you may have been lucid for a moment and then lost the lucidity, which is not only possible but extremely common. It is not only that you fully comprehend that you are sleeping and dreaming when lucid but also you are instantly in the same mindset and full knowledge of your ordinary day-to-day self and activities. You will remember what time of day it is in ordinary reality, where your body is lying, what you need to do when you wake up, what you planned to do when you got lucid—all of it.

The Feeling

Often, the moment of becoming lucid is accompanied by a sensory rush, or a sudden invigorating shift in the feel of the energy of your dream body, as well as a sudden increase in the crispness and clarity of your perception of the dream. I often refer to this energy body sensation as the "rain stick" effect. It could be described as a cascade of intense tingling that travels through the dream body in a sequential manner, much like the granules in the instrument known as a rain stick flowing enthusiastically down through it when you flip it over.

Some authors and teachers would say that this energetic vibrational state is an indication that you have projected out of body, and this may very well be true. There are a lot of overlapping symptoms between lucid dreaming and astral projection. Some experts, such as prolific astral projector and author Robert Bruce, would say that lucid dreaming may be an out-of-body experience that happens in the mental plane of existence.[1]

In this way, lucid dreaming is like an out-of-body experience in the astral plane but with differences in one's ability to sense the dream body. Also, it seems that astral projection can happen in real time in this physical reality as well as in other realities, whereas lucid dreaming happens in mental, or dreaming, realities. This does make it confusing to discern what has really happened sometimes. In any case, if I suddenly become

---

1. Robert Bruce, *Astral Dynamics: The Complete Book of Out-of-Body Experiences* (Hampton Roads Publishing, 2009), 218–219.

aware that I'm dreaming, whether I get the vibratory surge or not, and whether it's truly an out-of-body experience or not, I treat the experience as a precious lucid dream and try to get as much time immersing in the experience of its magick as possible.

On the occasions where there may not be an obvious change in sensation upon becoming lucid, there is at the very least a conscious feeling of revelation—an *aha!* moment where you realize fully that you are in a dream body. Even when it is not accompanied by a noticeable change of sensation in the dream body, it is usually accompanied by a sudden change in the clarity of one's perception. There is the distinct feeling of waking up mentally while realizing you are still in the dream scene.

How Lucidity Happens

There are two primary ways in which one can become lucid. The first way is that you can be fully asleep, already dreaming normally, and then have that realization of becoming lucid from within the established dream. This is known as a dream-induced lucid dream. The second, and more rare case, is when you intend not to allow the blackout stage of falling asleep to happen at all from the get-go and instead try very hard to stay mentally conscious through the process of allowing only the body to fall asleep. If you succeed in this with great focus, the mind watches the transition from waking alertness to patiently watching the gradual formation of a dream scene. This wake-induced method of attaining lucidity is possible but much more difficult, and it requires more focused practice of meditation techniques.

I have successfully cultivated wake-induced lucid dreams many times, but it is far easier and more common to experience dream-induced lucid dreams. I would say that going from fully awake straight into lucidity probably only accounts for about ten to twenty percent of my lucid dreaming experiences. Since it is much more common to create a predisposition to induce lucidity from inside of a regular dream that is already in progress, this is the approach upon which most magickal dreamers tend to try to focus. Both approaches will be outlined for practice in chapter 3, Reviewing the Basics. For now, though, let's pause and ignite some initial lucid magick by having you bless your dream journal.

ARCANUM
Blessing Your Dream Journal

· • ● ○ ● • ·

Consecrating an item is to give it special energetic distinction as a magickal tool. It can amplify the power of the tool as well as create a more personal bond between it and you. Blessing your dream journal is a form of consecration and a way to help you stay conscious of the sacred nature of the work you are doing as you try to cultivate lucid magickal experiences.

1. Place your dream journal on your normal altar or alternatively on any clean table or desk surface.

2. Standing in front of the journal, hold your non-dominant hand overhead with your hand palm up and hold your dominant hand with your hand palm down, hovering just over the book.

3. Envision a white shimmering and enlivening energy being drawn into your upraised nondominant hand. Imagine this energy flowing down your arm, across your shoulders and heart center and down into your dominant arm. Let the energy proceed to flow out of your dominant hand and into the journal.

4. Once you can both feel and envision this happening, say: "I charge this book to serve as my dream journal; to function as a sacred receptacle for all the dream memories I collect from my travels through the multiverse as well as my lucid dreams. By air, fire, water, and earth, this dreaming journal is hereby birthed! So, Mote It Be."

Always make sure your dream journal is near your bedside for easy access upon awakening and make sure to bring your dream journal with you on overnight trips. Get ready to make sure you have a solid habit of documenting everything you remember from your dreams in this book, if you aren't already doing this. The dream journal can also be used to document waking thoughts with respect to your dreams or your thoughts on dreaming in general. Just be sure to date your entries and have a way of distinguishing if the entry is a dream or just your waking thoughts.

Magickal Philosophies of Lucidity

There is evidence in multiple traditions from cultures around the world showing that our ancient ancestors understood the magick of the lucid space and valued the practice of lucid dreaming greatly. In an interview, esteemed scholar of culture and mythology Joseph Campbell was asked, "So the adept, the sage, works to perfect the ability to stay conscious in his sleep?" and he responded, "Oh, in fact that's one of the monastic disciplines, where you go to sleep pronouncing a mantra of waking knowledge—kind of a fishing line to carry you from waking to transcendent consciousness. But the fact that the Buddha means 'the waked up' teaches the main lesson here."[2]

My dream mentor, Robert Moss, states, "In the midst of the shamanic revival in our society, there is a good deal of confusion about who 'shamans' are and what they do. Many people seem to believe that shamans are people who hold sweat lodges and burn lots of sage. If you are a North American Indian, or wanna-be, this may be the case, but external rituals have little to do with the heart of shamanic practice, which is *dreaming*."[3] We know that the shamans, seers, and wise ones of many ancient and indigenous cultures were the clear dreamers of their communities. This tells us that dreaming has long been seen as a way to access spiritual aid, wisdom, and healing, and that those who could do this with clarity and purpose held special roles in this regard.

Most importantly for the occultist, there are clear Hermetic teachings that explain why learning to awaken within dreams really is a cornerstone to the famous Great Work. Italian philosopher Julius Evola states:

2. Douglas Auchincloss, "On Waking Up: An Interview with Joseph Campbell," *Parabola: Myth and the Quest for Meaning—Sleep*, Vol. VII, no. I (January 1982): 80.

3. Robert Moss, *Conscious Dreaming: A Spiritual Path For Everyday Life* (Three Rivers Press, 1996), 146.

"The nocturnal state of sleep can be considered that darkness that has to be thinned out of the Materia so that the inner Light can begin to shine."[4] He also states, "To arrive at the Light after the alchemical 'black' means to possess the capacity to complete this 'voyage' consciously, entering thus into the supernatural vigil."[5] It is through awakening in sleep that we transcend death, understanding the very nature of ourselves as spirits, and touching the mysteries of the living consciousness of the universe. There is a metaphoric parallel between day and waking as compared to night and sleeping, which relate to life and death respectively. Waking up in spirit form during sleep helps us explore the very nature of how conscious awareness persists beyond physicality.

This awakening into higher self is certainly akin to chrysopoeia, or the transmutation into gold after which the original alchemists sought. We know the alchemists' purpose of aspiring to turn base metals into gold held important metaphors for learning how to transform our base human attributes more toward enlightenment. It was thought that witnessing this mysterious process firsthand in the laboratory would carry over into the magician's innate understanding and then to their ability to perform this transformation within the self. There is constant debate among occultists over whether any of the famous alchemists ever succeeded in the final creation of gold, physically or metaphorically.

An important conversation in this respect revolves around the idea that there was a missing ingredient in the process—one which, if it were present, would be the final substance that tipped the experiment toward its end goal. This elusive missing ingredient was named the philosopher's stone. What if the missing piece in the sacred quest toward enlightenment lies in true lucidity? The philosopher's stone may be the substrate that is created when there is a combination of the magician's ability to become lucid in dreams and all realities with the disciplined practice of magick and spiritual practices within that lucid state.

---

4. Julius Evola, *The Hermetic Tradition: Symbols and Teachings of the Royal Art* (Inner Traditions International, 1971), 152.

5. Evola, *The Hermetic Tradition*, 153.

The space of lucid dreaming, then, becomes the naturally occurring laboratory for the firsthand witnessing of the magickal and spiritual mysteries. Gaining entry to this is not necessarily easy, and it certainly takes discipline, but all those who have had the great fortune to explore it deeply seem to attest to its sacredness. Let us aspire to be the magicians among the modern-day population of our species who reignite our personal and societal passions for engaging deeply with dreaming, as did many of our ancestors.

Accepting Dreams as Transpersonal and Transtemporal

There are many lucid dream authors and teachers who approach the experience of dreaming from the stance that everything encountered in the dreamtime is only a product of one's own mind. The reason for this is probably the scientific backdrop of the society in which we currently live, where we equate the mind to the finite workings of the physiological structures of the brain. With this science alone we cannot readily prove ideas about the collective unconscious, telepathy, communications with the divine, and the like.

It is often comical to witness metaphysical theories being shut down in the name of science when the very spirit of science is to explore the thresholds of the as-of-yet unknown. As magicians, it is important to remember that the very essence of magick is to embrace the notion that anything is possible, and that we seek to explore beyond what is seen and what is provable. The space of lucid dreaming gives us the opportunity to do this in ways no other magickal modality can.

Consider, for a moment, some essential philosophies of the Western occultist. We are given the idea of the Hermetic "All."[6] This is the sum of every possible conceivable thing in the universe. The All is made up of every object, being, situation, thought, concept, and reality that ever was, is, and could be, through all manner of infinite eternities. A crucial understanding of the concept of the All includes the idea that everything within the All is mental in nature. We have here a picture of an infinite and timeless universe

6. Three Initiates, *The Kybalion* (Tarcher/Penguin Group, 2008), 54.

wherein everything has awareness or intelligence of some kind, and where this infiniteness defines some kind of connected whole.

When you consider this along with the Hermetic principle of correspondence—that is, the idea that everything you can imagine has some kind of relationship or ripple to every other plane of existence—then we find ourselves considering the distinct possibility of our dreams as important realities that not only have an effect on this physical reality but which also have intelligent conscious awareness in and operating them. It then becomes impossible for you, the magician who entertains these philosophies, to stay confined within the idea of dream realities as being localized and contained solely within the mind of the individual dreamer, connected to nothing else.

What is consciousness, exactly? No one really has a concrete or scientifically provable answer to this question, but lucid dreaming is a way to explore this elusive secret directly. The motivated occultist is inspired by learning about the workings of the universe and the mysterious ways in which energy and awareness intersect to create magick, and there is no better classroom for the inspection of magickal experimentation and learning about the deeper nature of conscious awareness than the landscape of a lucid dream. This is because the lucid dream is a mentally responsive environment that allows us to reach out beyond ourselves and our experience of time as linear. It seems to be able to respond not only to your own thoughts but also to those of Higher Self, divine beings and guides, archetypes, the collective unconscious, and maybe even the sum of Universal intelligences, or Hermetic All itself.

Motivations for Inducing Lucidity

When I say that my lucid experiences caused me to understand that the dreamtime was more real than waking life, I also felt that it was, in many ways, more important. Some major motivating factors for the work of cultivating lucid magick exist around the concept that you can explore the mysteries of your being in ways that are both organic and transcend physical life. Usually, Witches and magicians are drawn to magickal practice because of a personal knowing that there is much more to life than meets the eye. We crave direct experiences that highlight to us the mysteries of magick, spirits, afterlife, energy, and consciousness. Lucid dreaming allows us to have these direct experiences.

Development of the Spirit

Being lucid in dreaming feels like functioning as an invincible spirit with every supernatural ability you fantasize about having in waking life. I believe that, in fact, we are all spirits who are working on our evolutionary development through eternity from one reality to the next, and that arguably, our overall course of development is more important than this one physical life we are experiencing right now. This does not mean that I think we should waste or undervalue physical life in any way. I believe we are here to learn and that we don't know what we don't know. We need to live well and be cognizant of using our magick and our dreaming to enhance this physical existence as best we can if we are to do our due diligence.

What I do know is that doing magick in lucid dreams feels like a way to progress our spiritual and magickal learning rapidly. It allows us to absorb lessons that would otherwise take eons to witness in physical nature, and this is the same mindset that the early alchemists had about witnessing important transformations in the laboratory. In lucid dreams as in the alchemy lab, our auric fields and subconscious minds get to have larger lessons embedded in them, and these become integrated into the very fabric of our beings.

Experiencing the Void

In addition to the clear parallels between spiritual practices within lucidity and alchemical philosophies and the experience of getting to understand oneself as an eternal and bodiless spirit entity, there is another major aspect of lucid dreaming that should appeal to you as an occultist. In lucidity, it is common to be able to have experiences of an accessible abyss, or void. This is an empty space that sometimes is bottomless dark, and sometimes feels like eternal light. These could be two separate things, but either way, it is possible to rest in these aware spaces and bear witness to the spontaneous birth of dream elements. It is as if these void spaces are the "chaos"—a potential name for the raw building blocks of conscious intelligence from which all experiences and all magick are formed.

The prospect of experiencing this should be an exciting thought, for it is often into the ethers of the chaos that one reaches when trying to access unformed energies for the purpose of magickally molding them into a customized end-result. Think of the possible benefits to the sorcerer's skill set in terms of being able to visualize the manifestation process after having been able to witness it firsthand in its purest form. We understand that the idea of the ancient principle "as above, so below" refers to the concept that all that is possible on the spiritual planes of existence is possible in some form here in our physical existence and vice versa. To be able to integrate this lesson firsthand from the nonphysical planes is a privilege that the serious occultist cannot afford to pass up.

Lucid Dreaming as a Magickal Support

At the time of the writing of this book, it has been fourteen years since the lucid dream with the stone creatures, and it still has not lost its wonder. Since that time, I have transitioned from working in the health care field to working full time for myself, running my own occult order in American Witchcraft, and providing magickal, psychic, and healing services to clients. It is not an easy or especially lucrative life path to take when carried out with integrity and authenticity, but one that I feel is my calling.

While my career and my magick have been busily becoming entwined as one, these past years have also been filled with lucid dream experiences that have helped to deepen my magickal skills and my spiritual growth in invaluable ways. I fully believe that my rare ability to succeed as a professional occultist has been greatly augmented by my lucid magick practice. You, too, can enhance waking magick that you do for the manifestation of life successes by using lucid dreaming to hone your magickal skills.

Access Other Realms

When you awaken fully while the body is still asleep and become fully aware of the nature of the reality of the dreaming realms, you will have access to the supernatural planes in a way that can't be achieved while waking. The realms of the dead, the fair folk, the gods, and all manner of spirits become directly accessible. It is possible to encounter numerous types of spirits firsthand, including ancestors, restless dead, deities, fairy beasts, and demons, to name a few.

Some of the energetic downloads from spirits, especially deities, can have direct and lasting effects on the literal energetic state of the physical aura that can be perceived ongoing during waking. Wisdom gained from these interactions also has a lasting influence upon the mindset, mental clarity level, and perceptual abilities of the magician, causing an increased effectiveness of function in waking life.

Ritual and Spellwork

In lucid dreams, it is possible to practice ritual actions that are used in ordinary reality, but with the benefit of being able to see and feel what the visible energetic effects are when not constrained by the physics of a material world. You can practice activating symbols such as pentagrams, planetary and alchemical glyphs, the runes, and the Ogham and receive their energies internally firsthand.

You can also witness the ways these types of symbols work externally when they are practiced and projected as purposeful streams of magick imposed upon a dream environment or a dream character. You can practice battle magick techniques to gain firsthand experience in their effectiveness. These lucid dream magickal practice experiences often result in acquiring repeatable sorcery skills that work in a parallel way in ordinary reality that you could not otherwise learn. There will be many examples of these experiments and the direct benefits to physical reality gleaned, which will be explained in this book.

Divination and Time-Space Communications

In the space of lucid dreaming, it is also possible for the magickal practitioner to ask and receive clear and truly unbiased answers to divination questions. You must experience this firsthand in order to understand how different and undeniably true lucid divinations feel in comparison to those performed in waking. In lucidity, you can play with shape-shifting, vanquish negative entities, and even time travel to a certain degree.

The lucid landscape can even serve as a classroom for conducting experiments in trying to summon and coordinate communications with the consciousness of other physically living dreamers. It is an amazing place in which to conduct shadow work or figure out how you might be serving as a spirit guide for others. In this space, you can get forthright directives and instructions on how to best serve your gods and spirits, and you can work on revisiting other lives and realities.

Empowering the Great Work

One of the most important ways in which I have engaged lucid dreaming magickally is using lucidity to enhance the endeavor of gaining conversation with the Holy Guardian Angel (HGA), and thereby uncovering important personal insights into the larger nature of existence and consciousness itself. The work of encountering the HGA is a goal written about in classical grimoires and is considered to be a pinnacle act of important spirit evocation in a magician's career.

More will be said in chapter 11 about the theorized nature of this guiding being. Because of the deep implications of all of this, I continue to always strive to increase and improve my lucid dreaming exploits, as I consider the practice to be a key part of my work and purpose here in this life.

The Challenges of Getting There

There are a lot of books on lucid dreaming out there that claim that all people are equally capable of cultivating lucid dreams. I would never claim that as a universally true statement, and while it may be theoretically true in some respects, I have seen many people try without success. If, for example, you have some unchangeable factor that prevents working on sharp mental focus or that prevents you from cultivating decent regular night dream recall, then it may be less likely that lucid dreaming is going to be something you can purposefully induce and foster routinely. That said, even the cultivation of a few deeply meaningful experiences makes it well worth the effort.

There can be a certain amount of natural talent and predisposition involved with lucid dreaming, just as there is natural talent involved in other types of specialty skill development in life. We don't all have the bodies to be professional basketball players, or the innate musical talent to play Beethoven's Piano Sonata No. 29, and we don't all have the unique type of mind that is most naturally suited for frequent lucid dreaming. The thing about this is that you won't really know if you are suited for lucid dreaming and its magick until you give it a significantly disciplined, long-term effort. In this effort, you, the magician, have an advantage that other would-be lucid dreamers don't, and that is the ability to utilize magick to help you achieve your lucid dreaming goals.

Sometimes, even if you don't achieve the exact thing that you set out to do, you learn a whole lot of other unexpected lessons and insights along the way. There is much to be learned simply from the practices needed to cultivate lucid dreams, even if you don't actually have one. The irony is that undertaking the practices outlined in this book with humility and a releasing of expectation tends to increase mental clarity, which then increases the chance of becoming lucid.

The Distillation

You now have a clear idea of what lucid dreaming is, how to identify a dream as fully lucid, and the primary ways in which lucid dreams occur. You have considered some of the specific magickal philosophies that relate to lucid dreaming as well as some of the magickal benefits and motivations specific to you as a magician. It is hoped that you also understand that while this can be a challenging aspect of magick to master, your efforts are well worth the challenge no matter the specifics of the outcome. With this attitude in mind, let us take the next chapter to ensure that full value is being placed on spontaneous dreams during the process of trying to birth dreams of the lucid variety.

WHAT ABOUT
NON-LUCID DREAMS?

When we dream, our cerebral cortex fires in all the same ways that it would if we were experiencing the dream actions in waking life. This means that the brain and the nervous system of your physical body experience the activities of the dream almost as if they were happening in waking. When you dream, you don't normally realize that you are dreaming until after you have awoken, and because of this, those dream experiences are simply things that your consciousness has now undergone.

These experiences can greatly inform the development of your magick, even if it is in a less direct manner than if you had experienced a fully lucid dream. In fact, it is essential to pay close attention to spontaneous night dreams to continue to work on effectively understanding the nature of one's reality, and this is the key to lucidity: truly awakening, in all realities. We must awaken more acutely to the nature of our physical reality if we are to have solid hopes of awakening to the full nature of dream realities.

Non-Lucid Dream Intention Setting

Though it was mentioned previously, it needs to be impressed in more detail that it is extremely important not to forget to prize your routine non-lucid night dream encounters. Not every occultist will succeed in developing a practice of frequent lucid dreaming, but even so, all the magickal concepts considered in this book can be helpful when alternatively applied to spontaneously occurring, or non-lucid dreams.

Any of the suggestions for lucid dream plans mentioned throughout the book can just as well be enacted as bedtime dream intentions. That is to say that instead of only reiterating to yourself for example, "My lucid dream plan is to have a face-to-face encounter with the goddess Brigid," you could also say to yourself prior to falling asleep, "My non-lucid dream intention is to have a face-to-face encounter with the goddess Brigid." In this way, you are intending to cultivate a spontaneous dream experience where this happens, even if it is not carried out during a bout of lucidity. A detailed discussion of lucid dream plans will be given in chapter 3, Reviewing the Basics.

To stay engaged with your non-lucid dreams, consider trying to set a dream intention every night—that is, stating the type of dream experience you'd like to incubate—and repeat it nightly until you get at least a semblance of it to happen. Be sure to write your dream intention down in your dream journal prior to going to sleep. Then, when you wake up and journal any recalled dreams, you will be able to directly assess any bearing that your intention had upon the resulting experiences. This is a lovely parallel practice for use in non-lucid dreaming to have going alongside the setting of lucid dream plans.

Remember that these processes do not need to be mutually exclusive. You can absolutely be intending to cultivate lucidity and have a lucid dream plan ready to go and simultaneously be setting intentions or asking questions of your non-lucid dreaming life, making the best of both worlds. If you become lucid, fantastic! If you don't, you are still gaining huge magickal learning experiences from your dreams.

Non-Lucid Dream Divination

Another excellent practice that can be performed with respect to non-lucid dreaming is divination. The intention here is not simply to interpret the meaning of random dreams that have been recalled but to carry out a very purposeful divination process. The method for this is as such: Instead of simply trying to cultivate a particular type of night dream experience because it's something you specifically want to engage in, try stating a divination question to the dreamtime upon going to sleep rather than just setting a straight intention. For example, you might say, "What would it look like if I were to accept the new role being offered to me at work?" Write your divination question down in your dream journal. When you awaken, record your dreams, and accept the material in the first recalled dream of the night as the response to your question.

It is often not easy to interpret your results initially, and it can take time to develop confidence in the skill of doing so. It can be explained in terms of treating the recalled dream as if it were a tarot card that you pulled in response to the question. Sometimes a pulled card does not appear to have a direct relationship to the question asked, but the skilled practitioner will be able to intuit what the vibration of the card is likely to have to do with the request at hand. Similarly, the dream you recall may seem odd and unrelated to the question. Even if you can't figure out the message initially, if you write it down in your journal as the dream responding to the question, some correlation will likely come to you synchronously at some point soon, if not immediately.

Here is an example of a fruitful dream divination process and how it can be directly beneficial to the advancement of one's magickal practice: The question I posed was: "What is the deeper meaning of the Ogham symbol Muin?" The first dream of the night that I recalled involved a very close friend and me walking outside and encountering a very scary bear that we had to carefully make our way around. There was a feeling of confidence in our ability to survive successfully.

Upon waking, my intuition regarding the dream with respect to the initial query was that the dream was demonstrating a truth about how it is easier to work through hard things together with those you love and trust than it is to do so alone. This knowledge then helped me to understand that in my sorcerous use of Muin, it might work well for inspiring trust, for fostering connection to others, or for facilitating effective teamwork.

I have successfully used non-lucid dream divination to gain intuitive insights regarding all kinds of magick, spirits, techniques, and symbols. The point here, again, is that you can use the lucid dream plan ideas presented further along in this book to also inspire your spontaneous dream quests and questions even if you haven't yet cultivated a purposefully executed lucid dream.

ARCANUM
Setting a Non-Lucid Dream
Intention or Divination

· • ● ○ ● • ·

Follow these instructions in order to become more confident in purposefully accessing your non-lucid dreams. You may use this guideline to set an intention for a dream experience you'd simply like to have or to ask a specific divination question for the seeking of advice.

1. Grab your dream journal right now, no matter what time of the day it is.

2. Think of either an intended experience or a divination question to which you would like to dedicate tonight's upcoming dreaming. Maybe you have a specific question on which you'd like advice or insight. Maybe you just want to set the intention that you fly in a dream or have a dream that allows you to have fun.

3. Decide on your intention or question and write it down in your dream journal with today's date.

4. The next time you have reawakened from sleep, journal your dreams. Designate the first dream remembered as the response to your intention or question.

5. Document your results and any perceived meaning that you glean from them.

Remember that it is okay if you don't initially see the correlation between your intention or question and what you documented from your dreaming. It can take time to understand the language of your own dreams, but in doing this you are off to a great start.

Types of Spontaneous Non-Lucid Dreams

It is important to consider the possibility that dreams may occur in an infinitely wide variety of possible types of realities and forms. Understanding some of the different types of dreams you are likely to have can help narrow down the meaning or implications inherent in your experience. Over the past twenty years, I have journaled my dreams every single day without fail, and because of this it has been possible for me to look back and recognize trends that occur and be able to associate most dreams with a recurring category.

⋅ The following categories are not based on any universally acknowledged system but come from my own overview of the patterns witnessed over decades of dreaming. Keep in mind that it is certainly possible for a dream to overlap into more than one of these categories.

Precognitive Dreams

A certain percentage of dreams are either literally, partially, or metaphorically precognitive, meaning that they are indications of something that is to come to pass in ordinary reality. Most people don't realize this because they don't have a reliable dream journaling practice. Without preserving recalled dreams in written form, most of them will soon be forgotten with no way to look back and review your experiences. A person who has been logging dreams for a good number of years will come to see that there are intermittent life circumstances that occur where you feel as though you've previously dreamed that which is happening in ordinary reality. If you have the documentation, then you can go and verify this.

Precognitive dreams seem to come with palpable emotion that lingers upon waking—a possible signal to the fact that there is a link between the dream and your experiences in waking reality. Precognitive dreams can serve as a means for going forward in time for the purpose of rehearsing that which we will need to be able to carry out in life. In addition to these qualities, precognitive dreams, once recognized, show us personal proof that our conscious awareness can move forward in time, beyond the moment and place where the physical body currently resides. These glimpses into the nonlocal nature of consciousness are invaluable for you as a magician who is seeking to understand and explore the mysteries more deeply.

Several years ago, four girlfriends and I were trying to organize a weekend trip away together. We had an email thread going where suggestions for destinations were being discussed. There was talk of Vermont, Atlantic City, upstate New York, and various options in or near New England. One night during the time when this back and forth was happening, I had a dream of being with these same four ladies on a lovely slate patio that overlooked the ocean, waves crashing down below. We were all wearing white bathrobes and had wine glasses in hand. I awoke and journaled the dream but decided not to say anything about it, and not to offer any real opinion about where we should go for our trip.

I had the feeling that the dream was precognitive, and as an experiment, I decided to stay quiet and see if I could just watch it play out rather than insert my own influence into the situation. After a bit, it came to light that one of the women's families had offered us the use of their home in Maine. We went there and as it turned out, we spent one whole day at a nearby spa where they give you white bathrobes to wear and you could relax and wait for each other in between appointments with wine or champagne out on the ocean-view patio. Finding myself in the exact situation I had dreamed of was thrilling to say the least. I had personal proof that my awareness had been able to move ahead in time from where my body was and experience a glimpse of what was to come.

Sometimes a precognitive dream is not exactly literal as to how the scene will play out in ordinary reality but is still a version or reflection of what is to come. One night, I dreamed of walking along the top of a cement retaining wall with my mother walking a few feet ahead of me. We were up high and balancing as we went, and I could see just beyond my mom that we were about to come to the end of the wall, where it just ended at a drop-off. My mom showed no signs of slowing down and almost seemed to be stumbling toward the edge. Not wanting her to fall off and undoubtedly become seriously injured, I lurched forward, grabbing her around the waist, shouting "Mom, stop!" I woke with a start, my body physically lurching forward and the words still actively in my throat.

That very morning in ordinary reality I went to work, where I was employed as a physical therapist in a skilled nursing facility. It was early and the unit I was on was quiet as I documented patient notes at a nursing station. I looked up to see one of our very impaired patients outside in the parking lot, hobbling around on her own. She wasn't supposed to even stand up on her own let alone walk or go outside unattended. No other staff members were in sight, so I ran out the door to try to catch up with the patient. She was on an island in the middle of the parking lot, about to stumble forward off a cement curb, when I was able to run up behind her and catch her around the waist, shouting, "Mary, stop!" I successfully prevented her Parkinsonian gait from causing her to trip off the curb, and I carefully supported her as we walked back inside.

In this instance, the dream I'd had was not exactly literal to the events that unfolded in waking, but the parallels were uncanny. In the dream, the cement was much higher and more dramatic, and the character was my own mother, not a nursing home patient. It was as if the dream heightened the experience and provided me with the necessary emotional investment by having me carry out the rescue for my own mom, which would be needed to prepare me for the important event of the day.

In addition to the obvious benefits of becoming more aware of precognitive dreams, if you were to find yourself lucid within a dream scene that seems like it may have a connection to ordinary reality, you could ask right on the spot, "What do I need to know about this dream's bearing upon my waking life?" and, dropping all expectations, see what ensues. If you could lucidly find out that a dream is, in fact, precognitive before its events play out, perhaps you could stop it, alter it, prepare for it, or even invite it in, if the dream is a desirable experience.

Emotional and Symbolic Message Dreams

Some dreams do not seem to mimic events that we could encounter in ordinary reality, especially when it seems obvious that they are largely symbolic. While not every dream is meant for emotional analysis and unpacking necessarily, sometimes it can feel as if the main point of a dream is a personal message or a learning opportunity. Some examples of these can be where you are struggling to cope with being naked or partially clothed in front of others; seeing animals in odd ways that wouldn't be possible in waking, such as a tiger in your bedroom; or seeing overly dramatized versions of things that you personally already view as symbolic. Examples of such symbolism could be water signifying emotions, a house signifying the state of your affairs, or elevator rides signifying the need to rise to higher levels.

These are only a few examples of many infinite potential dream symbols, of course. Some personal message dreams require symbol interpretation in this way, and some don't. I have had some obvious personal message dreams, such as one where I was walking along in the dream and noticed a piece of paper lying on the floor. Upon picking it up, I looked at the message written on it that stated, "Just be yourself, Nikki." It doesn't get much more obvious than that! However, any magician or occultist would certainly benefit from improving the skill of symbol interpretation, as this translates over into other magickal disciplines such as scrying, tea leaf reading, omen reading, and other modes of divination as well.

You might be wondering who emotional or symbolic dream messages may be coming from, and there are many possible answers to this. Sometimes you may get a strong feeling that a dream message came to you from a specific known guide or deity. It is possible to encounter symbolic dream messages that seem to originate from loved ones in spirit or even from your own Higher Self. Some dreams of this nature may simply be a product of your own personally developed language with the universe.

We don't know why we are drawn into all the various dreams we encounter, but it's possible that sometimes we end up in a symbolic dream in order to get better at interpreting this mysterious language that exists between ourselves and the rest of existence.

Logging your dreams and paying attention to those that seem to have symbolic messages is a great way of developing a personal set of symbol correspondences. I have had wise teachers who have recommended that a dreamer never use prefabricated dream dictionaries in the interpretation of their dreams. I agree with this advice because it has become very clear that various symbols do not mean the same things to all people. A dream dictionary might list a fox as a sign of trickery, for example, because of some popular correspondences with this animal as a symbol. Imagine, however, that Jane was bitten by a fox as a child, whereas her friend Joe has a fox as his primary animal guide. When Jane dreams of a fox as a symbol, it could pertain to dealing with fear, and when Joe dreams of a fox as a symbol, it could be an important moment of remembering to drum up spiritual inspiration.

Journaling can help you notate any recurring symbolism you notice in your dreams and begin to see what they tend to represent for you personally. This is much better than a symbol dictionary written by someone else, and helps you develop your gut response to symbols in a way that will enhance your other divinations. You will also be developing a potential personal language for reading omens and synchronicities from the waking world around you. This is not to minimize the fact that personal emotional and symbolic dreams are useful to us in the general sense of using them to cultivate personal growth, expand our abilities to understand our challenges, and regulate our emotions.

The intuitive symbol interpretation skill is merely being stressed here as a major benefit for your development as a diligent occultist. In lucid dreaming, when you ask a divination question aloud to the dream, you may very well be given a cryptic response in the form of a symbol or an image. If you have been paying attention to symbolism in your spontaneous non-lucid dreams, then you will be more apt to understand the potential meaning behind these types of lucid dream responses when they occur.

Dreams of Other Realities

As you know, I take the stance that it is highly likely that many dreams are access points into all kinds of iterations of an infinite number of different possible realities that could exist materially or immaterially. Even some theoretical physicists postulate that there is an infinite number of potential versions of reality that spring forth from every moment of this reality. Expand and apply that concept to the moments of other nonphysical realities also and we are well beyond the number and types of realities our minds are capable of conceiving.

Think about the number of times you might be documenting a non-lucid dream that goes something like, "I'm in my house with my family except that the house is different," or "I'm on vacation with a woman I know to be my mother except that she looks different than Mom in ordinary reality," and so on. It seems that an exorbitant number of our dreams involve scenarios that are not supernatural in nature but which differ in various ways from ordinary reality. We could think of these as being some of the many possible versions of realities that somehow relate to this one but did not end up manifesting physically.

Sometimes it can be hard to tell if such dreams are precognitive. When in doubt, look for things that still have a possibility of happening. For example, if you have a dream of being with your kids at ages three and five but in ordinary reality they are already adults, then the dream could be an alternate version of this reality that didn't play out, and the ages of the children might rule out the possibility of the dream being precognitive.

One of the tricky things that we need to consider is that in other versions of reality it is possible that many facets could be things that don't exist here at all. Often, if I don't know any other category that a particular dream seems to fit into, I realize that it makes sense as an example of an adventure in another plane or reality. This means that even the most mundane-seeming dream can be viewed as an opportunity to experience a different way that things could have gone, or a reality that is somehow akin to this one and connected to you but has unique differences. This allows you to have a potent forum in which to study the mysteries in a multiverse format, which can encompass many possible personal truths.

Another very intriguing idea that has come up with respect to studying these types of dreams is that of identifying locations that seem to recur in dream scenarios. For example, I have dreamed numerous times about the church and graveyard near the town center of my childhood hometown. In these dreams, this location is often slightly different looking or feeling than the way I know it to be in ordinary reality, yet I know that it is meant to represent the corresponding location from physical reality.

In one dream of this place, I became lucid, and before I was able to execute my lucid dream plan, I witnessed what could only be described as the Wild Hunt, or a Faery Rade, surging past. This is a folkloric phenomenon that has various versions but generally is a stampeding swarm of spirits who seem to be hunting or in pursuit of something. It is considered to be dangerous and often an ill omen. I intuitively knew to duck to avoid its violently surging stream of force as the beings whooshed by me.

Upon waking, I realized that it was possible that the reason I dreamed of this place frequently was because it was a permeable place where dreaming and waking realities seemed to easily intersect. I suspect that there are a great many of these special spots that could be identified in dreams and then visited for follow-up magick in waking or used as portals for subsequent waking journeys or lucid travel attempts.

Visitations from the Deceased

Dreams of the deceased could be nestled in or overlap with other categories, but in terms of inspection by the occultist, spontaneous dreams involving spirits of the dead deserve their own category. If we take the view that dreams are actual realities to be experienced and are spaces of congregation by multiple conscious beings, then it is not a hard jump to presume that dreaming of our deceased loved ones can be actual visitations or interactions.

Many times, I have been contacted by clients, friends, or students who wish to relay a dream experience involving a deceased loved one. In most of these instances, the person is adamantly sure that the interaction was "real." I don't doubt this at all. Just as precognitive dreams can have a lingering emotional connection here in this reality, dreams of the deceased, when they are actual interpersonal communications between the dreamer and the spirit, have an emotional energy signature that is palpable and recognizable.

If you become lucid within a dream where you are already interacting with the spirit of a deceased person, your mental wakefulness could then allow you to purposefully steer the communications in a direction of healing. You could have conversations you didn't get to have while they were alive or learn more about them or other more distant ancestors, to name a few examples. Alternatively, you could purposefully induce lucidity and then carry out one of these types of tasks by summoning the desired beloved spirit, which will be talked about later in the lucid dream plan setting section of chapter 3.

Dreams of the deceased do not only involve the spirits of people we have known in this life. On one occasion, I had a poignant dream where I specifically understood that some of the characters were dead and some were not. Upon journaling this in waking, I noted that the deceased characters tended to be much less vocal and communicative than the characters who seemed to represent people who continue to be physically alive in my waking life. When I realized this trait, I looked back through years of journals where I mentioned dream characters unknown from ordinary reality. Very often there were trends where they would have limited or no speech, and I realized that there could be all manner of spirit beings appearing in dreams.

If, like me, you make note of dreams where you don't know some of the characters from ordinary reality, it's quite possible that some of them are actually spirits of deceased beings. Take note of any behavioral characteristics that may recur, and you may be able to start to recognize trends that clue you in to character types in the moment. If you become lucid within a dream and you recognize any of these trends, then you will be able to ask the dream or the characters directly about their relationship to you. If you are finding yourself in dream realities where these spirits are your allies, then it is worth your time to consider whether these allies may be able to be involved in further waking magick as well.

Dreams as the Outside Observer

This is an extremely fascinating dream category to be sure. Not everyone seems to have these types of dreams, though I have met a handful of people who report having these experiences just as I have had. In this type of dream, you experience the feeling of watching a story or a scene play out. You witness it as if watching a movie but are somehow not a part of the action or of the scene at all.

The dreamer awakens from these experiences with the odd realization that they have been privy to something of which they may not be a part. It is sometimes possible for a dream to begin this way and then transform to become a situation where the dreamer has, indeed, become part of the dream. There could be lots of potential reasons to explain why our awareness may have been drawn to witness a story as an outside observer. It could simply be a story or a scene with an important message to consider, or a poignant learning opportunity.

Another possible explanation is that we could be monitoring situations involving beings for whom we, ourselves, serve as spiritual guides. This may seem far-fetched at first to some, but let us revisit the old Hermetic teachings of "as above, so below…as within, so without." Why is it feasible for us to conceive of having guides ourselves but difficult for us to imagine that we might be simultaneously serving as a guide for others?

I have experienced dreams that started off as watching a scene from beyond it to finding myself somehow able to step in and function on behalf of the good of one of the characters, thereby changing the outcome from how things seemed to be going. I usually don't have a clear memory of how I was able to do that or of being conscious of the type of vested interest I may have had in the story that caused me to get involved.

These experiences do, however, tend to give me pause and spark a process of introspection into the nature of the dream that encourages an expanding personal belief system regarding the nature of our consciousness and of ourselves as spiritual beings in general. The direct experience and then contemplation of this is very beneficial to the magician who functions often within the spirit model of magick.

If you gain your own experiences in aiding or guiding another being, then it can deepen your understanding of why your own guides may be vested in helping you in turn. Everything in magick is about relationships, whether it is your relationship to a guide, to a nonhuman energy, to a nature entity, to an ancestor, or to yourself. As you gain skill, you will have realized that a deeper understanding of spirit relationships is crucial to eliciting an increase in magickal effectiveness.

The Distillation

We have taken time in this chapter to highlight the essential need to value and inspect our spontaneously occurring non-lucid dreams. Though the overall focus of this book is one of helping you to bring lucid dreaming into your magickal practice, you must make the inspection and engagement of your non-lucid dreams an equal priority throughout this process.

You can now strive to look through your dream journal and get better at recognizing dream types and qualities that present as trends for you. You should also be taking advantage of the spontaneous nature of non-lucid dreams for the practice of setting bedtime dream intentions or divinations. Interacting with the juice of your non-lucid dreams will also help you to get ready to do the work of chapter 3 in setting lucid dream plans.

REVIEWING
THE BASICS

Here we will dig into the foundational skills and practices that generally need to be present to predispose oneself to lucid dreaming. This will include examining your rate of dream recall and looking at factors you can adjust to ensure its robustness. We will also discuss how to use reality checks to work toward dream-induced lucid dreaming, as well as discuss specific techniques you can try when attempting wake-induced lucid dreaming.

We will discuss some of the common challenges of holding on to the lucid state when lucidity does ultimately occur. Lastly, we will cover the concept of setting lucid dream plans so that you are fully prepared not to waste any valuable lucid magick opportunities.

Creating a Predisposition

So how, then, do you create this predisposition for dream-induced lucidity? First, there needs to be a steady habit and reliability of routine recall of regular non-lucid dreams in place. One thing that is very important in cultivating an ongoing practice of daily dream recall, as well as in the prompting of lucid dreaming, is the practice of meditation in your day-to-day waking life. One of the qualities that many lucid dreamers seem to share is a very keen, clear, alert, and perceptive mind, and an ability for excellent mental focus as well as emotional regulation.

When you awaken from sleeping, for you to be able to recall what it is that you were just dreaming, you need to have enough clarity and present-moment focus to be able to stay aware of what was happening in the dream while simultaneously finding yourself transitioning back into an awareness of ordinary reality. Anything that distracts from that fragile moment, such as being awakened by a startle or jarring alarm, random loud noises, someone instantly needing your attention, feeling sick, and so forth, can detract from your ability to harness that memory.

Being able to have focused mental effort upon the moment of waking, such as is enhanced by the skills developed through regular meditation, can help with this greatly. There is no effort gone to waste for you, the occultist, in generating a meditation practice to enhance your lucidity, since meditative focus will also greatly enhance your practice of every other type of magick as well.

In terms of dream recall, there are a lot of factors that can either help or hinder this ability to remember dreams upon waking. People who engage in the creative arts have been shown to have greater recall than those who do not.[7] People who test more highly on indicators for open-mindedness, people with better visual memory, and people who simply value the content of dreams and the idea of dreams in general are all more likely to have greater recall, for example, than those who don't.[8]

There was a study conducted that showed that females tended to have slightly higher rates of recall than males.[9] There have also been findings showing that recall tends to go down with advanced age.[10] There was even a study done that showed variations in dream recall rates between popu-

---

7. Michael Schredl, "Creativity and Dream Recall," *The Journal of Creative Behavior*, vol. 29 (1) (1995): 16–24.

8. Veronica K. Tonay, "Personality Correlates of Dream Recall: Who Remembers?" *Dreaming*, vol. 3 (1) (March 1993): 1–8.

9. Michael Schredl, "Gender Differences in Dream Recall," *Journal of Mental Imagery*, vol. 24 (1–2) (2000): 169–176.

10. Edwin Kahn and Charles Fisher, "Dream Recall in the Aged," *Psychophysiology* 5, no. 2 (1968): 222.

lations of people with different political persuasions.[11] The variables are so many that it can be difficult to tell just what is hindering you when you find that recall is lacking.

If you look at the indicators and commonalities for good recall, the common thread within the previous list of indicators, as well as most other theories, is that they are all things that tend to increase our mental clarity. I have found that basically everything that improves your overall health helps to improve your mental clarity as well, thus having a big potential impact on dream recall. This can include how cleanly you eat, your meditation practice, the healthiness of your overall sleep routine, your exercise regime, how you handle stress, having access to supportive friends and community, and more.

The fact that there are some unchangeable factors to dream recall, as evidenced by some of the studies cited previously such as age and gender, can help us each to understand why we have the unique trends we have in our own dream recall histories. However, we will focus on some of the factors that we can, in fact, change readily.

The following are several practical tips that are helpful for anyone looking to enhance their basic dream recall. Be sure to consider the following practices as essential basics and take an honest inventory of how well you have integrated such practices for yourself thus far. Do your best to patiently develop these instead of rushing forth to the lucid magick. The efforts will pay off greatly and prevent frustrations in failing to become lucid that can ensue when a predisposition has not been solidly created.

Meditating

Having 20 minutes of daily quiet stillness meditation is one important recommendation, not only for the would-be lucid sorcerer but for all humans. There is possibly no better way to hone the skills of mental focus and emotional control than through a routine of dedicated meditation practice.

Meditation helps one to become better and better at present-moment awareness. When you are routinely in the habit of noticing the depth and

11. Kelly Bulkeley, "Dream Recall and Political Ideology: Results of a Demographic Survey," *Dreaming*, vol. 22 (1) (March 2012): 1–9.

quality of the moment you are in, you will become more likely to also do that when dreaming, which could lead to the revelation of lucidity since you are inspecting the very nature of the present moment as you experience it.

Meditation also has been shown to directly enhance basic dream recall, with your chance of remembering a dream the next morning being noticeably increased if you meditated the day before.[12] As I have mentioned and will further discuss in the next pages, regular daily dream recall is a prerequisite for the development of a lucid dream practice.

There are many approaches one can take to meditation. Although guided meditations or mantra-based meditations are better than no meditation at all, I suggest that aspiring lucid magicians adopt a method that aims to hone a high level of sharp focus. This means that you should consider a classical method that has you choosing one singular point of focus and making it your goal to keep your attention on that focal point for the length of time of your sitting. Your focal point could be the breath, the sensation of your hands or feet, or a point of light or darkness behind your closed eyelids, to name a few examples.

ARCANUM
Single Point of Focus Meditation Technique

· · ● ○ ● · ·

There are many single point of focus options when choosing a meditative style, but the following meditation technique is specifically well suited to the lucid magician. Focusing on the space of the third eye in the inner vision will have the added bonus of later enhancing your ability to stay alert during the unique transitory state between waking and sleeping known as the hypnagogic state. For now, though, use the following as a waking daily meditation practice.

1. Find a comfortable place to sit where you can be relatively undisturbed for 20 minutes. You may lie down,

---

12. Henry Reed, "Improved Dream Recall Associated with Meditation," *Journal of Clinical Psychology* vol. 34 (1) (January 1978): 150–156.

but it is not recommended if you are already tired or tend to struggle with falling asleep during meditation.

2. Set a timer for 20 minutes.

3. Start the timer and close your eyes, bringing your focus to a point in the center of the back of your closed eyelids, just above the level of your eyes. You may begin to perceive this spot as a point of either light or darkness, and you will then notice that this lighting perception will shift and change. The challenge is to not try to identify what is happening or follow the shifts to any real thought processes, but to just try to watch that point.

4. Every time that you feel judgments or external thoughts creeping in, rein your awareness back to simple attention upon this point. You may need to do this hundreds of times within the space of the prescribed 20 minutes, and that is not only okay but also very normal. This is the work of meditation—the practice of choosing where you put your focus.

5. One of the potential pitfalls for Witches and magickal practitioners in this style of meditation can be the temptation to follow morphing imagery in the mind because it feels like a tantalizing psychic rabbit hole to explore. When this happens, remind yourself that you can do a more psychically exploratory or divinatory practice later, and that this is your time for a no-thought, present-moment awareness style of meditation. Psychic meditative visioning does not nurture the same skill set as a single point of focus practice. Redirect your attention back to the point behind the eyelids as many times as needed.

When the timer finishes, congratulate yourself on your success, for the success here lies in showing up to meditate at all. Try to avoid making judgments about the nature of the experience itself or assessing how well you think you did. If you sat and tried, then you did well.

Setting Intention

Another way to improve dream recall is by simply developing the habit of stating the intention to remember your dreams just before falling asleep at night. I say to myself "I remember my dreams," and I literally take a moment to picture myself awakening in the morning and mentally perusing and writing down the dreams I have just awoken from.

As a magician, I believe that it is important to phrase these intention statements in the present tense, so as not to keep the result perpetually hanging in the unattainable future state. If you are always saying "I *will* remember my dreams," it could contain a subconscious implication of remembering them someday as opposed to imminently, always keeping them just out of reach.

Journaling

In chapter 1, we discussed the need for a dream journal as well as the potential blessing and charging of this important tool. You might be wondering how you can journal your dreams if you are still struggling to get enough dream recall to even have anything to write down. The answer is relatively simple. Keep your journal and pen near the bedside. When you wake up, write down everything you can remember from your dreams. Even if all you have upon waking is a vague memory of a scene, a little dream fragment or a snippet, write that down.

If you don't even have a glimpse or a fragment, still take a moment to write the date and simply note how you felt upon awakening. Make a habit of writing something at that waking moment, even if it isn't a dream.

In doing this routinely, you are teaching your mind to focus on this exact moment. You are showing your mind that you value the transition from sleeping to waking and you wish to explore it more deeply and to examine it routinely. You are creating and ingraining the habit of being more and more acutely aware of that momentary transition so that you bring your dream memories with you as you wake up.

You might write as little as "I woke with a start, feeling groggy and unrested" or "I awoke to the chirping of birds only to find there was no such sound audible from my bedroom" or "I remember being near water in my dream." Sometimes I wake up with a song or a word in my head, but I might not specifically remember the dream experience that led me to that. I will still write that down and value it for the clue to my dreaming that it is.

If you do awaken with recalled dreams, do your best to write down as much detail from them as you can remember. It doesn't necessarily matter what tense you write your dreams in. I tend to use the past tense as though I'm retelling the story of my experiences to a friend. That said, you may prefer to write in the present tense in order to remind yourself of the "all time is now" feeling of dreams in the multiverse.

One common challenge with dream journaling is this: The dreamer will awaken in the middle of the night remembering their dream but feeling so tired and craving that luscious descent back into sleep they decide that they will just wait and write it down in the morning. This rarely works, and the dreamer awakens to find that the experience they intended to save and write later has vanished. It takes work and perseverance, but when you wake up in the middle of the night with some dream material, do your best to write it down in that moment.

I get a lot of questions on whether it is okay to use electronic, typed documentation of dreams or voice-recorded dream transcriptions. My feeling is that it is fine for the average person who just wishes to increase recall a bit and have a basic low-level access to their dream material. For magickal purposes, however, I do not feel that it is as good as writing the dream by hand in a paper journal. There is a slowing down of the reliving of the dream experience that happens with mindful physical writing that increases your present-moment awareness. Also, the journal is easy to flip back through in order to look for keywords, drawings, symbols, and other things that could easily get lost in lists of saved electronic files. I prefer rifling through pages in leather books rather than having to click on lists of file names to find what I want. Also, your handwriting contains something of your energy signature, so some of the energy of the dream is brought more tangibly through into a handwritten journal.

Reality Checks

Let's assume that you have developed the skill of daily dream recall and return fully to the topic of how one works to become lucid in dreams.

There are numerous approaches, some more common than others. The main concept to begin with is that of creating ingrained habits of constantly examining the nature of reality. Reality checks can be done in lots of different ways, but the most important thing is that they need to be done very frequently throughout the day in waking reality. The goal is to make reality testing such a habitual part of yourself that you will be prone to occasionally checking the nature of reality even when you are dreaming.

Examining Your Hands

One very common method made famous by the author Carlos Castaneda in *The Art of Dreaming* is to try to look for and then examine your hands as often as possible.[13] To ingrain this habit while waking, you literally pick up your hand throughout the day and carefully examine the back of it, turn it over to look closely at your palm, and then flip it back to the original side again, making sure nothing has changed since your initial inspection.

Often, in dreaming, if you examine something with such scrutiny, it will tend to morph and malform before your eyes. In establishing the habit of close inspection in this way, the hope is that examining your hands will become so routine and automatic that you will eventually also do it in your dreams. When you do, it is likely that the level of focus will cause you to notice something awry, or some type of visual aberration will occur that is common when dreaming. When this happens, you'll be able to have that sudden realization that you are, in fact, dreaming.

Pinching Yourself

Another method is that of simply pinching yourself. There is a reason that phrases such as "pinch me so I know I'm not dreaming" became popular. If you pinch yourself and you are dreaming, you may not feel any pain or sensation, or your fingers may squish through your arm as if it isn't solid. Again, the visuals and sensations of the dream may morph as they are wont to do, and when the pinch doesn't work as you expected, you have a great chance of becoming alerted to the fact that you are dreaming. If you

13. Carlos Castaneda, *The Art of Dreaming* (Harper Perennial, 1993), 21.

do adopt this as your favored method of reality testing, please be sure not to hurt yourself.

Pinching Your Nostrils Shut

Another reality check that I favor involves pinching both of your nostrils fully shut and then trying to take a deep breath in through your nose. The reason I like this one is because it can be done frequently and in public without people really noticing what you are doing. This method is a bit more subtle than stopping to stare intently at your hand while turning it over and back again.

If you try pinching your nose and breathing in through it often enough, when you finally test it in a dream, you will be delighted to feel that the clean and refreshing sensation of the full breath moves through your nose even though you know it's effectively blocked. You'll realize that you are sleeping in your bed and that your physical nose isn't pinched. You will know that your brain felt the full breath even though you pinched your nose in your dream body, and you'll likely become lucid.

Checking Your Environment

Another major way to check the nature of your reality is to practice looking for incongruencies. This means frequently scanning your environment for anything that seems odd, out of place, unnatural, or new and foreign to you. If you make a solid habit of this, then you might be more inclined to also do it regularly in dreams. Dream realities can include lots of things that would not be a normal part of ordinary reality, so try to develop the habit of being acutely perceptive as to the details of your surroundings.

You can also simply try to constantly ask yourself in your mind if you are dreaming, though this should not be considered your primary reality check habit because merely thinking about it doesn't seem to work strongly enough on its own. There are many times that you could find yourself within a dream, thinking about the nature of dreaming, and yet not realize that you are *actually* dreaming at that moment! Waking up from these types of scenarios feels both ironic and frustrating, as the would-be lucid dreamer will instantly recognize it as having missed an opportunity to attain lucidity.

Cementing the Reality Check Habit

Whatever reality check or combination of reality check methods you choose, find a way to do them numerous times throughout the day. Once an hour should be a minimum, but more is preferable. Ideally you should choose one favorite reality check method that involves your physical body without accoutrements and try to implement it at least hourly. Take into consideration your lifestyle, how often you are in the direct presence of other people, and what types of tasks you are routinely doing, then choose something that can merge in with your particular routine.

It should be noted that these days there are applications for your smartphone that can be set to remind you to test the nature of your reality that are specifically aimed at inducing lucid dreams. Alternatively, even without an app, you could just program your phone to give you a gentle alarm at certain intervals throughout the day to help you remember to create the routine habit of reality checking.

Phone apps should not be the primary reality check you depend upon because that habit is then reliant upon your phone alerting you to do a reality check in your dream as well. If your dream doesn't include you having a phone present, your chances of successfully executing this kind of check are low, but if you have an ongoing habit of staring at your hands or trying to breathe through closed nostrils, you can happen upon that habit in any potential dream scenario.

Reality Checks Can Fail

I believe that one of the reasons reality checks sometimes fail is that things don't always work the same way in different types of dream realities. I have woken up from many dreams where I certainly did successfully do a reality check or two and yet they failed. Sometimes I just stopped and asked myself if I was dreaming, and because I looked around and everything felt normal and solid to me, I assumed that I wasn't dreaming.

Remember that usually when we are dreaming, we are just there, going about our business in this alternate-conscious reality, not questioning it! I have also tried to test for dreaming by levitating, and then woke up remembering testing it in the dream but having the ability to levitate fail, so I did not become lucid. As it turns out, floating and flying are not always possible in every single dream reality in which you might find yourself.

Different dreamscapes can have their own unique physics, densities, and experiences inherent to them. For example, in this physical reality that we are all currently sharing, a human being can't just rocket-launch their physical body up into the sky to fly without equipment. Our bodies are materially dense, and we have a strong gravitational field here. In some dream realities, a person can fly easily, like superman, soaring through the sky. In some other dream realities, this doesn't really seem to work, however, even under the same standards of lucidity, and a more extreme effort of a swimming sort of flying is needed to travel in the air. In some dream realities, the lucid efforts of flying don't seem to work well at all.

Because of these differences between dream scenes and realities, not every kind of reality check works equally well in every dream. If you wake from a dream more than once remembering that you executed a reality check without subsequently becoming lucid, it might be time to add a different reality check habit into the mix.

ARCANUM
Establishing a Reality Check Habit

· · ● ○ ● · ·

Take a moment to truly engage and practice some of the methods of reality checking discussed to see how they feel. The purpose of this exercise will be to see which one(s) you feel you are intuitively connecting with the most. It is advisable to pick no more than one or two initially and then intend to carry them out as frequently as possible throughout the course of each day.

Technique 1

Lift your dominant hand and stare at your palm. Inspect its lines and details, count your fingers, and notice if you are wearing any rings. Now flip your hand over and look at the back of your hand. Keep your attention sharply focused upon it, noticing your fingernails and rings, and counting your fingers again. Once more, flip it back over to look at the palm side again. Has anything changed since your initial inspection? Notice how well you were able to focus on this activity.

Technique 2

Take your dominant hand and gently pinch either your thigh or your opposite arm. Notice the sensation of the pinch. Could you feel it? Was the pressure felt in keeping with how much force you think you used? Did the density of the limb you pinched feel as you expected it to, or did it feel harder or softer than usual? Did anything odd happen? Notice how well you were able to keep your focus on this activity.

Technique 3

With your dominant hand, reach up and pinch your nostrils closed. Next, attempt to take a deep breath in through your blocked nose. Focus on the sensations involved in what it feels like to do this. If you are waking, no air should move through. Do you feel any sense of airflow? Now release your nostrils and take a good breath in through the nose and feel the contrasting sensation that occurs when breath is flowing freely there. Notice how well you were able to keep your focus on this activity.

· • ● ○ ● • ·

Which of the previous three practices felt most engaging to you? Consider taking your favorite and intending to use it from here on out, a couple of times an hour at least, all day every day. Remember that it is okay to also do mentally based reality checks such as just contemplating the nature of your reality or looking around for incongruencies. The point to take in is that you do need to have at least one physical action–based technique that does not rely on a device or on thinking alone in order for you to experience optimal results.

Wake-Induced Lucid Dreaming

Having talked about some things that can make it more likely for you to spontaneously become lucid while already dreaming, I will now review the technique of trying to remain conscious from waking straight into dreaming. This method is more difficult, but it is certainly possible.

For some in the Buddhist tradition, wake-induced lucid dreaming is an important goal because it is believed that if one masters the ability to stay conscious while transitioning from waking to sleeping, that one will be able to stay conscious while transitioning from living to dying, thereby allowing for the fullest and clearest immersion in the divine evolution of that process. Again, in some traditions like this one, wakefulness is correlated to living and sleeping is correlated to dying, metaphorically.

Even if you don't succeed at wake-induced lucid dreaming, the act of trying sure can teach you a lot about the workings of the mind and what is possible in the hypnagogic state. This is that liminal state of consciousness that can be experienced when you are not fully awake but also not quite yet asleep. It is rich with magickal imagery, messages, spirit communication, and many other mysteries to explore. I find it easier to work on holding experiences of the hypnagogic state in that drifting space of the morning when you wake and stretch a bit but then allow yourself to slip back into sleep, as opposed to the process of initially going to bed at night. When you are tired and your body and mind are in true need of deep sleep, it is a much harder feat to stay consciously aware through the process of falling asleep.

Counting Method

One method for wake-induced lucid dreaming that I have tried is to begin counting slowly, with an affirmation of being awake or knowing you are dreaming stated between each number, such as "One…I am dreaming… Two…I am dreaming…Three…I am dreaming…" and so on. The goal is that eventually you will start to slip into a dream where you will be continuing to state that you are dreaming and be able to stay lucid to this fact as the dream scene forms. Counting gives your awareness the job of paying attention to the numeric sequence, which helps add that subtle layer of wakefulness that the mantra alone does not tend to provide.

Focusing on Darkness Method

Another method that has worked better for me than the previous one is to simply focus very intently on the blank, dark space on the back of the closed eyelids while drifting off to sleep. When you do this without the intention of creating any purposeful images, keeping your mind as clear of intruding thoughts as you can and just watching that space patiently, often you will start to first see patterns of light emerge and then what seem to be various textures.

If you can be alert and patient enough for a long enough time, those textures will become three-dimensional and often details will start to emerge, such as walls, windows, doors, or a landscape.

You must continue to be very patient, as you will witness the dream scene forming before the point when you are likely to be able to anchor within it with an actual dream body. Once you see the scene, you can carefully and gently see if you can pick up your dream hands to look at them. This can often help you to gain awareness of your dream body as it materializes within the scene. If you move too quickly, you are likely to lose hold of the scene entirely and wake up.

If you do succeed in patiently watching a dream scene form and then waiting until you are in it, you will still be aware that this is a dream, never having blacked out into unconscious sleeping. You will be able to go ahead and make use of your lucid dreaming time. It should seem obvious that part of the point of your daily meditation practice is to enhance this very focusing skill that is needed to stay alert to the hypnagogic state for efforts in wake-induced lucid dreaming.

Picturing a Familiar Place Method

Another method to induce a lucid dream that has worked for me is to picture myself in a very familiar place in ordinary reality, and then mentally walk around, imagining in my mind's eye every detail I can recall of the scene. The key is to really focus on inner visualization of the remembered details of the place and to move slowly and purposefully in the mind's eye, tapping into as many sensory aspects as you can recall from this well-known mental walk.

For example, for a good number of years I used to rent a unique office space in an old historic factory in my town. I became so familiar with the feel of opening the exterior door and all the details of the long walk down several halls to my space that it turned into a good lucid dreaming induction technique. I would imagine the feel of the cool metal of the door handle, the color and weight of the old door as I pulled it open, and the feel of the cement threshold beneath my feet. I would imagine pulling the door wide and stepping in onto the old wood floors, knowing where some of the creaks, dips, and worn places were, and remembering them while really trying to feel the sensations of it all mentally.

I practiced the internal visualization of luxuriating in the sensory aspect of this familiar walk many times, and eventually I would have an occasional wake-induced success where I would see that the factory hallway had solidified from an internal imagining to a three-dimensional dream scene in which I could anchor myself and continue along with lucid dream plan adventures. If you are especially fond of visualization exercises, then something like this could be a great wake-induced technique for you.

Timing Wake-Induced Attempts

You will need to experiment with finding the best timing for wake-induced practice for you, personally. It certainly takes a decent amount of willpower to do this. The idea is to set an alarm that wakes you up somewhere between 3:00 and 5:00 a.m. and get up for a bit. Go to the bathroom, have some tea or a light snack, journal what you remember of your dreams so far and maybe read for a bit, returning to bed in about an hour. Upon your return to bed, implement your choice from among the wake-induced methods just discussed.

The well-timed interruption in your sleep seems to cause a phenomenon sometimes called REM loading, where the REM cycle suddenly seems to pop in earlier and for longer, possibly to somehow atone for the interruption. Because of this, it is a much more conducive time to try wake-induced lucidity methods.[14] When REM sleep is close at hand, the hypnagogic state

14. David Jay Brown, *Dreaming Wide Awake: Lucid Dreaming, Shamanic Healing, and Psychedelics* (Park Street Press, 2016), 55.

feels more active, and it is therefore easier to keep one's mental focus upon that imagery in a meditative way for long enough to be able to witness the actual formation of dream scenes.

If You Don't Succeed

Even though most people begin their lucid successes with the more common dream-induced lucidity experiences that come from reality checking within a dream, I highly recommend that the enthusiastic lucid magician also try to conquer the difficult challenge of the wake-induced lucid dream. I have found that when I become lucid spontaneously from within a dream, that once I awaken and the dream has dissipated, I cannot easily re-enter a state of lucidity at will.

On the other hand, after having a wake-induced period of lucidity, I find that I am quite often able to revert to the same type of meditative focus on the hypnagogic state that got me there in the first place. This often results in successfully restoring lucidity repeatedly, sometimes anywhere from seven to ten times in a row over a period of two hours. Imagine how many lucid magick experiments you might possibly execute over such a period!

Even though you might not succeed in walking straight from full wakefulness into a wake-induced lucid dream, trying routinely helps deepen the imprint of the habit of trying to be awake to the reality you are in, thus also increasing your chances of a regular dream-induced lucid dream. Meditative exercises such as these wake-induced lucid dream techniques also tend to help beef up your mental focus abilities across the board for magick and for life, so again, it's a win-win situation, or what I call a virtuous cycle.

You have set up a system of reality checks that you will strive to work on throughout the course of each day and can now also try to luxuriate in the hypnagogic state each time you are going back to sleep, maybe trying one of the wake-induced methods we recently discussed. Even though these techniques work best when paired with a wake-back-to-bed routine as described, you should attempt them when you are falling asleep for the first time at night, as well as when you get back in bed after getting up to go to the bathroom, and any time at all that you happen to wake up and then have the opportunity to let yourself consciously go back to sleep. This way, you could potentially be practicing your awareness of the transition from waking to sleeping multiple times every day, without even adding any time in your schedule to the efforts of this magickal practice.

Anchoring

Once you start to experience attaining lucidity, the next big thing to work on is your skill in anchoring solidly into it. Being in the lucid dream state can be very difficult to hang on to for long, and lots of factors can lurch you right back into waking if you aren't attentive enough to this eventuality. Even when you become lucid in the middle of a regular dream, if you try to do too much too quickly without really solidifying your sense of presence in the dream, you can easily lose hold of it. This will often cause you to either wake up or to lose lucidity and revert to being at the whim of the dream rather than awaken to the real nature of it.

I have found that having a surge of excitement or any other strong emotion, seeing or feeling something amazing or having any experience with lots of heightened sensation to it, will often result in instantly waking back up. This isn't necessarily a bad thing, though. For example, receiving an energetic infusion from a deity can have the most amazing, intense, and unique feeling to it, and when you allow yourself to be fully present and soak it in, you will likely lose hold of the dream scene after a bit and wake up. It is completely worth it, though, because you can often continue to feel the energetic results of the deity interaction affecting you for some time after waking.

Even though waking before you wanted to is a normal phenomenon, you certainly don't want to lose hold of your lucidity before you have successfully executed whatever plan you had in mind, and this happens all too often. I have lost my lucidity countless times before I wanted to, highlighting to me the importance of re-anchoring frequently to maximize time in this precious state. You should use an anchoring technique then, not only upon initially becoming lucid, but at intervals during your lucid dream as well.

Some authors, such as lucid dreamer Charlie Morley, say that they spin or move quickly to anchor into a dream scene, but this has not worked well for me.[15] I have found that the opposite is helpful—taking a moment that is very still and grounding and present within the dream body helps me to retain my place in the dream. I look around, trying to sharply notice the details and solidity of the scene, and then touch some of the physical surfaces in the dream. Then I will pick up my hands and examine them or rub them together, feeling a clear connection to my dream body.

Note that I prefer to use this as an anchoring technique, not to be confused with looking at the hands as a reality test technique. I may also look at my feet upon the floor of the dream, asserting my ability to move my dream body intentionally with respect to the dream scene. Then I will slowly start walking and moving around a bit to be fully engaged in the scene, reminding myself that I am dreaming as I go. It's also completely possible to lose lucidity without waking up and just slip back into ordinary dreaming, so continuing to remind yourself often that you are dreaming is not only useful but very important.

Your Lucid Dream Plan

As soon as I find that I can move my dream body in the scene without the scene becoming unstable, I execute my lucid dream plan. The lucid dream plan is a concise statement of what you wish to try to achieve during this lucid dream, phrased in a way that it can be spoken to the dream space as a command. This point right here is crucial to stay on top of so that you don't miss the opportunity to do magick in the lucid state: It's important to always have a lucid dream plan decided upon ahead of time so when you do become lucid you don't miss the small window of opportunity that you have in order to make the best use of it. In fact, you should formulate a lucid dream plan using the exercise that follows if you don't already have one because even the act of reading books about dreaming may help predispose you to cultivating a lucid dream.

The next time you become lucid in a dream, the goal is to instantly verbalize your plan to the atmosphere of the dream scene as soon as you have anchored yourself well within the dream. If you wait too long and get dis-

---

15. Charlie Morley, *Dreams of Awakening: Lucid Dreaming and Mindfulness of Dream and Sleep* (Hay House, 2013), 168.

tracted by the goings-on of the dream or get sucked into putzing around with flying and sex and controlling the landscape, you may find yourself awake before you have gotten the chance to work on an important magickal goal that you had in mind. You will likely get lots of cool ideas for lucid dream plans while reading this book, as I will relay many different types of magickal explorations and experiments that I have found to be possible and beneficial when lucid.

I have found, however, that not every lucid dream plan can be completed in every type of dream realm. If you attempt to cultivate a magickal experience by stating your command and it doesn't work, consider anchoring again and then rewording your request. When a lucid dream plan fails, it is also a good opportunity to practice clearing the mind and releasing any expectation around what you thought would happen. Sometimes the dream will not respond to your request if you are looking for something specific, but it may respond in very surprising, rewarding, and informative ways when you let go of preconceived notions and allow it to do so.

This release of preconceived notions also allows us to trust the information or experience that comes as a result of the lucid dream plan command. When you clear your mind after asserting your plan's statement, you can accept what ensues as an organic and divine response to the query and not treat it solely as the product of our own biased desire. This is a skill that can be developed, and one which is discussed further in chapter 4.

When I have been keeping the same lucid dream plan in mind for a while and have not become lucid, I have found that it is a good idea to go to my dream journal and formulate a new one. Sometimes the fresh energy of thought or enthusiasm toward another goal seems to reinforce and renew the ability to keep that idea more at the forefront of the mind. In this way, the likelihood for lucidity and the connection to getting that work to happen in the dreamtime increases. You can always put the prior lucid dream plan back in the rotation once you find you are successfully becoming lucid again, or consider doing divination to help you choose which lucid dream plan should be prioritized at the current time.

ARCANUM
Formulating a Lucid Dream Plan

· • ● ○ ● • ·

Take a moment to think about where you are in your own personal magickal and spiritual exploration. What is something that you would love to experience more deeply but is difficult to do in ordinary reality? Maybe you'd like to speak directly to a deity or a spirit or see visibly the results of ritual techniques you frequently use. You might have a divination question to which you have not yet received a clear answer. You will encounter many ideas for lucid dream plans through the magickal examples explained in this book, but for now:

1. Think of something you'd like to do the next time you become lucid in a dream and write it in your dream

   ournal. Try to make the goal statement simple and easy to say so you can easily mentally repeat it.

2. Repeat your lucid dream plan statement to yourself a few times and commit it to memory.

3. From now on, each time you are going to sleep, mentally reiterate this lucid dream plan to yourself until you get to implement it.

4. After having gotten to execute a lucid dream plan, create a new lucid dream plan, write that one in your journal, and continue on in that fashion.

It may seem obvious, but it is just as important to journal the results of your lucid dreams and lucid dream experiments as it is to journal your non-lucid dreams. Documenting the results of the execution of a lucid dream plan often helps give a logical idea as to what would be the most appropriate lucid dream plan to try for next.

The Distillation

This chapter has served to help you shore up a solid foundational base upon which to build your lucid magick practice. We discussed the importance of developing good dream recall and some of the factors affecting this as well as practices to enhance it. Meditation, journaling, and intention setting are some of the habits that help increase dream recall and also serve to support your ability to become lucid. We covered techniques of reality checking so that you are helping to predispose yourself to cultivate dream-induced lucid dreams. We also talked about methods for honing the more difficult wake-induced lucid dreams and the benefits of practicing these techniques.

Building upon the base skills for becoming lucid, we began to explore the idea of developing skill in anchoring into the dream effectively once lucid, and not losing the precious opportunity to use the space for magick. Lastly, you began working on formulating your current lucid dream plan statement and committing it to memory so that it will be the first thing you do upon becoming lucid. With your basic understanding of lucidity and core practices in place, we'll continue on to discuss some nuanced approaches to lucidity that are specifically important for you as a magician.

BEYOND THE BASICS–
LUCID SKILL DEVELOPMENT
FOR MAGICIANS

As a practitioner of magick aiming to use the lucid dream space as a place of magickal and spiritual development, there are some points and skills that need to be acknowledged and honed. While you certainly should gain enjoyment from your lucid dreams, that is far from our only objective here. You want to learn how to ensure that the results of the experiments and lucid dream plans you enact are trustworthy. You also want to learn how to align your actions in the lucid space with your evolving belief systems and spiritual evolution. In this chapter, we will cover some lucid finesse points specific to you, the dream sorcerer and lucid occultist.

Releasing Control

In order to be able to trust the results of your lucid experiments, one thing that needs to be discussed in more depth is the idea of being able to release control over the dream scene. Many people prize lucid dreaming because they enjoy the powerful feeling of being able to control the dream. I want to make it abundantly clear that often that is not at all what we are trying to do as magicians practicing magickal experiments within the dreamtime. It is, in fact, usually the exact opposite.

We do want to have control over our clarity of conscious awareness and how well we are anchored into the dream, but that is all. If you think deeply about it, what good would magickal experimentation be if we were just carefully orchestrating the results according to our expectations? That would be like doing a tarot card reading where instead of shuffling and seeing what organically comes up, you asked your divinatory question and then purposely went through the deck and handpicked the cards that show your personal favorite outcome. That is not magick; that is more akin to a self-soothing of the ego.

This is not to say that there aren't times when controlling the dream is an important magickal technique. As an example, in one instance when I became fully lucid, I was simply practicing envisioning bugs crawling up from within the ground of the dream and allowing them to crawl on me. Hundreds of little white bugs indeed appeared and prickled as they crawled up my legs. I imagined what it would be like if black worms were to start coming up as well and allowed them to swarm me too. Normally in ordinary reality I would be jumpy and quite grossed out if this type of thing were to happen, but the lucid state was an amazing place to practice calmly experiencing such an encounter without the need for fear.

If you use your imagination, you can probably come up with numerous ideas for ways a controlled environment would be useful for rehearsing skills you'd like to improve in physical life or for creating custom situations for overcoming fears as in the previous example. Even though these ways of controlling the dream are satisfying and useful, they are not always aligned with the work of the magician. To use the lucid state to master divination, magickal experiments, spirit summoning, and enhancing spiritual relationships, an honest release of control will be essential.

Psychic Skills

As an occultist, you probably already realize that there is the need to release control during waking psychically oriented activities as well. You must hone your waking psychic skills and mind-clearing techniques so they can also be applied with integrity during lucid magick. To use the lucid dream space effectively for magickal practice, talking with spirits, and the like, requires the practitioner to have some already well-developed psychic skills in place. This is not to say that you need to have extraordinary psychic talent because you don't. You just need to have good divination hygiene.

For example, when you do an awake meditation that is aimed at retrieving psychic or intuitive information, it is very important to be able to learn to grab the real psychic impulses that come through, filtering them out from the flow of your logical thinking, without feeling at all like you have created them yourself. It's important to be able to ask a question and then clear the slate of your mind and simply watch and wait to see what arises without inserting your will or your preconceived notions into the mix. You can practice using the exercise that follows. It takes a good length of time and repeated practice before the average practitioner really starts to feel confident in this process, but once they do, their divination skills usually seem to truly take off. A parallel type of process is necessary when using the lucid dream space for any kind of magick, spirit work, or divination.

Using these skills in a lucid dream, you first will want to anchor yourself and then clearly state your lucid dream plan, divination question, or perform the magickal act that you had intended. Next, purposely clear the slate of your mind and allow whatever naturally happens because of your actions or your request to happen on its own. Watch it happen, don't make it happen.

If you routinely orchestrate lucid dream plans and the results are always exactly what you expected them to be like, you may be inserting yourself and creating the results rather than letting them be true psychic findings. If this is so, then I urge you to take an honest look at your process and your mindset during that execution. The skills of releasing expectation can easily be practiced in the waking state. A simple way to do this is to practice divining for magickally significant images.

ARCANUM
Basic Image Divination Practice

· · ● ○ ● · ·

This exercise serves to help you develop the skill of posing a psychic question and learning to bring the mind to a blank, clear state where the response happens as a spontaneous impulse. If you practice this often, you will be able to use your confident mastery in this approach to create more effective psychic work both in waking and in lucid dreaming.

1. Close your eyes and bring your attention to the third eye, the Witch's eye, the mind's eye.

2. Next, state whatever is on your mind—maybe something such as "Show me a clue to the next step in my career process," or "Show me something about my relationship to the goddess Brigid." This can be anything you would ask in any normal divination process.

3. After clearly stating your request, take a deep breath, and on the exhale, imagine the slate of your Witch's eye being wiped completely clean.

4. Keep your attention on the quiet darkness of that blank slate until something spontaneously arises there.

5. Accept that image as the initial answer that you should be considering in response to your question. Be sure to accept it even if it seems to make no sense to you, or even if it seems to have a vibe that is opposite of what you would expect or want it to be. You don't need to be able to instantly figure out what it means, but you do need to be able to let go of expectation and the logical mind, accepting whatever happens.

6. Journal the question and the resulting response without the need for interpretation.

Keep in mind that if you are not an especially psychically visual person, you can still perform an effective variation of this exercise. You would still ask your question and clear your mind, but instead of specifically waiting for an image, you can rest in blank stillness until any impulse at all arises. This could be an emotion, a sensation in the body, a message being heard, or a knowing in the mind. Similarly, you would strive to simply accept whatever happens in response to your question as the initial answer, without the need to interpret it.

Ethics and Consent

A lot of years elapsed in which I was enjoying freeform exploration of the lucid dream realms, exercising my immense freedom to do magick there and trying anything I felt compelled to experience. It took me some time to learn to reconcile my waking principles of ethics with my evolving beliefs about the nature of dreams. By considering the following points, I hope you will benefit from the lessons I learned so that you can make consistently solid ethical lucid dream behavior choices from the start.

Lucid Sexual Encounters

Some of the things that many lucid dreamers enjoy most are sexual encounters. Sexual experiences in the lucid dream body are often much smoother, crisper, and more enjoyable than they are on the physical plane. Because of this, it can be an immense temptation to walk up to the first dream character you see upon becoming lucid and initiate a sexual encounter with them.

Whether you personally view dream characters as being separate spirits with agency or as being parts of your own psyche, wouldn't you want even your own internal sexual experiences to be consensual, so that you are treating yourself with respect? You likely wouldn't want any part of your subconscious to feel taken advantage of in any way. In addition to this thought, I started to wonder if some of these realities, which are dreams for me, could be the ordinary or main reality for any of these dream characters. In this case, I certainly can't just walk up to someone and start touching them sexually no matter how alluring this may seem, even though I know I'm dreaming.

Treat Lucidity as Real, not "Just a Dream"

It's so very easy to forget to be aware of this ethical viewpoint at first when you realize you are dreaming, because you may write the experience off as "just a dream," so you feel as though you can do whatever you want. This mindset comes about, in part, from the way our modern society has treated dreams—as flights of fancy that are not real. This oversight is hypocritical as a magician and spiritual seeker, as your lucid experiences will continue to reiterate the truth that these experiences are real beyond any doubt. They are conscious and intelligent experiences just as the nature of the universe is conscious and intelligent.

The experienced lucid dreamer realizes that this state of being is at least as real as anything that can be experienced in physical reality and is considered by mystics of many cultures and ages to be the optimal setting for the purposeful acceleration of spiritual development. If we accept this potential truth, then we need to respect the possible nature of any reality and the implications of our actions upon its residents. This means that any manipulative magick, violence, sex, disrespect, or nonconsensual activities of any kind may be perceived as completely real and potentially traumatic by other dream beings.

Put Yourself in the Dream Character's Shoes

This line of thinking should be extended to any acts that could be perceived as violent or having a significant or potentially harmful impact on the dream reality or its characters. One approach that seems to work well in finding a good barometer for ethical decisions is to turn the situation around and place yourself in the role of the dream character in question. How would I feel if someone—maybe someone I perceived as a spirit or a Witch—appeared in my room out of the blue? How would I want that interaction to go, even if I made the mistake of misinterpreting who they were? How would I feel if a random stranger approached me and performed magick upon me without asking?

We don't always know if dream characters are parts of our own subconscious, if they are other living beings having dreams, if they are beings from other realities, or if they are spiritual entities. It is likely that every one of these is a possible truth that can be encountered in lucid dreaming at various times. You must create your own personal guidelines for ethics in the other realities and ensure that your chosen actions are aligned not only with the magick you wish to create but also with your personal aspirations for spiritual development and wisdom seeking.

It is my belief that you can only gain wisdom and enlightenment from a lucid dreaming practice equivalent to the amount of reverence and value that you place upon it. Like all else in magick, your relationship with the lucid dreamtime should be treated as a respectful energetic exchange.

ARCANUM
Dream Journal Writing Prompt

· · ● ○ ● · ·

Your growing beliefs about the nature of dreams will have a direct effect on how you feel you should conduct yourself ethically in lucid dreams. Your dream journal need not only be used to document actual dream material and the setting of dream intentions and divinations. It is also a wonderful place to record developments in your own philosophies and depths of understanding regarding the nature of dreams in general.

Take a moment to open your dream journal to a fresh page. Write the date and the title "Today's Outlook on Dreaming." Then take 5 to 10 minutes to write your spontaneous responses to the following questions:

+ What kinds of realities do you seem to be visiting in your dreams?

+ What trends in dream categories or dream types seem to be present in your dreams?

+ Name something you've done in a dream that improves your outlook on or understanding of magick.

Consider revisiting this writing prompt again after finishing reading this book, and possibly at six-month to one-year intervals following that to witness the evolution of your thoughts and the richness of your practice.

The Distillation

In this chapter, we covered some key concepts that are specific to you as a magickal lucid dreamer. We discussed the benefits of learning not to try to control the dream while lucid so that your magickal experiments are natural and not contrived. We also talked about honing your waking skills in psychic impulse retrieval and mind clearing so that these same skills will be accessible to you in your lucid divinations. Lastly, we discussed some ethical considerations that are specific to the beliefs of occultism and that need to be addressed in order to be in right relationship to your own spiritual development as you access the lucid dream space.

It is time now to move on from the alchemical salt to the mysterious mercury. All of part 1 has been about ensuring that your lucid dream understanding is solid and that you have brought the necessary support practices into your waking physical life. With this base in place, we can proceed into the details of the depth of sorcery, spiritual growth, and the explorations of the mysteries that you can truly experience within your lucid practice.

Part Two

THE MERCURY– SORCERY WITHIN THE LUCID DREAM

This next section of the book is here to inspire and motivate your very spirit. The following chapters give a sampling of what types of sorcery are possible to execute as lucid dream plans. As you read about some of the magickal acts for which the lucid dream state is particularly suited, make notes on the types of things that you, personally, feel drawn to trying to accomplish. The descriptions provided are not solely intended as inspiration for what you might like to experience yourself. They are also provided so that you can consider some of the direct and amazing benefits that follow the magician from lucidity into the magick of waking life after certain lucid magick experiences.

Remember that while this section of the book does cover things you would do as your practice advances, it is necessary that you understand at this stage what types of things are possible. This will help you continue to improve at formulating and executing your own lucid dream plans and create the necessary motivation for working some of the magick of part 3. This section, the Mercury, reveals the fluidity and potential within your ever-evolving lucid spirit.

FLYING

Flying in lucid dreaming is wonderful fun, though it is not necessarily an action that directly impacts your magickal or spiritual development. It can impact it indirectly, however. It can be tempting to start flying every time you become lucid simply because it can feel so amazing, and it's something we don't get to do in ordinary reality in the literal sense.

Why Do It?

Even though you don't want to waste numerous ongoing lucid dreaming opportunities on flying necessarily, it is certainly worthwhile to get some experience with it. Flying is a classically beloved lucid dream activity in general, so if you haven't done it much, it is simply worth doing to help you understand more about the reality of dreams, lucidity, and what all the hype is about.

Lucid Flying Can Improve Skill in Waking Journey Work

You may think that there is no practical application to be carried over to physical reality from the experience of lucid dream flying. When you have gotten the feel of what it truly is like to fly over different landscapes, this can result in building skills that you can use to enhance your ability to fly in awake shamanic-style journey work. This is quite an invaluable ability to have.

Journey work takes practice and focus, and it isn't always easy for every magickal practitioner to confidently visualize the process of traveling around in non-ordinary reality. When you have a clear and awake memory of what it really feels like to fly, it becomes easier to recall these sensations and use this skill in visualizations that often come up in journeys or guided meditations.

Learning to Release Fear

The experience of flying can also help you to embody the fearless confidence building that can come from lucid dreaming. The awe of the dreamtime combined with the lucid knowledge that you can't harm your physical body through the actions at hand allow you to learn to move around in the dream realms with any supernatural movement you can think of. In doing this, you are gaining experiences that allow you to integrate the truth that you are a spirit yourself. This helps you to understand the nature of other spirits with whom you wish to communicate or learn from as a magician. More importantly, realizing you are a spirit means acknowledging that you exist beyond this life, helping release fear of death.

Learning to Change Locations without Losing Lucidity

Often when you suddenly find yourself lucid in a dream, you may not be in a location that you find suitable for the lucid dream plan that you have in mind. It can be extremely useful then to be able to move yourself to an open space quickly, with as little time wasted as possible. You could instead opt to mentally change the construct of the scene, try exploring and walking to another location or simply enact the lucid dream plan within the too-cramped space. With these options you run the risk of these efforts using up all the time you may have or causing you to lose your anchoring.

If you do call out a lucid dream plan in a cramped dream space, the surroundings can confuse or alter the way in which the lucid dream plan experiment may have been able to naturally unfold in the right space. Therefore, having the confidence and experience to be able to fly easily from one spot to another without getting too distracted by it can be a great skill to have, so it's worth doing it purposely at least a couple of times so you can get the hang of it.

Learning That Dream Realms Have Variance in Atmospheric Properties

The other interesting thing that happens with flying experiments is that you can come to realize that flying doesn't necessarily work the same way in every dream realm in which you might find yourself. In many of the dreams in which I have flown, I have been able to sort of rocket-launch myself right up and fly in a simple, soaring, superhero sort of fashion. Every now and again though, the effort required to fly seems much more difficult, despite having attained full lucidity. In these instances, I might have to do a vigorous swimming sort of motion, using much more physical effort to move through the air, or I might only be able to do a short levitation sort of float to get from one place to another. In some dream scenarios, attempts to float, levitate, or fly may not even work at all.

In any case, what I find useful and interesting about these findings is the idea that not all dream realms are necessarily alike. What I mean is that they don't all function the same or have the same set of physics, rules, or density. I've come to think of it with respect to our physics here on physical Earth—we know what we can generally do, what our gravity is like, and what the density of objects is like here.

I believe that in dreaming we can travel in and out of all different types of nonphysical realities, though they seem to have their own unique sets of physical-feeling experiences. Realizing that flying can work completely differently from one dream reality to the next can help you to learn firsthand some of this complexity about the nature of the dream realms themselves. It helps to cement the personal truth that we are moving between loads of different types of realities in our dream exploits and create an understanding of the idea of a multiverse.

Failing Is Also a Learning Experience

Some authors have postulated that a failure to be able to fly in some lucid attempts is due to personal doubt or having lost a degree of lucidity. I have practiced crystallizing my awareness of the dream after failed attempts to fly and reasserting my confidence in my lucidity and the goal and still found that it can be a struggle unless I ask to be transported to a different reality.

Understanding the nature of dreams only comes from truths you can accept personally because of your own firsthand experiences, not just from reading about them. If you learn on your own that not all dream realms work in the same way despite being fully lucid, it can help you come to your own conclusion about dreams being actual alternative realities that we are able to explore, as opposed to just the mental constructs of our own personal minds.

As an occultist, your confidence in such a personal truth creates more solid philosophical foundations upon which deeper magickal exploits may be based. Variations in flying ability that we may deem to be a product of the varying physical densities of different realities also help us to put our waking physical reality into perspective as just one of these many possible dream realities.

Implementing Flying as a Lucid Dream Plan

To execute the lucid dream plan of practicing flying, you don't necessarily need to shout your intended plan to the dream world the way that you might need to with certain other plans that are more divinatory or exploratory in nature. In the case of flying, simply start by trying to boost yourself up into the air to see if you are able to soar around. If this doesn't seem to work, see if you can swim your arms breast-stroke style and get yourself moving in the air that way. If this also doesn't work, see if you can gently levitate up and float around. You can also try adding a confidently worded command such as "I am able to fly!" if you think it might help.

If none of that works, then you can at least usually get some extraordinarily high, bounding jumps going, which can also be a great way of traveling quickly to another spot. This is still useful and indeed very fun to do.

Causing Other Dream Characters to Fly

Sometimes your actions in lucidity may impose flying upon a dream character other than yourself in a useful way. For example, in one bout of wake-induced lucidity, as the dream scene formed, the figure of a recognizable television personality appeared on top of me, as if to force himself upon me sexually. Since I was lucid, I wasn't worried about it. I took the time to carefully lift my dream hands to inspect them and help the dream to stabilize.

Once I had done that, without thinking, I did a flick of my wrist in a dismissive motion that you would use as if you were brushing something off and shouted "Fly!"

The immediate result was that the inappropriately behaving man went hurtling off into the distant recesses of the dream space, spinning head over heels out of his own control. This freed up my dream body and my own space to continue forth into the dream without him impeding my agenda. Later, upon waking, I made note of the "wrist flick and fly" technique as something that could easily be used in the moment in dream or waking realities upon encountering a negative energy, even more quickly and flippantly than constructing a banishing pentagram, for example.

Another interesting thing with respect to other dream beings and flying is that it can serve as a means of learning about the very nature of the beings around you. When you become lucid and realize that you can fly, asking characters around you if they can join you in flight is a fun experiment. Quite often they will look at you in awe and confusion and not show any indication that they could consider flying. Occasionally, a happy dream character will confidently join you. These wildly varying responses have caused me to question whether the beings who could fly are also people who, like me, are currently aware that they are dreaming.

Lucid Versus Non-Lucid Flying Dreams

Many folks have spontaneous, non-lucid dreams of flying. These have value as well, for you may wake up with the recall of the invigorating and fearless empowerment of the experience, and it becomes obvious that this is a dream memory to be cherished. If you can remember how the sensations of flying felt in a night dream, then this, too, can help with the journey work skill set described previously. The differences between lucid and non-lucid flying benefits lie in the magician's ability to decide consciously in the moment what they might like to learn from a particular episode of flying.

When lucid, you can decide if you want to practice different methods to test out the relative density of the reality you are in. You can decide if you'd like to practice trying to land on different surfaces to see if you can do so and remain anchored within your dream body. When lucid, the sensations also seem to feel crisper and more intense than the sensations recalled from non-lucid flying, making them easier to remember and recall in future imaginal states.

The Distillation

After reading this chapter, you should be able to decide whether or not you'd like to spend a lucid experience or two on experiments related to flying. You now know that lucid flying can carry over to the visualization skills needed to fly in waking journey work, and that lucid flying experiences help you to release fears of bodily harm in dreams because you are experiencing yourself as a spirit. Your lucid flying practice can help you understand how to be better at moving to other locations within the dream that suit your plans without losing your grasp on the dream and waking prematurely.

In this chapter, we also discussed some ways that engaging flying with other beings in the dream can be useful or revelatory. We compared some of the parallel benefits to flying in non-lucid dreams as well. Now that we have covered all of this, let's get ready to practice some more advanced lucid magick in the next chapter.

CEREMONIAL MAGICK
TECHNIQUES

Performing acts of sorcery in lucid dreams has immense potential to help you hasten the development of your magickal skill level. In some cases, acts of lucid magick can also have direct energetic effects upon you or some circumstances of your life. In this chapter, we will talk about some commonly known ceremonial ritual acts, such as energetically signing pentagrams, the Qabalistic Cross, and the Lesser Banishing Ritual of the Pentagram. We will be reviewing instructions for performing these actions and discuss the possible benefits to you of carrying them out.

Signing Pentagrams

For any classically trained magician, one of the first ceremonial actions learned is the signing of the invoking and banishing pentagrams. This generally involves learning to draw a star in the air along a particular pattern with your hand or with a ritual casting tool. The star is drawn in a certain way to denote whether it is for cleansing or attracting, and there are even varying directions for drawing the pentagrams for invoking and banishing that differ depending on which primary element is being used to do the work. To get a feel for this, refer to Figure 1.

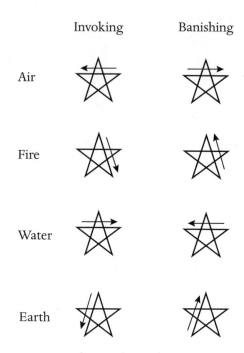

	Invoking	Banishing
Air		
Fire		
Water		
Earth		

Figure 1: Invoking and Banishing Pentagrams

While tracing the proper star in the air, energy is projected out of your arm as you envision the energetic tracings of the design hanging there in the air before you so that they can influence your environment. Since we live in the dense physical reality in which we do, we can't always visually see the energy or its direct action, but rather we must envision the star as well as the actions of banishing or invoking happening in our mind's eye and try to feel their effects with our subtle clairsentience.

If you practice simple ritual actions such as this within a lucid dream, however, you may get to see and feel the visual energetic results of the efforts since you are in a dream reality that may not be beholden to the same rules of physics that we have here.

Signing a Pentagram as a Lucid Dream Plan

At a time when you become lucid and your current lucid dream plan is to practice signing pentagrams, ensure that you are anchored in the dream with your feet solidly on the dream ground. Use your dominant, or casting, hand with your index and middle finger out and the others tucked in as you would in waking. Project energy out of your arm while motioning the shape of the elemental pentagram of your choice into the air before you. You may accompany the energetic signing with a proclamation of your efforts if you wish, such as "I cast the invoking pentagram of air!" Once you have energetically drawn the shape, wait and watch to see what effects are wrought upon the dream scene from this act.

Creating a Neural Groove, or Dream Muscle Memory

This type of lucid experimental rehearsal is helping you to do what I call "creating a neural groove." It's like muscle memory but for subtle energetic sorcerous effects. You are carving out a deeper learned familiarity with the subtle experiences of magickal acts. The forgiving classroom setting that is lucid dreaming allows you to have a crisp and tangible experience without having to imagine what is happening—it actually happens there, unimpeded by the physics of a dense material reality. Then, when you go to replicate the signing of a pentagram in ordinary reality, your preconceived understanding of what it should feel like increases your ability to cast it with confidence, despite our physics limiting the visual effects of the magick.

Results of a Pentagram Rehearsal

In one experience where I became lucid while dreaming, I found that a creepy stone angel statue was moving toward me in a way that felt sinister. I wasn't scared, of course, because I had already had the revelation that I was dreaming. As it continued to approach, I kept my wits, stayed anchored, and decided to try out a simple banishing pentagram signing upon the being to see what would happen. I raised my right arm, which is my usual casting hand in ordinary reality, and with my hand in a traditional benediction gesture, motioned a banishing pentagram of air into the space between myself and the nefarious moving statue.

I didn't really see the whole shape of the pentagram hang in the air, as I had thought I might. Instead, I saw the air sort of just shimmer and ripple where I had drawn the star. The clear ripple (sort of how heat waves look as they radiate up from hot pavement) began to naturally flow toward the statue. It then appeared as if the stone creature began to be pushed by this invisible energetic force away from me steadily, and off into the distance.

It was quite satisfying to see the results of the magickal force of the pentagram being enacted upon this dream character firsthand. The experience also served to give me confidence in the energy that lies behind the signing of my pentagrams. I am now able to better envision the shape of a star as I cast it and the changing clear ripple of the atmospheric energy that contains the dynamic action of the gesture.

Ideas for Pentagram Lucid Dream Plans
Various experiments could involve trying to sign the differing elemental pentagrams in the corresponding elemental energetic colors of your tradition to see the unique effects they have upon the landscape of the dream. Try both banishing and invoking pentagrams under different sets of lucid circumstances and be sure to keep detailed written records of your results. You can then use this knowledge to improve your awake usage of these ceremonial magick actions.

ARCANUM

Practicing Pentagrams in
Preparation for Lucid Usage

·   ·   ●   ○   ●   ·   ·

To be ready for your lucid pentagram experiments, make sure that you already have the confident and accurate ability to smoothly perform the pentagrams of your choice at a moment's notice. It is worthwhile to practice ahead of time, and this is never wasted time even if you already have familiarity with the elemental pentagrams. As a magician, you can always improve the depth of connection between your ritual actions and the intensity level of the energetic effect that then occurs.

Refer to Figure 1 to learn the differences in the direction of the pentagram when drawn for each element if you don't already have these differences in detail memorized. Practice the following banishing pentagram of air exercise for starters.

1. Stand tall with your feet solidly beneath you, shoulder-width apart. When practicing, you may face east just to reinforce the correspondence between the direction of the east and the element of air in Western magick, even though compass directions may be completely irrelevant in many dream realms.

2. Lift your casting arm parallel to the ground and bend in your thumb, pinky, and ring fingers so that it your pointer and middle fingers are extended together. These two fingers will serve as your casting tool. This is often referred to as benediction pose. You could also practice this with a physical casting tool, such as a wand or an athame, but it is worthwhile to practice feeling the energy as it comes directly from your hand. Also, you want to re-create the action as closely as possible to the way you want to practice it in the dream, and you may not want to waste valuable time summoning a wand when you become lucid.

3. Take a deep breath in and imagine shimmering yellow energy flowing down into your crown and into your heart center. Feel the yellow energy traveling from there out through your casting arm and allow it to flow from your fingertips. You can envision a different energy color if you wish. Yellow is the color associated with air in American Witchcraft and much of Western magick, but do what will benefit you most in the magick of your tradition or practice.

4. Trace a banishing pentagram of air in the space in front of you with the hand that is held in benediction pose. Make the pentagram clear and large, as wide as your shoulders and as tall as the distance between your waist and the top of your head. Do your best to envision the energy trail coming from your fingers and causing a

shimmering yellow construct that hangs in the air in front of you in the pentagram shape.

5. When you have imagined it clearly, lower your arm and try to sense any effect your technique has had upon you or the atmosphere around you. This will prepare you to do the same type of curious information gathering regarding resulting effects once you get to perform this in lucid dreaming.

After gaining familiarity with this exercise, you can repeat this process using the banishing pentagram of fire to the south while envisioning red energy, water to the west while envisioning blue energy, and earth to the north while envisioning green energy. You can then go back to the element of air and practice making the invoking pentagram of air in yellow, invoking pentagram of fire in red, invoking pentagram of water in blue, and the invoking pentagram of earth in green.

Make sure to document for yourself in writing the differences in sensations and emotions created by each of these separate actions. Once you feel familiar with this exercise, you are ready to conduct detailed pentagram experiments in lucidity to deepen the relationship of your auric field and your inner knowing to this magickal skill.

Qabalistic Cross

Many magicians will likely also be familiar, at least in concept if not in practice, with the idea of the Qabalistic Cross. This is a very well-known portion of the famous Lesser Banishing Ritual of the Pentagram (LBRP), a basic ritual procedure from the tradition of the Hermetic Order of the Golden Dawn. The LBRP is discussed later in this chapter in more detail. The overall purpose of the ritual actions of the LBRP are for cleansing and setting up sacred space and are taught to many would-be ceremonial magicians.

The Qabalistic Cross is the first section of the LBRP but can be done on its own as a personal centering and energy-balancing exercise. It is the part of the LBRP that has a more internal effect upon the magician, where the other components have more outward effects upon the ritual environment. It involves intoning some sacred Hebrew phrases in sequence while touching spots on the body in a cross formation: head, down to sternum, then right shoulder, over to left shoulder to complete the cross shape, then hands back over the heart to finish.[16]

ARCANUM
Practicing the Qabalistic Cross

· · ● ○ ● · ·

Try practicing the following instructions for the Qabalistic Cross. It takes at least a few trial runs before you start to get the knack of coordinating the gestures with the words. The meanings of the Hebrew words of this act are given in parentheses, but they are not spoken. Voice only the words given in all capital letters, and say them as a vibration, or intonation. This means that you would take a deep breath and then powerfully hold out the sounds of the word for the entire length of your exhale, allowing the sound to vibrate through your body and energy field.

1. Stand tall, your feet hip-width apart and firmly planted on the ground.

2. With your dominant hand in benediction pose, touch the forehead and vibrate ATEH (*thou art*).

3. Touch the sternum over your heart center and vibrate MALKUTH (*the Kingdom*).

4. Touch the right shoulder and vibrate VE-GEBURAH (*and the Power*).

5. Touch the left shoulder and vibrate VE-GEDULAH (*and the Glory*).

6. Clasp the hands over the heart and vibrate LE-OLAM (*forever*) AMEN.

16. Lon Milo Duquette and David Shoemaker, *Llewellyn's Complete Book of Ceremonial Magick* (Llewellyn Publications, 2020), 297.

After having completed this, stand firmly in your spot, quietly pausing to sense how you feel. Performing the Qabalistic Cross is an intentional act of establishing the pillars of the Tree of Life within oneself and can have some profound effects upon you. Be sure to document anything you notice and include the entry in your dream journal if the performance of the Qabalistic Cross is an upcoming lucid dream plan you may have. In this way, you can learn by comparing the waking and lucid dreaming results of this magick.

Results of a Lucid Qabalistic Cross Rehearsal

In one lucid dream experience, when I became fully aware that I was dreaming, I decided to perform the Qabalistic Cross as my lucid dream plan. I aimed to see if there were any energetic effects amplified in the dreamtime that would help me to better understand and feel how it ideally should be so that I could increase my ability to replicate its effectiveness in ordinary reality. I vibrated the words while touching the proper spots, and I did indeed experience a column of white light descending downward from above my crown and moving fully down through me to the ground as a cylinder of purity existing in myself. It did not form an actual cross shape of energy as I had postulated, though I was at no point standing with my arms fully outstretched in the "t" position. Maybe doing this would have changed the direction of movement of that white light somewhat.

The effect of the Qabalistic Cross was quite peaceful, though I would not describe it as particularly intense, unlike some of the magickal experiences you will see me describe in the coming pages. Having had this experience, I learned that, for me, the Qabalistic Cross is a great technique to involve in routine day-opening practices but not one I would choose where a particularly exaggerated energetic effect is needed. It felt centering and purifying internally, though not extremely empowering or invigorating. Perhaps this is exactly what it is meant to do! These results may or may not ring true for you, personally, but it would be a good point of discernment for you to make for yourself as you assess your own results.

Lesser Banishing Ritual of the Pentagram

The well-known ritual called the Lesser Banishing Ritual of the Pentagram (LBRP) involves beginning and ending with the Qabalistic Cross as described, but also includes the integration of banishing pentagrams energetically signed to each quarter, accompanied by the intonations of certain Hebrew names for God. The names of the archangels of the cardinal directions are also activated to help bless the space.

While the Qabalistic Cross can be used alone as previously described, when combined with the fuller actions of the complete LBRP, it is used to extend the energetic effects outward from the self. Now the magician, centered and stabilized within the energies of the Tree of Life, emanates and calls upon divine energies to the quarters so that the cleansing and hallowing effects encompass the entire ritual space. This ritual is commonly used as a foundational way to set the space on its own but is also used as the first step preceding other ritual actions.

ARCANUM
Practicing the LBRP

· • ● ○ ● • ·

To practice the Lesser Banishing Ritual of the Pentagram prior to executing it in a lucid dream, walk yourself through the following instructions. In waking ceremonial magick, this ritual is meant to begin facing east, and then orients to each of the quarters for certain actions. Again, there may be no meaningful compass directions within your lucid dream space, so when you get to the point of conducting this there, simply rotate your body clockwise ninety degrees each time you would be turning to face the next direction. When waking, however, make an attempt to orient yourself to the compass directions as indicated.

1. Stand tall, your feet hip-width apart and firmly planted on the ground.

2. With your dominant hand in benediction pose, touch the forehead and vibrate ATEH (*thou art*).

3. Touching the sternum over the heart space, vibrate MALKUTH (*the Kingdom*).

4. Touching the right shoulder, vibrate VE-GEBURAH (*and the Power*).

5. Touching the left shoulder, vibrate VE-GEDULAH (*and the Glory*).

6. Clasping the hands upon the breast, vibrate LE-OLAHM (*forever*), AMEN.

7. Turning to the east, make a banishing pentagram (that of earth). Vibrate IHVH (pronounced: Ye-ho-wau).

8. Turning to the south, the same, but vibrate ADNI (pronounced: Adonai).

9. Turning to the west, the same, but vibrate AHIH (pronounced: Eheieh).

10. Turning to the north, the same, but vibrate AGLA (pronounced: Agla).

11. Return to face east and extend the arms in the form of a cross.

12. While vibrating the angels' names, say, "Before me RAPHAEL; Behind me GABRIEL; On my right hand MICHAEL; On my left hand AURIEL; For about me flames the Pentagram, And in the Column stands the six-rayed Star."

13. Repeat steps 1 to 6, to close with the Qabalistic Cross.

When you have enacted all of these words and actions, pause quietly and make note of any feelings, knowings, or subtle energy sensations you can perceive. Document them so that you can compare your results to future outcomes witnessed by performing this ritual in a lucid dream.

Benefits of the Lucid LBRP

Whether you are new to this ritual or you have been accustomed to using it for some time, it could be extremely beneficial for you to execute it within the space of lucid dreaming. You will have the chance to experience and possibly even see the energetic effects that take place within you as well as those extending through the atmosphere around you. This is important so you can understand if the effects of the banishing pentagrams and divine names at the quarters produce a gentle cleansing or a strong wiping of the space to a clean slate or even an onslaught of spiritual energy. Seeing and feeling it firsthand and knowing what your real influence is will help you decide more accurately when it is the appropriate waking ritual to choose according to what your imminent goal may be in the moment.

Another possible benefit of conducting this ritual while lucid could be related to the development of your relationships to the archangels of the quarters. It is possible that when you vibrate the angel names, you may actually witness these beings showing up upon your direction. This could be a humbling and life-changing experience, or the angels may show up just looking like an average Joe. Either way, you will be learning something amazing about this ritual. On the other hand, when you vibrate the angel names, it may simply produce an energetic effect in each of the quarters. Alternatively, you may even see a representative from among their legions arrive to stand for them in lieu of the angels themselves.

There are many magicians and Witches who are now using various modified versions of the LBRP. When a ritual like this has stood the test of time and been made available to the public, it is only natural that its structure has then served as a source of inspiration for customization. This growing and diverse use of the ritual creates a powerful and dynamic group consciousness that exists around it. When you use it, you are tapping into an already existing well of power.

Customization of the LBRP

Many practitioners, like me, use versions of this practice that call upon polytheistic deities and their energies instead of using the original angelic and Qabalistic techniques. One lovely example of this exists in John Michael

Greer's Welsh druidic version of the LBRP.[17] Another that has been created specifically for use with the ancient Irish goddess the Morrigan is described in Stephanie Woodfield's *Priestess of the Morrigan*.[18] While it would be interesting and beneficial for you to execute the original ritual in the lucid space to enhance your general knowledge as a magician, it is always worthwhile to practice the actual ritual methods you use most in your practice within the lucid dream as well. Your memory of how it felt to do so will increase that energetic muscle memory and increase your effectiveness when you then return to using the ritual while awake in ordinary reality.

The Distillation

In this chapter, you have been given instructions for some classical ceremonial magick actions to prepare you for practicing them in lucid dreams. We have discussed the concept of laying down a groove, or deepening familiarity with the subtle energetics of ritual actions, and how this can be done in lucidity in an unimpeded way. You should be beginning to understand that there is a catalyzing of one's magickal skill level that can happen by practicing magick in a setting where the density of the physics of material existence does not inhibit the results. We will be proceeding forth now to extend these concepts to the magick of entire magickal alphabets and other occult symbols.

17. John Michael Greer, *The Celtic Golden Dawn: An Original and Complete Curriculum of Druidical Study* (Llewellyn Publications, 2013), 31–34.
18. Stephanie Woodfield, *Priestess of the Morrigan: Prayers, Rituals, and Devotional Work to the Great Queen* (Llewellyn Publications, 2021), 141–147.

THE SORCERY OF MAGICKAL ALPHABETS AND SYMBOLS

In general, a symbol is a powerful connector to the energetic vibrations for which it stands, and so any means of activating that symbol can bring the consciousness of that symbol's stream of energy flow into yourself, your atmosphere, or a magickal working. Having mastery over the sorcerous usage of symbols can provide you with a thorough toolbox of options for creating all manner of magickal effects.

Symbols, whether we are talking about alchemical, astrological, alphabetic, or otherwise, hold great power through the group consciousness created by the shared understanding of their meaning. One immense benefit of alphabetic or other small, simple, or easily drawn symbols is that they are useful on the fly as a means of quick magick. Individual symbols that are signed, intoned, or gestured allow you to create your choice of internal shifts or external changes upon the atmosphere around you.

Norse Runic and Irish Ogham Alphabets

The Norse runes and the Irish Ogham are just two of many existing magickal alphabets containing symbols with which it is possible to deeply explore and augment your sorcerous usage through lucid dreaming. Examples of lucid dream plans involving the letters of these two alphabets are discussed here because these happen to be the two systems in which I have diligently trained.

As a devotee of guides and deities that hail primarily from the Irish and Norse pantheons, I have been naturally drawn to the magick of these alphabets. You may feel their pull as well, or you might end up taking the teachings here as examples and applying the concepts to other alphabetic systems that may better suit your personal practice.

I am extremely fond of mastering the sorcery of an entire alphabetic system because letters provide such diverse magickal options. Firstly, there is the basic fact that they are used to express language, and the familiarity with the letters of a language begins to help you understand the magick of its culture of origin. Then, there are the sound building blocks that letters represent that can be magickally intoned on their own or put together in customized vibrational combinations.

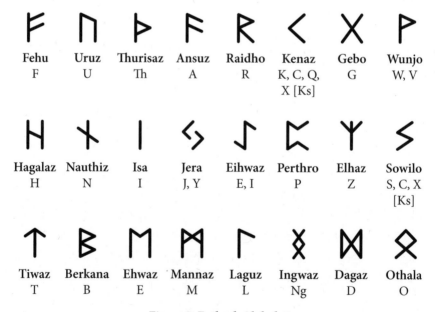

Fehu	Uruz	Thurisaz	Ansuz	Raidho	Kenaz	Gebo	Wunjo
F	U	Th	A	R	K, C, Q, X [Ks]	G	W, V

Hagalaz	Nauthiz	Isa	Jera	Eihwaz	Perthro	Elhaz	Sowilo
H	N	I	J, Y	E, I	P	Z	S, C, X [Ks]

Tiwaz	Berkana	Ehwaz	Mannaz	Laguz	Ingwaz	Dagaz	Othala
T	B	E	M	L	Ng	D	O

Figure 2: Futhark Alphabet

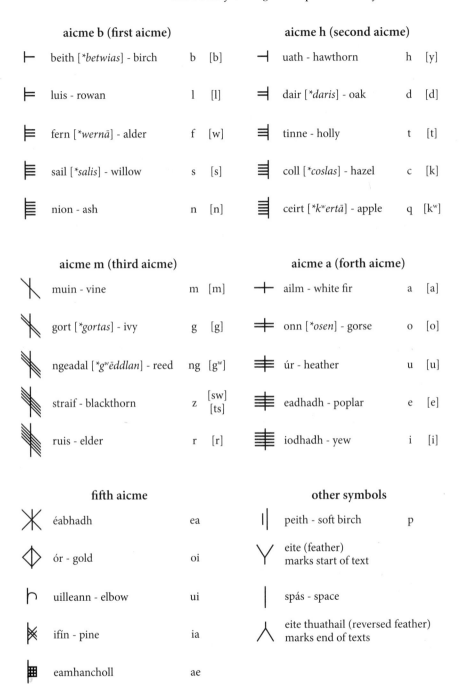

aicme b (first aicme)

⊢	beith [*betwias] - birch	b	[b]
⊨	luis - rowan	l	[l]
⊫	fern [*wernā] - alder	f	[w]
⊞	sail [*salis] - willow	s	[s]
⊟	nion - ash	n	[n]

aicme h (second aicme)

⊣	uath - hawthorn	h	[y]
⊐	dair [*daris] - oak	d	[d]
≡	tinne - holly	t	[t]
≣	coll [*coslas] - hazel	c	[k]
≣	ceirt [*kʷertā] - apple	q	[kʷ]

aicme m (third aicme)

⋏	muin - vine	m	[m]
	gort [*gortas] - ivy	g	[g]
	ngeadal [*gʷēddlan] - reed	ng	[gʷ]
	straif - blackthorn	z	[sw] [ts]
	ruis - elder	r	[r]

aicme a (forth aicme)

✛	ailm - white fir	a	[a]
	onn [*osen] - gorse	o	[o]
	úr - heather	u	[u]
	eadhadh - poplar	e	[e]
	iodhadh - yew	i	[i]

fifth aicme

✳	éabhadh	ea
◇	ór - gold	oi
ᚅ	uilleann - elbow	ui
⋈	ifín - pine	ia
▦	eamhancholl	ae

other symbols

‖	peith - soft birch	p
Y	eite (feather) marks start of text	
│	spás - space	
⋀	eite thuathail (reversed feather) marks end of texts	

Figure 3: Ogham Alphabet

Letters are easily transcribed into hand gestures that then allow you to use quick magick techniques in any situation in as subtle a manner as needed. Most importantly, each letter of a magickal alphabet has an assigned or associated meaning with energy that is brought forth just by the activation of the letter, whether this be vocal, by gesture, signing, carving, or writing.

The runes and the Ogham each contain a set of letters whose meanings are very complex, often with many layers of nuance and associated correspondences. It can take a while for a studious magician to master an alphabet as a system of sorcery, but lucid experimentation with magickal activation of such symbols can greatly help in cementing a personal relationship with the dynamic vibrations of each letter. Pictured in Figure 2 is the version of the runic alphabet I use, known as the Elder Futhark alphabet, and in Figure 3 is the Ogham alphabet.

Symbols Are Connectors

Whenever you activate a magickal letter symbol, you are tapping into the flow of its energy in the universe. If you gain firsthand experience as to what this energetic output looks like and feels like while lucid, you are then able to clearly picture this when you activate the symbols in ordinary reality, and your connection to that flow that exists in the universe will be much more effective.

I have heard other Witches say, "Where your mind goes, energy flows," and I believe this to be true. When you organically experience the result of activating a magickal symbol in lucid dreaming, you develop a memory of it and a familiarity with the action. Your ability to replicate that effect by having begun to forge a groove of resonance with the outcome is greatly enhanced.

When you conduct a magickal act in the moment or when you add the use of any symbol to a magickal working, you are looking to add that layer of sympathy to the energetic output of the spell. By using any of the technique examples discussed, you are activating your connection to a vibration with which you have a relationship. In addition to hand gestures, signing, vocal sound intonations, and carved and written depictions, you can even activate the magick of a letter simply by stating or chanting the letter name itself.

Hand Gestures

Hand gestures are some of the most useful forms of quick magick that an occultist can use. You don't have to have any magickal tools with you, yet you can generate energetic effects using hand gestures whether you are in a ritual space or acting on the fly. It does take practice for your energy body to learn to equate the hand gesture to the desired energetic effect, however. This is where lucid dream magick practice of this skill is extremely effective. When you practice a hand gesture while lucid and witness the resulting effect with such crisp clarity, it becomes easier later while waking for your mind to know what the magick should feel like and to then create the remembered effect to link to the gesture.

There are some different systems of established hand positions for the runes, and I use the ones taught by Edred Thorsson in his training guide *The Nine Doors of Midgard,* since I studied that system of runic sorcery.[19] A chart of these hand gestures for the Elder Futhark alphabet can be found in the appendix.

A Kenaz Lucid Experiment

When I found myself in a lucid dream and was at the point of being ready to explore more deeply the nature of the rune kenaz, I started off by simply verbally stating aloud in the dream scene, "I would like to experience the energy of the rune kenaz!"

Figure 4: Rune Kenaz

Remember that you can always simply ask to experience the energy of the magickal symbol in question first if you can't think of the best way to activate it in the moment of executing your lucid dream plan.

---

19. Edred Thorsson, *The Nine Doors of Midgard: A Curriculum of Rune-work* (The Rune Gild, 2016), 116–123.

In the Elder Futhark, kenaz is known as "the torch" and tends to be considered a rune of fire and illumination. This is, of course, putting it in extremely over-generalized terms for the sake of this conversation. Each rune has immense and dynamic depth to its energy, meaning, and powers, but I am simply mentioning the most well-known associations here so that you can compare what is generally accepted as the rune's vibration with the outcomes of the experiments I describe here.

In any case, after shouting out my request, I started to become infused with a very warm, tingly energy. It filled my body and lifted me up off the ground a bit so that I was hovering over the area. Managing to stay lucid, I decided to practice moving the kenaz energy with hand gestures.

Kenaz can actually be made using either a one-handed or a two-handed version of its shape. I first made the one-handed version as indicated in Figure 5, and a small but steady stream of orange and white energy flowed forth from my hand.

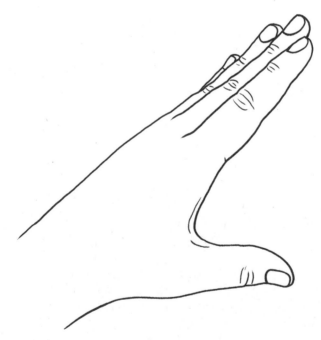

Figure 5: Hand Gesture for Kenaz

To compare, I then used both of my hands to make the shape of the rune, which looks like a "less-than" sign from mathematics. I opened my two hands forcefully from a closed position of being palm to palm, to opening into the kenaz form. Refer to Figure 6.

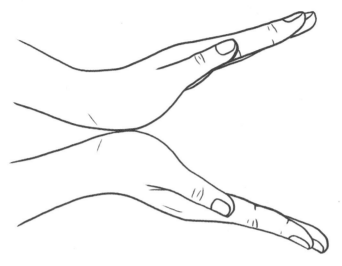

Figure 6: Two-Handed Gesture for Kenaz

This action produced one large but well-formed ball of the same orange and white energy that was released from the motion of creating this hand gesture. You can see that in the case of this runic experiment, the energy did seem to be warm and fiery as you might expect, yet the results were not ostentatious or overwhelmingly powerful.

If I'd had a preconceived notion of what it would feel like to shoot fire from my hands, this was not as dramatic as all that. I would have imagined shooting fire as something redder, hotter, and more aggressive.

Since this trial, I have found that using these hand gestures in magick even in ordinary reality where the element of fire is needed, especially in a dynamic or flowing way, has been extremely useful and effective. The direct benefit is that my memory of the experience allows me to visualize the type of energy created by my unique energy body when I do this action, making a more solid connection to its placement and flow even though it isn't noticeably visible when executed in physical reality.

If you gain experiences such as these for yourself, your instant magick (sorcery skills) will also be greatly enhanced. If you decide to try this same lucid experiment, you might find that your activation of this runic hand gesture creates a very similar effect to mine, or you might find that it is completely different. The point is that we all have different energetic constitutions, and so it is important for you to explore your own energetic relationship to the underlying vibratory effects of any given symbol.

Since you may not yet know how often you are likely to become lucid for the conducting of such magickal experiments, make sure to prioritize practicing the gestures you feel that you would be drawn to use frequently in your own practice. There is no need for you to feel you must work through an entire alphabet unless you feel called to do so. Having taken the time to do this myself, I have found that even though I had practiced with all the letters lucidly, there were many I never tended to activate while waking. You can make the most of your precious lucid time by choosing to work on practicing with the symbol gestures that call to you the most.

Signing

To "sign" a rune, or any other symbol for that matter, means simply to use your arm and hand to motion the drawing of it in the air while projecting a stream of energy out of the drawing arm. This is the same concept used in our magickal drawing of pentagrams and hexagrams and such in ceremonial magick, but I wanted to give another example with a rune, so you can truly see how it is possible to develop this type of sorcery skill with any magickal symbol, and therefore to help to fuel the creativity of your own personalized lucid dream plans.

Something to note upon the consideration of experiments in signing is the distinct pattern that emerges when differentiating the results of signing a symbol versus making the hand gesture with the simple intention to experience it. The signing is created by projecting an outflow of energy, and so it is more likely to have an external effect on the world around you, where the simple holding of a hand gesture may be more likely to have you drawing the experience of the symbol to yourself inwardly, like an antenna. These are important distinctions to make so that you can improve your efficacy as a sorcerer in this reality by choosing the techniques that will most effectively bring you the desired outcome.

A Gebo Lucid Experiment

In one dream where I became lucid, I was at the point of experimenting with experiencing the magick of the rune gebo through signing. Gebo is the rune known as "the gift" and brings teachings of connection with others and an awareness that the true gift of life is loving relationships. Refer to the image of gebo in Figure 7.

Figure 7: Rune Gebo

I projected energy through my right hand, which is my casting hand, and used it to draw gebo in the air before me. The effect of this action was exerted on the whole atmosphere around me. The air in the yard where I stood in the dream scene took on a silvery watery shimmer with a little bit of a glowing waviness to it, and these ripples in the air were also filled with lovely glittery sparkles.

This runic experience was very beautiful and inspired feelings of awe and wonder. It felt like a fantasy movie scene where the magick of love and beauty is made manifest in a supernatural way. This lucid dream experience taught me that even though the sparkles wouldn't be visible to the naked eye when this was executed in ordinary reality, I could use this signing to have a beneficial effect on the waking atmosphere. I realized I could use the effect to help myself and others experience the unity of awe and love that comes from true appreciation of one's existence and of connecting to others with compassion in the present moment.

As you consider lucid dream plan examples such as this, begin to think about which letters or symbols you'd like to gesture or sign in a lucid dream. Your own experiments will help you find nuanced understanding of these symbols whose meanings are often speculative due to their ancient age and the fact that few writings survive to teach us of their true origins.

ARCANUM
Practicing Signing

· · ● ○ ● · ·

To prepare for a lucid dream plan that involves signing, choose a symbol, a rune, or an Ogham letter that you feel you may like to learn to use as an instant magick technique.

1. Stand comfortably with your feet planted solidly, hip-width, beneath you. Hold your casting arm straight out in front of you, parallel to the ground with your index and middle fingers extended and your thumb, ring, and pinky fingers tucked in.

2. Take a deep breath in, and upon your exhalation, draw the symbol in the air before you. Imagine that your breath can help you project a stream of energy from your hand.

3. Envision the energy trail depicting the symbol hanging there in the air the way a skywriter leaves marks in the sky.

4. Pause and take note of what color you perceive the energy to be. What is the feeling of the energy in the space around you now? Notice anything you can sense physically or psychically.

5. Be sure to document the intuited results of this waking practice so you can compare them to the results you gather later from executing the same signing while lucid.

Practicing this intermittently in waking while waiting for the opportunity to carry it out in lucidity will have you prepped and ready to execute symbol signing as a lucid dream plan. Not only will you have familiarized yourself with the movements but also with the habit of pausing just afterward to take in your assessment of their effects. You will be able to do this in an efficient and unbiased way without wasting any precious lucid time.

Chanting

Chanting or intoning a runic or Ogham letter name within a lucid dream tends to elicit dramatic results compared to the activation of the letter with hand gestures or signings alone. This is likely because a lot of natural force of energy is expelled through the combination of breath and voice, whereas the hand gestures and signings rely more on envisioning the symbol and associating it with the subtle energy of the action.

Another interesting note about chanting experiments is that they are less predictable in terms of whether the magickal effect will occur internally upon the magician or externally upon the atmosphere or both. Where this may become a bit more obvious with respect to subtle hand gestures creating internal energy flows and signings being more projective, it can go either way with chanting. The vibratory nature of the breath and voice are exerted both on the environment and the magician's dream body.

Chanting in a lucid dream is also different than the experience of chanting to raise magickal energy while awake. In waking chanting practices, it is very common for a magician to use hundreds of repetitions of a mantra or other magick words to build up an energetic resonance with the desired effect.

In lucid dreaming, on the other hand, you will find that because the environment is so crisp and responsive it only takes a few repetitions to have a noticeable effect. Sometimes a magickal response is even elicited with one decent intonation of a word.

To be time efficient and lower the chances that you will lose lucidity prior to completing your experiment with a runic or Oghamic name chant, I recommend carrying out such a lucid dream plan as follows: take in a deep breath and then bellow out the sound of the letter name for the entire length of your nice, long exhale. You will likely start to see an impact upon yourself or the dream realm right away. If not, try a few more repetitions of the intonation, then pause and assess yourself and your surroundings to see what you can perceive.

A Beith Lucid Experiment

In a lucid magick experiment while chanting the name of the Ogham letter name beith (pronounced BAY-uh), the symbol for the letter hung in the air in shimmering white energy, intensifying as I sang the sound of the name a few times. Beith appears in Figure 8.

Figure 8: Ogham Beith

Then, the resultant effect upon the dream scene was an immediate shift of the dream from daytime to nighttime. It was as though the energy created an instant reset of the atmosphere. I found this to be an interesting manifestation of this letter, which is often associated with purification and new beginnings, and is the first letter of the ancient Irish alphabet.

I would have personally been more prone to thinking about beith's purification specifically in terms of cleansing, and I would not have thought of a temporal or cyclical reset on my own. If we think of the deep dark of night as the metaphorical dark moon of the daily cycle, then it would, in fact, be the place to come back to as the empty point that is primed and cleansed and ready for a new beginning.

This experiment greatly enhanced the depth of my understanding of beith because my relationship to the light and dark aspects of the daily cycle as a metaphor for the lunar cycle and the female hormonal cycle are philosophically rich. The dark moon is the menstruation, or purging of that which no longer supports life. If the dark of night is the corresponding point on the daily cycle to the dark moon in the lunar cycle, it makes great sense to me that beith would encapsulate the same energies of the dark moon, and this is powerful magick to engage. In this way, I now see beith as the thorough cleansing that precedes a new beginning, but not necessarily the impetus for the new beginning itself.

ARCANUM
Letter Name Chanting

· · ● ○ ● · ·

This exercise will familiarize you with the acts of creating sustained, powerful vocal sounds and learning to assess their resultant magickal effects. Such rehearsal will prepare you for execution of chanting within a lucid dream so that you are ready to perform it and have something to which you can compare lucid results.

1. Choose a rune or other magickal letter name whose magick you would like to master further.

2. Set a timer for 5 minutes.

3. Stand upright, feet planted firmly on the ground and hip-width apart.

4. Take a deep breath in and confidently vibrate the rune or letter name aloud, holding out the sound of the name to prolong it for the full time it takes you to complete your exhale.

5. Continue with the deep breaths and the chanted vibration of the word name through each exhale for the whole 5 minutes if able.

6. When the timer is done, pause and notice the energetic quality of the space around you as well as how your own body and auric field are feeling.

7. Document any perceived effects that you can intuit so they can be compared to the results of later lucid dream plan experiments.

You may perform this exercise in a sitting position if you are prone to lightheadedness or have a limited breath capacity. Performance of this exercise on a regular basis can actually help to improve your lung capacity and ritual projection performance, but you should consult your doctor about doing prolonged breath work if you have any cardiopulmonary issues.

The Distillation

In this chapter, you have seen the benefits of practicing the activation of symbols and magickal letters in lucid dreams. By practicing hand gestures, signing, or chanting in waking, you can develop practical sorcery skill while preparing to use them in lucidity. Eventually the lucid practice of these actions will help you to put an adept level of polish and understanding on this type of instant magick. This is a true catalyst for the enhancement of indwelling sorcery skill.

Again, remember not to simply take my experiments as truths regarding the magickal nature of these letters, but instead perform your own experiments with them to see what the specific effects will be when you personally activate these symbols. Remember also that you can expand your experiments to substitute other things. You can sign the symbol of Mercury or chant Hebrew letter names. All of that said, there is no harm in trying to apply the insights I have gained experimentally in your own works of sorcery and manifestation in the interim, while you work on cultivating your own lucid magickal exploits.

PROJECTING
RAW ENERGY

It is very useful to experience the nature of your own naturally projected streams of energy in lucid dreaming. When I talk about raw energy, I'm talking about exploring the ways in which you, as an individual, organically emanate energetic forces that are unique to your own auric constitution.

We know that each of us has our own energy signature, and the qualities of our energy are perceivable in their own combinations of color, vibration, and sensory details. These subtle energy qualities can be difficult to perceive in physical waking reality but are often easily experienced in lucid dreaming. When you understand more about the natural ground-state, or energetic neutral of your constitution, you can then become better at influencing your projections when you need to shift their qualities for specific magickal aims.

Protection Projections

As a priestess who is a long-term devotee of the Morrigan, an ancient Irish goddess of battle, I am accustomed to being asked to help in vanquishing a negative entity or preventing it from continuing to wreak havoc. I have often carried this work out in the space of lucid dreaming, where it is easier and safer to directly interact with summoned negative entities. In lucid dreams, you can engage unknown spirits without the same level of risk to the physical body and mind than you might encounter if you summoned them while waking.

In such situations, the ability to shoot fire or send a blast of raw energy as a form of battle magick within lucid dreaming can be very useful for the magician with missions and assignments. Just as the experiences of flying can help you to improve how well you navigate that task in various journey realms and variable dream densities, so the experiences of blasting energy can have similar skill carryover as well.

It is important to experience how your energy tends to manifest when projected. If you might need to use energy projection skills in lucid missions, then you need to gain familiarity with your skill level beforehand. This way, when you do have a lucid dream plan that involves dealing with a negative entity, your energy blasts will not be unpredictable or unreliable in nature. Prior experience can also help you to re-create the sensation of it in ordinary reality when needed, even if the result of your efforts is not visible to the naked eye.

There are times when creating a blast of energetic force is necessary for protection against an entity, including cleansing an area of dense energetic negativity, performing powerful exorcisms, or moving stagnant energy. If you've already gotten to feel what it is like to do this in the dream space, your mind can better help you repeat it with subtle energetic projection when it is needed in waking. It is also very useful to know what your own energetic effects are without the added influence of runic or symbol techniques in the case that those things are not part of your personal practice.

The Look and Feel of Your Energy

I have had numerous occasions in lucid dreaming where I encountered an adversary or simply wished to practice producing energy blasts. Often, when I would put my hands up and intend to project, it wouldn't be fire that would seem to come out of my hands even though that is what I would have expected and was what I was literally envisioning. Most of the time, what emanates naturally from my hands when I shoot energy from them looks like an opalescent sparkly rainbow of energetic light. It is powerful and can push back an enemy, don't get me wrong, but it looks embarrassingly pretty for such a badass form of battle magick.

It is humbling, because here I am in a lucid dream knowing that technically I should be able to control such details if I forced them, but instead I decided to let things happen organically and take it as a learning opportunity. I realized that unless I really focus hard, activate the fiery rune kenaz, the Ogham symbol tinne or onn, or verbalize the literal word "fire" when I try to shoot a blast of energy, that I will simply produce the opalescent type of energetic flow that naturally comes from me and my own energy field. Now I have the choice of using it as it naturally is or adding magickal techniques to finesse the quality of the emission.

Thinking back on it, I realized that throughout my life, my aura had been described in that same way to me by numerous psychics—as having a vibrant sparkling glitter to it. Having received this literal validation in lucid dreaming to the descriptions of my aura given to me in ordinary reality by others caused me to go down a rabbit hole of exploration regarding the wildly differing natures of the energy fields between one person and another. I learned things about the nature of my own spirit and energy that are unique and that I might never have thought to consider otherwise.

Not only can you practice the projection of energy to help you become more effective in future endeavors where that is needed but also your experiments may teach you something about the nature of your own inherent energy field, and how you need to act if you want to change its emanation in the moment.

ARCANUM
Projecting Raw Energy

· · ● ○ ● · ·

Ideally, practicing the projection of energy while awake is best done with a partner so that you can get feedback regarding what your energy projection is like naturally. It is important to conduct an exercise such as this with another magickally minded individual whom you trust. You want to know you will have their honest responses to these trials, and that they are invested in working on magickal skill building together with you in a high-integrity manner.

1. Stand a few feet away from a friend who is willing to do energy experiments with you, facing one another.

2. Take a deep breath in, and on the exhale, thrust your dominant arm and hand forward with your palm facing out, intending to allow a surge of energy to flow down your arm and out toward your partner.

3. Feel the energy push forth without attempting to envision its color or qualities.

4. Once you feel that the result of your combined exhale and intention has been fully released from you, lower your arm.

5. Pause and give your partner a moment to see what they feel, and what it is like to be on the receiving end of that subtle energy projection.

6. Ask them to answer the following questions automatically without thinking too much about it: What is the first color that comes to mind when they consider how the energy felt? Did it have a subtle temperature or quality that was perceivable? Were there tingles or any other sensations?

To see how variable this can be, be sure to allow your partner to try it too. Reversing roles and practicing clearing your mind and pausing to grab psychic sensations and impulses in situations like this without applying analytical thought is great practice for unbiased organic sensing in the lucid state. It is also possible that your unaltered energy projections may differ under various circumstances, so try to practice with your partner on a few different occasions.

Logging the descriptions you get may help you to make sense of what your energy is like when you successfully surge it forth in this way later within a lucid dream. Combining your understanding of your waking and sleeping projections creates a virtuous cycle within the development of your energy skills.

The Distillation

This chapter has reviewed the concept of exploring the natural state of your energy and the projection of it in lucid dreams. You have seen that gaining these types of experiences through lucid dream plan experiments with your energy can have benefits upon your skill level in future magickal endeavors. These include being prepared to effectively project your energy to protect you from negative entities, cleanse dense spaces, and perform other acts of sorcery in response to your environment on the fly. Ultimately, you should also now understand that it is always advisable to work to gain a better understanding of your own unique energy constitution. The more experience you gain with your own energetic ground state, the better you will be at finessing it as the need arises.

WORKING WITH SPACE, TIME, AND SHAPE

Lucid dreaming is the perfect, and maybe the only, place where we can directly experience more dramatically supernatural magickal actions. Conducting lucid dream experiments with things such as time travel, astral projection, or shape-shifting can serve to deepen your understanding of time, space, and being. Consider some of the following concepts as potential future lucid dream plans and you will be building a more solid foundation of philosophies that you can personally accept as true regarding the mysteries. The more you understand about how things work beyond this body and these physics, the more effective your magick can be.

Time Travel

Time travel is certainly an elusive thing. Generally, the closest experience outside of dreaming I have come across for magickal practitioners to achieve that can be time travel oriented is shamanic-style journeying. In this practice, the trained adept can travel beyond this physical reality and move through spiritual realms to access other planes and times. This is sometimes done for the purpose of bringing back information, serving as a mediator to the spirits, or facilitating healing from traumas that stem from the past or will affect the future. This is generally done in an awake but trancelike state and is dependent on the internal psychic skill of the magician for it to be done accurately and well.

I was asked by one of my students if I had ever achieved time travel specifically through lucid dreaming as opposed to just within journey work. At the time I had not, simply because I had never thought to implement it as a lucid dream plan. Naturally, I then put it on the priority list of magickal experiments to undertake.

The Salem, Massachusetts, 1692 Time Travel Experiment

When the time came that I next found myself in a lucid dream and was ready to enact this quest, I yelled out to the dream, "Take me to Salem, Massachusetts, in 1692!" This time in history is significant to me due to my connection to my eight-times great-grandfather Samuel Wardwell, who was hanged in the Witch trials of the time.

After calling out my command, the scene before me wavered, blurred, and reformed itself. I was pleasantly surprised that I had not been sucked into a black vortex of swirling motion as often can happen if you put such a dynamic request out to the dreamtime. When this happens, the results are often so disorienting that it becomes too difficult to maintain that all-important sense of being anchored in the scene and can cause waking.

So, in this case, as the scene re-formed and I looked around, I saw that I was standing near a rocky coastline. There were odd anchors, wooden boxes, and things that looked like ship parts, and the area was quite rural. I clambered about along the rocks, exploring a bit, and came upon a woman who was also out walking there. She was not dressed in the clothes of colonial times but was in a modern style of dress, including typical jeans and a T-shirt. I approached her and said, "Excuse me, but can you tell me where we are?" She looked at me as though I were insane and, seeming slightly scared of me, replied, "Uh, we're in Salem," as though it were completely obvious, and that I must be off my rocker. I thanked her and continued exploring for a bit, trying to work out the reality of what was happening.

The Realization of What Really Happened

It seemed that the space I had managed to enter was a dream reality of Salem. I was not, however, in the physical world version of Salem. It became clear to me that perhaps this might not be at all possible. It makes sense that as your sleeping body lies, you can only enter dream realities, since you are traveling there only with your conscious awareness and not the body.

I awoke from that dream into a face-palm moment where I realized that which should have been obvious to me from the get-go: In dreaming, you can travel to other times, but they will be parallel dream or nonphysical versions of those times, and not the literal physical reality you might be imagining. I realized the woman I had met in the dream was quite possibly another dreamer. Not being lucid, she probably didn't realize she was dreaming and, though she recognized the area as Salem, obviously familiar to her by her tone and response, she likely had no inkling that this was an iteration of a 1692 dream reality version of Salem.

This experience taught me that I could have refined my request further. Perhaps I could have clarified the command such that I would enter the closest version of a physical historical time possible. I could have also asked to witness specific scenes in history as an outside observer.

Part of me is happy and comforted by the idea that a magician cannot easily go back to the past in this reality, as I have met far too many angry people who would take advantage of that potentiality for the purposes of changing history to suit their own goals, narratives, morals, or desires. Well-intentioned as this could be, we have all entertained the utter chaos that could ensue in the present if history were changed such that we or those we love were never born. If you have not spent enough time considering such concepts, perhaps it is time for you to indulge in watching some classic *Doctor Who* episodes, where a lovable time-traveler deals with these very issues.

ARCANUM
Preparation for Lucid Time Travel

· ·˙ ● ○ ● · ·

In practicing this exercise, you will be preparing your mind for the concept of time travel in general. You will be increasing your chances of executing your lucid dream plan smoothly and without losing your anchored solidity within the space of dreaming. You will also be giving yourself an experience that you can then use to compare to the results of your future lucid experiment. You will be able to learn from the differences that existed in your conscious preconceived notions about time travel and the qualities that arose organically through lucidity.

1. Decide on a time and place that you would like to try to travel to in a future lucid dream.

2. Sit or lie down comfortably so that you can begin to relax your body and close your eyes.

3. Breathe deeply, allowing your internal attention to gently be brought to your Witch's eye, your inner place of seeing and sensing. Perform the following psychic visualization exercise.

4. Imagine that you are sitting in your own familiar home. Take a moment to envision your surroundings. Look at the walls, furnishings, and decorations. Imagine getting up and mindfully walking toward the door that leads outside. As you imagine moving through your home in this direction, say to yourself, "When I walk out the door, I will arrive in the time and place of my choosing." Continue to reiterate this to yourself until you imagine yourself opening the door and stepping outside. When the door opens, prepare to see the scene you wish to time travel to. Step out of the door and take note of what you see. What are the details of your surroundings? Are there any people here? If you need to, walk forth and explore to gather more information about this place. Take your time, mindfully walking and gathering spontaneous insights. Feel free to talk to characters you may encounter along the way.

5. When you are ready, imagine turning back around and finding the door to your home. Imagine the feel of the handle, opening the door and stepping back inside and over the threshold. Imagine walking back into the room

where you were when you started the visualization. Mentally sit yourself back down. Take a deep breath, gently releasing the effort of the visualization and allowing your attention to transition back to the sensations of the breath and the body.

6. Journal any details you gathered about the time and place that you visited. What draws you to want to explore this time and place more directly? What more would you wish to know?

This preparatory visionary experience can serve to heighten the inspiration and motivation that you have for successfully carrying out this time travel in a lucid dream. It may also help you to feel emotionally prepared for the shift so that you don't lose your anchoring upon the lucid dream plan command.

Shape-shifting

Shape-shifting is another magickal skill that also has possibilities for application within lucid dreams. Lucidity offers a space where the experience of shifting one's form is engaged literally and felt in a physical way. Being able to remember the sensations of the transformation can help the practitioner to envision this happening more effectively for waking journey work applications.

In shamanic-style journeying, the skilled traveler of the spiritual realms can learn to travel forth in various forms, depending on the needs of the mission and the landscape at hand. The practitioner can also directly learn pieces of wisdom that can only be gained by experiencing the vantage point of a different type of being, creature, or guide from the first-person perspective.

While shape-shifting can be profound and very useful to do in waking psychic work, there is nothing like achieving firsthand shape-shifting within the space of a lucid dream. I highly recommend this as a potential lucid dream plan for those of you who can execute it. If so, I recommend shifting into the form of an animal that is important to you, or which may serve as some type of guide to you, so that you can gain a deeper understanding of its nature. It could also be productive to shift into the form of an animal that has a connection to a deity you admire.

The Raven Shifter Experiment

As an example of shape-shifting as a lucid dream plan, I once called out the command "I wish to shape-shift into the form of a raven!" It was a very strange sensation indeed, as I felt my arms not really disappearing, but sort of melting and merging in with the general shape of my torso. I felt the shape of my face change and could no longer see the edge of the outline of my human, skin-covered nose, but my peripheral vision showed the edge of a black beak there instead. I had wings and was covered in feathers, and it was truly a wild metamorphosis to experience.

The change was gradual, over the course of maybe twenty to thirty seconds, and was not painful. From there, I was able to move my wings around, and to lift myself into the air for flight. It was amazing to still feel entirely aware as my usual conscious self, but to be in this new form with all the sensations that come with it.

As I flew a bit, I was most surprised by the feeling of it, for it was nothing like any of the other many episodes of lucid dream flying that I had previously experienced. This felt floaty and buoyant, like bodysurfing over gentle rhythmic waves of ocean water, and yet I was in the air. My wings felt like paddles and the air felt as if it helped to suspend me quite naturally. I began to realize that maybe this is what it feels like for birds when they fly—their anatomy as well as their sensory organs must allow them the sensation that the air is a supportive medium in which they have natural navigational skill.

Realizations from the Experiment

I had honestly never thought about birds' flight before in this way, so it was an amazing realization to have. The relationship of birds to the air may be akin to what our human relationship is to the sea. This provided a lot of food for thought about the nature of the very elements themselves. I also began to wonder about all the times when I had to "swim fly" instead of just launching through the air in various dream realities. Were those realities waterier by their elemental nature? Or was I more of a birdlike being in those dream realities? These are big exploratory concepts for a dream sorcerer to consider.

ARCANUM
Preparation for Animal Shape-shifting

· · ● ○ ● · ·

Think about what animal form you might take if you could enact shape-shifting in your next lucid dream. What would be your motivation for choosing that form? Is this the form of an animal guide you have come to know? Is the animal one that corresponds to a deity or a type of mythology that you love? Choose an animal form that makes your heart feel happy.

1. Begin to prepare by looking at images of the animal online. Note the details of its body shape, face, and claws. Imagine the textures of this animal and the nature of its behaviors and movements.

2. Take a moment to close your eyes and relax. Breathe deeply, letting some of the tension flow out of your body. Feel the outline of your shape, the quality and weight of your body where you rest.

3. Envision what it would be like for you to experience being your chosen animal firsthand. How would your feet and legs change? Imagine them morphing into the form and texture of your animal. How would your arms and torso change? Again, feel your body and imagine it morphing into the animal form. Lastly, how would your head change? Slowly allow yourself to feel all the parts of your body having changed form.

4. Imagine getting up and moving around now in this form. How does it feel? What is your movement like? Do you have abilities now that you don't normally have as a human being? Take your time enjoying exploring this form.

5. When you're ready, imagine sitting or lying back down in your animal form. Gently begin to reverse the transformation. Imagine your head becoming human again, then your torso and arms, and lastly your legs. Feel your body literally in physical reality, breathing deeply and wiggling your fingers and toes. Open your eyes when you are ready.

6. Document your thoughts so that you can later compare them with the experiences gained once you have carried this out in lucidity.

You will benefit from conducting this exercise even in waking, spending time trying to understand a beloved animal form better. When you get to perform it in a lucid dream, you will then get to learn unexpected new things from the experience.

Astral Projection

It is not uncommon to experience occasional unintentional bouts of astral projection while attempting to cultivate lucid dreams, especially when practicing wake-induced methods. There can certainly be some gray areas between lucid dreaming and astral projection, as both states offer crisper -than-usual awareness, wakefulness within bodily sleep, and supernatural sorts of abilities. Astral projection, however, is considered to be a true out-of-body experience, whereas lucid dreaming is presumed to be an experience of the conscious awareness awakening within a dream realm while the energy body most likely remains in its location in the physical body. As discussed in chapter 1, we can grossly discern them by looking at lucidity and dreams as happening in mental realms and astral projection as happening in an astral, or energetic realm.

Some practitioners warn of dangers involved with astral projection. These can vary from warnings of side effects of disorientation or astral energy loss all the way to the legend that if one allows the astral body to stray too far from the physical body that death could result. I have never noticed any negative effects of astral projection, and occult authors Melita

Denning and Osborne Phillips also assert that the astral body never fully detaches itself from the physical in an out-of-body experience.[20]

If you remain unconvinced that it is safe but do wish you could experience astral projection, then attempting it from within a lucid dream may provide an extra layer of protection. You may be able to specify that you would like to project out of your dream body within the dream realm, leaving the layers of your auric field undisturbed in bed in the physical body while your conscious awareness benefits from the experience.

There have been several times when I realized that in trying to become lucid, I had popped out of my body and was experiencing ordinary reality in real time with just an astral form instead. It felt different from lucid dreaming in that I had less attachment to any sort of dream body and felt more like a floating specter. In those situations, I floated around and explored my environment. I tried to notice things such as what birds, weather, or wildlife were outside at the moment or what my husband was doing at the time. In each instance, I was then able to return to my body and physically get up and go validate that what I had witnessed as an astral body was indeed part of the active conditions going on in real time.

Many people prize astral projection for the unique experience that it is, and they have been able to expand their skills to learn things about the mysteries and the nature of consciousness and the universe. Due to my proclivity for lucid dreaming and the revelations regarding the diverse nature of experiments that are possible when we are talking about dream realities as the medium of practice, I have kept my pursuits primarily upon this modality. Despite this, I did have one amazing experience wherein I orchestrated a lucid dream plan that was to succeed in astral projection *from within* the already lucid state of dreaming. I had my doubts about whether I would be able to do both in one sitting but figured it was certainly worth a try. I will relay the experience here to spark another potential lucid dream plan idea that you may wish to try yourself.

20. Melita Denning and Osborne Phillips, *The Llewellyn Practical Guide to Astral Projection* (Llewellyn Publications, 1980), 35.

Astral Projection from within the Lucid Dream

Upon becoming lucid, I began to project energy out of my dominant hand and traced a large vertically hanging circle in the air in front of me. I traced over the circle numerous times, intending the energy circle to stay there, intensify, and form a portal. As I continued strengthening the circular portal, I said aloud, "When I enter through this portal, I will leave my physical body." When I felt that the portal was well defined, I dove through it, and lo and behold, I entered the endless black abyss that some authors describe as the lucid void.

I no longer had my dream body and felt like I was just a point of awareness experiencing a neutral eternal conscious state. It was neither pleasant nor unpleasant but was certainly fascinating. I was not able to hold on to my experience of this state for very long before I found myself returned to my physical body and awakening.

For the magician interested in cultivating some experiences of astral projection who has potentially struggled with being able to directly separate as an astral entity from the physical form, the lucid practice may present an ideal way to circumvent some of the challenges inherent in shifting consciousness that would be necessary for that experience. Also, this method of moving from a lucid dream into the void may be desirable for the magician wanting to develop firsthand experience in witnessing the chaos, or raw etheric building blocks of universal intelligence that the void may represent.

ARCANUM

Astral Projection Technique

· · ● ○ ● · ·

There are many proposed techniques out there for preparing for astral projection. One favorite method I have had some success with is the Rope Projection Technique, which I discovered some years ago through the works of Robert Bruce.[21] This exercise represents my own modified version.

---

21. Bruce, *Astral Dynamics*, 172–174.

1. Lie down on your back and breathe deeply. Focus on your exhales for a few minutes, allowing yourself to soften and relax further with each out-breath.

2. Patiently conduct a body scan with the intention to relax each segment of your body even more deeply.

3. To perform this scan, start at your feet and place your awareness there, feeling the sensation of your feet becoming more released, heavier, and more relaxed. Continue upward, doing this along the length of the legs, through the hips and lower back, and through the belly and chest. Place your awareness on the hands and continue letting yourself relax more deeply, your hands, arms, and shoulders allowing tension to melt away, your whole body sinking into the support of your spot. Lastly, feel your scalp, head, and face, and relax these areas deeply. Allow softening and releasing to pervade your facial muscles and jaw so that everything feels loose.

4. Next, imagine that there is a rope that hangs down from the ceiling above you, its end directly over your solar plexus.

5. Letting your body stay still, soft, and relaxed, imagine energetic versions of your arms and hands reaching up from out of the physical body to grab hold of the rope.

6. Begin to pull yourself, hand over hand, up along the rope. Mentally envision and feel your energy body lifting out of your physical body, doing this climbing.

7. Allow yourself to continue up the rope through the ceiling and roof. Finding that the rope continues straight up into the sky, continue climbing your astral body up into the sky along the rope.

8. If you lose concentration, start again from the bottom, trying to see how long you can climb without becoming distracted. Eventually you will either fall asleep, experience interesting sensations in your energy, or find yourself having astrally projected out of the physical body.

9. Whether or not you succeeded in lifting yourself astrally out of the physical body, it's important to develop the habit of coming full circle at the end of your practice. If you did not fall asleep but are feeling done with the practice, take a moment just to mentally imagine yourself sliding back down the rope, your energy body recombining fully with your physical body where you lie.

10. As your body awakens, whether from sleeping or not, be sure to journal your experiences.

Even if you failed to accomplish an out-of-body experience with this technique, familiarity with it can give you a head start. You could even use the rope technique from within a lucid dream, and your ability to energetically climb right up and out of your dream body will be greatly enhanced in that setting.

The Distillation

This chapter has covered the notion that some very coveted, advanced magickal practices can be practiced firsthand in lucid dreaming. Each such experience brings with it amazing opportunities for learning about the nature of things like time, space, yourself as a spiritual being, the elements, and your understanding of other beings. Your lucid experiences and the knowledge gained from them can then enhance greatly the skill with which you approach some of this magick in waking.

In order to be able to successfully carry out these or similar experiments of time, space, or shape, you must choose one as your lucid dream plan, writing down exactly how you will word your request to the dreamtime so that you are prepared to execute it. Use the exercises provided to give your mind advanced training and techniques that can carry over to the lucid space, helping you keep your concentration when you get there. Doing the suggested exercises helps you keep your lucid dream plan in the forefront of your mind as well as increases your chances of becoming lucid.

COMMUNING
WITH DEITIES

In the world of magickal practice, it is often considered that intercession by spiritual beings with whom you have contracted or allied yourself is one of the primary ways of getting sorcerous manifestation work to happen effectively. Working with spirits is an excellent way, and for many practitioners the primary way, to facilitate the effective accomplishment of magickal goals, especially when your personal flow of energy is not going to be enough on its own.

In my tradition and practice, I have found that the more strength and depth you can build in the relationship between yourself and any deity, guide, or other helping spirit, the better the magickal work together will be as well.

Considerations of Spirit Summoning

For some occultists, there is a prized goal of achieving actual spirit evocation ritualistically. This means that the magician hones their own focus and ritual skill for years to a point where they can command a spirit to appear in a literal summoning in a specially cast manifestation triangle within the ritual space, in waking reality. It is not an easy undertaking, but one of the reasons it is a desired feat is because there is the idea that being able to be face-to-face and directly experience the presence of an elevated spirit being can have a vibrational raising effect upon the mind and energy body of the magician through proximity and resonance. It is thought that this is a way of quickening one's own spiritual wisdom and evolution through advanced magickal practice.

Full evocation is also considered somewhat dangerous due to the idea that encountering such intense energies firsthand could possibly be disorienting, fraying the nerves of the energy body, so to speak, and potentially leaving the caster addled or mentally off from that point forward. This danger can be bypassed by working to summon elevated beings in the lucid state. In this way, the wisdom can still be experienced firsthand, and the energetic effect can be brought forth to the physical body but is filtered through the dream body and the space between the worlds. The spirit's unique vibration is still encountered but is possibly gentler in nature, without the risk. Instead of functioning as a physically incarnate being summoning a spirit, you are simply functioning as a spirit summoning another spirit.

You may conduct a myriad of summonings of many different types of spirits within the fully lucid space. These include classically known deities, fae, spirits of place, spirits of the dead, spirits of other living people, plant spirits, familiar spirits, and even the elusive Holy Guardian Angel. We will talk about some of these specific spirit type nuances in chapter 11. Summoning entities in lucid dreaming is an amazing way to gain a better understanding of spirits and to set yourself up to have much more effective relationships and jointly executed magick in tandem with them.

I have found that some of the benefits of summoning a deity in lucid dreaming can include deepening your personal relationship, receiving wisdom, prophecy, asking for advice, learning more about the nature of deities, facilitating spiritual revelation and deeper understanding of yourself as a spiritual being, and receiving direct physical healing, empowerment, or other energetic infusions, to name a few. The act of deepening your relationship with a deity is incredibly gratifying and rewarding, and doing it in the lucid dream space takes the potential intensity of your interactions to a level that is normally not able to be accessed in waking reality.

Lucidity for Deepening Relationships with Deity

One major reason for wanting to summon a deity in a lucid dream is simply to learn more about them and to deepen your relationship with them. As magicians, we often have preconceived notions about deities that are based only on the mythology that we have access to. Assumptions about beings based purely on old literature can be problematic on many levels. Firstly, we have no way of knowing how much of the writings were influenced by Christian writers who were often transcribing things they didn't understand and therefore painting the ideas in a biased light. Also, we can assume that there is a lot missing from the extant literature of old that leaves us lacking in insight and information regarding the nuances of spiritual beings.

If we return to our discussion of Hermetics, we must consider also the idea behind the Principle of Correspondences.[22] This principle states that anything which happens on any one plane of existence has some correlation and ripple effect through every other plane of existence, at least metaphorically if not directly. If we take this to be true, then deities must be able to learn, evolve, and change just as we can. We need to be open to the idea that every sentient being is on their own path of evolution. With this mindset, it becomes extremely important to learn what is important to a deity now, and not to make presumptions based only on their old stories if we are to develop truly deep relationships.

Highlighting this need to broaden our view, over the course of a series of lucid dreams involving the summoning of the god Odin, I encountered him in numerous ways and forms. He has shown up as an elderly man just as easily as he has shown up as a young, hip guy wearing jeans and a T-shirt. Sometimes he has sent an assistant in his place and has offered the use of technology to help me to reach him when he was otherwise engaged. Odin has shown up in a form that emanated life-changing levels of fatherly care as well as in different forms where he has seemed sexually attracted to me. Over time, I have been able to put together all of the experiences I've had with him to allow a broader understanding of this

---

22. Three Initiates, *The Kybalion*, 65–80.

complex being, and I feel we see eye to eye because of this. Ironically, he has never come to me with only one eye!

In a specific example of deity summoning, one lucid dream plan was to summon the Morrigan. I had, at the time, already succeeded in meeting up with her in lucid dreams in numerous other ways, but it had been a while, and I sensed it was time to reconnect in this space. When I became lucid, I yelled out to the dream, "I wish to meet with the great Irish goddess the Morrigan!" From somewhere off in the distance of the dream scene I began to see something in the sky rushing toward me. It was undoubtedly her, and I could see her face and her long black wisps of hair blowing wildly as she flew, her flowy black and gray garments trailing from her in vapors that faded gradually the farther they were from her head. She was a being that seemed to be made of wind and illusion—an airy sky creature lacking in any solidity or physical substantiveness.

It is not uncommon for me to experience the Morrigan without a physical body in lucid dreaming, so I wasn't too surprised at that, but I was surprised by her face. As she got closer, I could see her expression—eyebrows raised in anticipation and excitement, as if she couldn't wait to see me, with a hint of a knowing smile. As she finally reached me, rushing toward me for a windy sort of all-encompassing embrace, she erupted into emotional sobs of relief. It shook me deeply and I began to sob as well, for I could feel her heart. It was almost like a scene where a distraught mother had been reunited with a child who she thought had been in danger or that she had somehow lost, or like two long-lost loves being reunited after a painful period of separation. Both crying audibly, we then merged, not in a true hug, as she was not made of physically substantial stuff in this dream setting, but in an energetic recombining that certainly had the emotional and energetic vibration of a strong and empowering hug to it.

This experience certainly allowed me to gain direct, firsthand validation about the deeper nature of our connection, how we feel about each other, and how much we mean to one another. There is something about connecting with other spiritual beings while lucid that allows a very direct download of knowing and experience even without much in the way of verbal communication happening. It was also a very important experience to have because it taught me that I cannot assume that the Morrigan is only a tough, justice-delivering battle goddess. In engaging directly, I was witness to her deeply emotional and compassionate side, which went a long way in building our bond.

Receiving Direct Deity Energy Infusions

One of the greatest things that can be experienced in lucid dreaming, in my opinion, is what I would refer to as an energy infusion that is delivered to you by a god or a goddess. It is one thing to receive omens, messages, or divinations with deity or to learn about your relationship with them through meditations and journeys while awake. All of this is useful and essential work for the magician, of course, but if you have the means to have a direct energetic experience like this with a deity or a guide, it will impress itself upon you in ways that the other methods of exploration simply cannot do.

It is one thing for you to be told in journey work that you are loved by deity. It is another thing altogether to experience that through a direct emotional and energetic download while you are completely mentally alert but also in a dream setting that allows you to transcend your normal limitations of connection and communication. The magician that has had such an experience goes forth with improved confidence in the day-to-day magick that is then enacted in concert with such a spirit, knowing the true feel of the nature of the relationship and therefore the level of vested interest that this spirit can bring to the table magickally. An energy download can also filter through the dream body and have lasting effects upon the state of empowerment of the auric field of the magician in waking.

One of the most epic experiences I have ever had was the one where I truly felt I had experienced the Morrigan in lucid dreaming fully for the first time. I became lucid in the middle of having a normal dream, and when I had myself well-anchored, I called out to the dream, "I summon the great Irish goddess the Morrigan!" I was expecting and hoping for some semblance of a being to appear and was very surprised when instead I was met with the onslaught of a violently whirling tornado that seemed to be made up of blurred crows and bats and other black, blurry things that couldn't be made out due to the speed at which it simultaneously spun and hurtled toward me. This spinning energy made a deep rumbling and shaking sound as it approached, and the whole thing was formidable and intimidating.

Knowing with full clarity that I was dreaming and couldn't be hurt by this, I stood there and allowed it to penetrate completely into my dream body and fill me. The energetic penetration blasted through me and continued to rumble and vibrate every fiber of my being and the sensations of my dream body with an indescribable level of intensity. I stayed relaxed and allowed it—I knew it was the energy of the Morrigan, and so I gave myself over to it fully.

The power that was being conducted throughout my dream body continued to flow and my body lifted off the ground until I was floating in the air as if lying on my back, parallel to the ground, this energetic current of forcible magnitude still thrumming through me. The raw power caused me to snarl audibly like an animal and to writhe involuntarily. I understood that the effects of the growling and twisting were also manifesting in my physical body in ordinary reality in simultaneity with the dream experience, as I lay in my bed. Breathing deeply, I allowed the power flow to run its course and subside and then chose to wake myself up and assure my husband, sleeping in the bed next to me, that I was all right and that my snarling like a wolf was no cause for alarm.

This sharing of power and energy from the Morrigan was not at all what I had expected might happen in response to summoning her. I was completely floored by it, immensely honored, and still vibrating energetically when I woke back up to physical reality. In fact, an infusion such as this one can sometimes be felt tangibly for many days in waking life in the aura of the physical body following its receipt. It often results in an immediate and direct improvement in the overall feeling of vitality and raw power that the magician can access through the energy body.

Deity energy infusions may spontaneously happen at random intervals when you try to summon deities, or you can purposely ask for one as a lucid dream plan. Infusions can happen from the same deity multiple times and manifest in different ways and with different energetic qualities. As you would expect, energy infusions from varying deities can be wildly different from one another. They all have their own unique vibrations and modes of transmission, but they always feel like an amazing gift that somehow helps to transfer some of the resonance of that deity's energy into your knowing and your ordinary reality.

Every divine energy infusion feels like a sacred gift, or an exchange given in return for devotion and attention. Even though this magick can feel mind-blowingly humbling and undeserved, it is also a way for us to walk the energy of the deity through our physical world, which could, in turn, be quite helpful and beneficial for them. It is possible that you may need to try numerous times in your lucid dream plans involving deity summonings or infusions to achieve an experience of this intensity level, but you will learn something from every attempt, and they will all have been worth it.

The Benefit of Things Not Going as Planned

Not all attempts to summon a deity or experience their energies or their teachings in a lucid dream will succeed or seem to go as planned, and this is okay. Do your best to word your call and/or request to them as clearly as you can but remember that there is lots to be learned when unexpected results ensue. You may have been hoping to talk with them face-to-face, but maybe that is not what they had in mind for the moment. Spirits can communicate with us in many different ways, including things such as silence or metaphor.

No Response

At times when you summon a deity and they don't appear, try not to get frustrated and lose hold of your lucidity. It is wise in situations like this to look at your dream hands or feet for a quick re-anchoring and then rephrase your request with more specific wording. If there continues to be no response, look at your hands or feet again, and consider switching to a new lucid dream plan.

For example, on one occasion I said, "I would like to speak face-to-face with the Morrigan," and I patiently waited and watched the dream scene around me. Nothing happened; no one appeared. Still lucid, I decided to alter the specificity of my request and stated, "Please, then, may I experience the goddess the Morrigan." I proceeded to receive a direct and intense energetic infusion instead.

In the situation where you ask again and you still receive no response, pause and check in with what you feel in the dream environment. Does it feel like the space is bereft of the deity's presence or not? There could be a telepathic download available for you to access. Alternatively, you can pause and check in with yourself. Are there qualities of this deity you can sense within yourself? Sometimes requests to interact with deity come with riddles and challenges of discovery or introspection.

Unexpected Appearance

Deities also can take many unexpected forms when called upon in lucid dreaming. It may seem as if they are not responding, yet they are. Not only can a deity show up in a form that doesn't match at all what you might expect of them, but sometimes they show up or respond by changing the atmosphere around you.

If you follow the psychic clearing method used in the image divination practice in chapter 4 and wait and watch with a clear mind and expectations released, you stand to learn all kinds of revelations you would never have imagined. Upon one summoning of Hekate, instead of arriving herself, I saw women, including myself, being lifted up into the air in various spots all around the distant landscape. I understood this was a metaphor for how she arrives energetically to lift women up when needed, and it was an emotional realization to witness this message firsthand.

Dream Landscape Factor

Sometimes when a deity doesn't show up when called upon in a lucid dream it may be because they can't materialize in some dream realities as easily as they can in others. Juat as flying is not necessarily manageable in the exact same way in every dream scenario, so the summoning and appearance of deities and spirits can have very different execution results and possibilities from one dream reality to the next.

One example of this was a time that I called for Odin and, because he couldn't come to where I was himself, he sent an assistant with a tablet and offered to use technology to communicate with me instead. This was such a shock to me that I knew for sure I hadn't imagined this outcome, and it expanded my knowledge of what was possible in dreams on a deep level.

ARCANUM
Preparing for a Lucid Deity Summoning

· · ● ○ ● · ·

The following exercise is intended to maximize your chances of having successful experiences in lucid deity summoning. Prepare by sitting down with your journal. Take the time to consider the following points and use them as writing prompts.

+ I would like to summon <*insert deity*> in a lucid dream. I would like to get to know this deity more deeply because...

+ When I summon this deity, to avoid confusion wherever possible, my specific lucid dream plan statement will be...

+ When I currently picture this deity in my mind, I envision them as...

+ A question I would like to ask this deity, given time, is...

After journaling out these points to clarify your thoughts and plans, consider taking time to sit in quiet meditation. Set a timer for a short sitting, maybe 5 minutes, which will serve as a calibration meditation. The idea is that to convene with deity properly, we need to raise our vibrational level, and a deity needs to lower theirs.

We increase our level with meditation. Dedicate this simple quiet time to calibrating yourself with the deity you hope to summon in your lucid dream. Say aloud or to yourself, "<*Insert deity name*>, it is my will to quiet my mind, clear and still. While I'm in my stillness time, I invite your energy to attune with mine." Proceed to sit quietly, keeping your awareness focused on your breath until the timer indicates that you are done. At this time say, "I thank you, <*insert deity name*>, for sharing this space with me. May we both go forth, pleased and fulfilled by the experience. Blessed Be."

After performing this waking work, you are now much better prepared for the successful execution of your deity summoning lucid dream plan. Clarifying your motivations and intentions with the previous prompts fuels the importance of this quest and increases the likelihood that you can make it happen. Proceed to write in your dream journal exactly what wording you would like to use for your current lucid dream plan where you call upon this deity. Next time you become lucid, anchor in and call it out. Then watch and wait with a clear mind and accept whatever comes.

The Distillation

In this chapter on deity summoning, we discussed the benefits of attempting to call deities to you in a lucid dream. There are benefits of relationship deepening; learning about the mysterious, unwritten nature of deities; receiving direct downloads of energy or wisdom; and receiving their teachings in various ways. We talked about deity summoning being potentially quite unpredictable and yet making sure to be ready to learn from all of the ways in which your results may vary from what you expected. Let us now move on to expand our potential lucid dream plans for the inclusion of a host of other types of spirits as well.

SUMMONING
OTHER SPIRITS

Deities are far from the only types of beings with whom you may wish to engage in lucid encounters. In this chapter, we will discuss the benefits of summoning other types of spirits in lucid dreams. Each magickal practitioner has different talents, priorities, and emphases in their own practice, which could lead to placing a higher priority upon deepening their work with various kinds of spirit allies. Here you will encounter descriptions of and advice regarding summonings involving plant spirits, ancestral spirits, spirits of other living humans, familiars, and the elusive Holy Guardian Angel.

Plant Spirits

So many Witches and magickal practitioners love to work with the talented and inspiring intelligences of nature, and, often, this involves bringing various plants and herbs into the mix. Everything in magick is about communication of some sort, and when you include plants in your spells and workings it is more effective when you truly have an established relationship with the energy of the plant, rather than just following a magickal spell recipe or looking up a plant correspondence for your goal and throwing it in.

The lucid state is great not only for convening with plant spirits in order to build relationships but also for allowing you an unbiased way to understand the deeper magick of your favorite plant allies and how to more effectively incorporate them into magickal workings.

Consider Both the Energy and the Personification of a Plant Spirit

Mugwort is a very well-known dream herb, and it is a plant that I have used in many forms for all kinds of psychic, dream, and intuitive enhancement work over the years. A time came when I decided to execute a lucid dream plan for the purpose of meeting the spirit of mugwort itself. Upon this occasion of lucidity, I commanded to the dream space, "I wish to experience the spirit of the plant mugwort!"

I waited with a clear mind, watching the dream scene before me. The wind picked up and the sky darkened, and I was surrounded by swirling gusts of air. I watched the airy, spiraling nature of the weather energy and it eventually just died back down. I woke up, feeling that my request was answered, but without form, with energy alone. I was confident that I had experienced something of the nature of mugwort's energy, but I still wanted to get to know it more tangibly.

I was able to fall back asleep and calmly wait through the hypnagogic state for the dream scene to reappear. This time, choosing my words more carefully, I stated, "I would like to meet a *personification* of the spirit of mugwort!" Upon this request, a great, fanciful bird appeared on the branch of one of the trees in the dream scene. The bird did not look like any bird that is known to exist among the species of birds on planet Earth that I know of. It was quite large, with proportions of height and width like a pre-teen human. It had long, swooping, many-colored tail feathers with purples and pinks being the dominant hues. The bird appeared to have femininity in its eyes, and she looked over her shoulder at me coyly. She held an air of mystery and magic but was also very self-assured at the same time. We spent a few moments just intimately connected through our gazes, and then I awoke.

Upon waking, I felt much more satisfied that I had gotten a deeper glimpse of the nature of the spirit of mugwort. The personification of a bird, even though I did not expect to see that at all and honestly had been expecting a humanoid being if anything, reinforced the airy nature of the plant hinted at in the prior dream. The whole scene reminded me of a teaching from the works of Agrippa that states, "Whence it is, that many philosophers were of opinion that Air is the cause of dreams, and of many other impressions of the mind, through the prolonging of images, or similitudes, or species...."[23] Though I had not been thinking about the element of air in any way prior to activating this lucid dream plan, the nature of mugwort was certainly validated to me personally in an airy way.

ARCANUM
Plant Spirit Attunement

· · ● ○ ● · ·

Try the following exercise to help prepare your connection to a plant spirit you are interested in summoning in a lucid dream. For this exercise, you will need some physical form of the plant whose spirit you will be contacting. This could be a small clipping of a fresh plant or a tree, some dried plant matter, or an essential oil, for example. You will also need to look up the scientific name of the plant you are working with in advance if you don't already know it.

1. Sit in a comfortable position with the plant matter in your hands. Take a moment to relax your body and breathe mindfully.

2. Feel the energy of the plant in your hands and notice its quality. Begin to engage all of your senses, taking time to smell the plant matter, inspect it visually, and feel its texture. Do not engage taste unless you know fully that the plant matter is ingestible in this form.

3. Take a deep breath in, and then exhale your breath directly out upon the plant matter. Imagine that the plant stuff

23. Donald Tyson, ed., James Freake, trans., *Three Books of Occult Philosophy: The Foundation Book of Western Occultism*, written by Henry Cornelius Agrippa of Nettesheim (Llewellyn Publications, 2007), 17.

is also breathing, and that it now breathes out while you breathe in. Take in the exhaled stream of energy of the plant with your inhales, and then share your exhales with the plant as it takes in the essence of you in turn.

4. After doing this shared cyclical breathing with the plant for a few minutes, whisper, "Speak to me, speak to me, spirit of *<insert common plant name, scientific plant name>*," repeating this three times as a gentle incantation.

5. Then, take one more deep breath and after your exhale, clear the mind and wait for a response from the plant spirit. You may receive energetic sensations in your body or energy field, knowings in the mind, or visions, or you may feel yourself having a verbal psychic conversation with the plant spirit. Be sure to accept whatever form of response occurs, releasing the need to understand what it all means right now.

6. When you feel finished with the communication, be sure to say thank you. Put the plant item down and document the experience so that you will be able to build on or compare it to what you receive in future lucid dream interactions.

You are now ready to try executing a lucid dream plan where you undertake to meet the personality of this plant intelligence. Success in this endeavor will cause the effectiveness of involving this plant in future magick to multiply. You may also find, as I have, that it seems as if the plant is getting to know you as well and could use this familiarity in its future dealings with you.

Spirits of the Deceased

I'm still not wholly sure of the reason, but I have sometimes found it more difficult to purposely summon spirits of the human deceased in lucid dreaming than other types of spirits. It seems as though it may be even more potentially unpredictable than dealing with deities, who may be stronger entities or have a presence across a greater variety of realities.

Some of the benefits of summoning spirits of the deceased include getting to know distant ancestors, understanding your lineage better, and making magickal allies. There are, of course, also the obvious motivations of summoning beloved dead so that direct conversations can happen, sharing messages that may have been unsaid in life, and simply being able to be in their presence because you want to.

Distant Ancestors

Each situation is unique, but it is possible that it may be more difficult to summon spirits of the deceased who have died long ago than it is to summon those who have passed more recently. In my attempts to summon my relative Samuel Wardwell from the Salem Witch trials, the results were often odd and difficult to interpret. I have had attempts to summon him with no response, one where all that showed up was a horse, and another where Samuel seemed to be stuck lying on the floor. He definitely seemed to struggle somewhat in getting himself through to me.

Even with such results, you can piece together the details of all of your experiments combined and this will often teach you something about your connection to this ancestor. Such summonings can also teach you a lot about the nature of dreaming as a reflection of life after death. When you get glimpses of distant relatives arriving in different forms or dressed in clothes from different times, it broadens your ability to accept the kinds of evolution or adventures that may happen after physical death.

The Recently Deceased

In contrast to such experiments with the summoning of distant ancestors, you may find a much greater ease in summoning the spirit of a recently deceased friend or loved one. Often there is an existing familiar connection that you have to the recently deceased that seems to make it more natural to draw them to you in a lucid dream. There are also emotional ties and the desire to make sure they have transitioned well and are thriving in their new state.

When I summoned a deceased friend within a few months of her death, she repeatedly showed up easily and clearly. We were able to have direct and coherent conversations. This contrasted greatly with my attempts to reach

Samuel, who was killed in 1692. The greater temporal distance between our time and his time of physical incarnation in the form of which I am aware may have a bearing on the greater difficulty in summoning him. For these reasons, I recommend that you first try to summon a deceased person that you know who has not been gone for too very long. It may set you up to have success as well as an emotionally rewarding experience, helping you to gain confidence for the execution of more elegant lucid dream plans down the road.

While the summoning of the dead can be somewhat more challenging than the lucid dream plans involving deities, it again provides a valuable potential teaching to the aspiring occultist. It gives food for thought regarding the nature of the conscious awareness of a recently deceased physical being as compared to the potentially evolved skills of a spirit we think of as a deity. Perhaps there is a prowess for dream navigation and multidimensional travel that is honed as one evolves. In the tradition of Vodou, for example, it is believed that human spirits can sometimes succeed in evolving on a path of apotheosis, eventually acting as a lwa, or tutelary spirit. My comparison of the abilities between deceased human spirits and spirits of deities in the dreamtime causes me to consider that this theory could be a reality in terms of the advancement of each of us as a spiritual being.

ARCANUM
Photo Gazing with the Deceased

· • ● ○ ● • ·

This exercise is intended to prepare you to forge and enliven a strong connection to a deceased friend or a loved one with whom you would like to communicate in lucid dreaming. You will need a decent photo of the person's face, ideally at least 5x7 inches or so.

1. Sit comfortably with the photo of your deceased contact in your hands.
2. Relax your body and breathe deeply and mindfully, doing your best to be present and still.

3. Say, "Spirit of <*insert name of deceased*>, awake and draw near. With the gaze of my eyes, I invite you here."

4. Hold the photo at eye level so that you are looking into the face of the person, making eye contact.

5. Allow your eyes to soften and your vision to blur. Begin to unfocus your eyes so that it feels like you are looking at something that lies beyond the back of the photo and not at the photo itself. Try not to blink, as this often resets the desired blurring effect.

6. While holding your deceased contact's photo in this blurred state, you may put forth conversational questions you wish to ask. With any query, be sure to pause just after and quiet your thoughts so that you can allow organic responses to come to you through your connection to this spirit.

7. When you feel you are finished, express love, thanks, and farewell as appropriate.

8. Put the photo down and blink your eyes open and shut a few times purposefully to reset the lubrication of your eyeballs and restore your vision to its normal style of function.

9. Be sure to document any results or insights from your conversation. You may wish to follow up on these when you get to converse with them face-to-face in a lucid dream.

Using a method such as this one to keep psychic channels open between you and a desired spirit serves to keep your lucid dream plan regarding this spirit of the dead fresh in your mind. It fuels ease of summoning and a likelihood that you will act on the plan with a high level of efficiency when you become lucid, increasing your chances of success. Write down the exact words you will use when you activate a lucid dream plan to summon this spirit so that they are concise and easy to remember.

Spirits of Living People

It is possible to summon in lucid dreaming the spirit of someone you know who is currently physically living. Interestingly, this often proves even more difficult than trying to summon deities or spirits of the deceased. As with my accounts of summoning deities and deceased spirits, and even less predictably, there have been times when I have called out something like "Jane Doe (a living friend), I call you to appear here before me!" and been unsuccessful. Sometimes I have called out for a friend and an entirely different friend shows up out of the blue.

One reason for wanting to summon a living person in lucid dreaming may include the desire to perform deep magick together at a level that transcends what can be done in the material world. You may wish to simply have face-to-face time with a person that you do not get to be with directly in daily life. You also may wish to share your passion and joy of lucid dreaming with someone who is dear to you.

Though it can be trickier to successfully summon the living, there are interesting points regarding the nature of consciousness that can be discovered through your attempts. Some experiments seem to hint that it is only easily feasible if the other person also happens to be sleeping and dreaming simultaneously in real time. Attempts made while the other person is in a meditative state have some lesser degree of success, while attempts made while the other person is fully awake and moving around in the world have proven most difficult. This can give food for thought regarding the levels of consciousness of two beings having a bearing on how well they can connect.

To summarize this, maybe when a person is completely and consciously awake and alert to this very dense, solid, physical reality, their ability to have a thread of their conscious awareness drawn away into a nonphysical state is more difficult than when both people's consciousnesses are settled into a similar vibratory state of disconnection from the physical body through dreaming or meditation. This could explain part of the difficulty that exists in attempting to summon the characters of living people—they might be awake and therefore too tethered to physical reality to have a response. Perhaps there is also a parallel in this that can explain some of the inconsistencies in dealing with the deceased, other spirits, and deities as well.

Familiar Spirits

Many Witches relate to the idea of having a familiar, and this can mean many different things. Some just use this term to denote a nonhuman spirit ally who helps them in their magick, some use it to describe the spirit of a physical animal with whom they feel magickally bonded, and some use it to refer to a complementary spiritual "other half." I refer to the last as the "true familiar" and see this kind of being as the anima to my animus, my nonhuman spiritual partner in crime to whom I am naturally connected.

You may use lucid dreaming for attempting direct communication with any spirit that you perceive as a familiar. If you are trying to summon the spirit of a bonded animal who is currently physically living, though, you may have the same difficulty as described in the section on summoning the spirits of living people. Unless the animal is also asleep and dreaming, the ability for you to link awarenesses in the lucid dream in the moment could be quite difficult. That said, you should be able to have success with the summoning of any familiar spirit who is not currently an incarnate being, no matter the type of spirit they are.

Summoning the True Familiar

At one time, I enacted the lucid dream plan "I summon to me my true familiar!" When this male being arrived so quickly, clearly, and easily, it was astounding how natural the process was, especially in contrast to the body of unpredictability inherent in my history of summoning all types of other beings before this point. I was brought to tears with the feeling of deep and natural connection that was obviously tangibly thick between us, and I was able to understand lots about him from a few quick initial questions. I was also able to summon him easily on repeated occasions, which allowed me to continue to get to know him more deeply.

I recommend that, when you are ready, you consider implementing a lucid dream plan such as this to meet your true familiar. The nature of such a being—your spiritual other half—seems to make the summoning natural and swift. It is as if they are already always there, and the request to summon them just enables them to manifest in whatever dream reality you find yourself.

If you start with a lucid dream plan such as I used, where you say, "I summon to me my true familiar," then you will get to see who spontaneously shows up without any expectation or specific influence of your own. When you do this, ask their name upon meeting them. This will serve to enable you to have easy conversations outside of lucid dreaming with other methods of divination and will allow you to be able to call upon them in your magickal workings as well.

Summoning Other Types of Familiars

If you aren't feeling ready to dive into a relationship with the true familiar but would just like to meet a magickal ally, consider implementing a lucid dream plan asking about this, such as "Show me a spirit who fits the definition of a familiar for me!" Another great lucid dream plan to use here may be "What is the name of the spirit familiar I need to become aware of at this time?" If you do already have an idea of the identity of such a being in your life, try summoning them by name. Once you have a spirit's name, the summoning can be more precise and tends to give smoother results. You can begin to see here how you might formulate a progression of lucid dream plans with a familiar to understand their nature and develop a friendship.

The Holy Guardian Angel

The seasoned occultist will have heard of the prized magickal feat of attaining the knowledge and conversation of the Holy Guardian Angel (HGA). There is debate in the occult world concerning what exactly the true nature of the HGA is. Some feel that it is one's Higher Self, presenting in its enlightened form, and others feel that the HGA is a separate being from oneself altogether—a special guide of a higher order to whom one is spiritually connected. No matter which belief is held, it is considered a great boon to one's spiritual evolution to be able to succeed in the summoning of this being and is said to result in greater ease for the magician afterward in manifesting blessings and abundance of all sorts.

In traditional approaches, the magician would work their way up to a full waking evocation ritual to summon the HGA and experience this energy firsthand. The concept is most well known through classical grimoiric reference, most especially from *The Book of the Sacred Magic of Abramelin the Mage*.[24] The process is rigorous and builds over the course of many months and sometimes years before the magician can succeed.

A solid lucid magick practice can support your efforts in contacting the HGA in amazing ways. While not a replacement for the experience of the full working, the HGA can be summoned directly in lucid dreaming ahead of the waking evocation. This can enable you to come into your ritual efforts with a name, a preexisting familiarity with the being's energy, and even some details of how they may present visually.

Executing a lucid dream approach to summoning the HGA is not meant to serve as a substitution for the experience of working toward a successful evocation in waking, as that experience certainly brings the energy of the spirit into the physical plane and your waking life like nothing else can. Because the HGA is defined in different ways by different people, it is important to be very specific with your lucid dream plan wording in this endeavor. The command I initially chose to use was "I summon the being who would be known to me as the Holy Guardian Angel in classical occult terms!"

I was stunned and humbled when a regal being entered my dream shortly after putting out this request. I was able to take in his appearance and successfully ask for his name. I continued to keep this lucid dream plan for numerous successive lucid dreams as well, continuing to amass more information and familiarity with him. When I did eventually succeed in my formal evocation ritual, I credit some of my success to the fact that I had already started establishing our connection consciously in the lucid space.

If you decide to explore the HGA and work toward its summoning, you should not consider lucid summoning to be a cheat in this process. The reason for this is, as an avid lucid magician, the amount of personal work you put into meditation, mental clarity, spirit relationships, and other magickal skills prior to that endeavor creates many of the same skill

---

24. S. L. MacGregor Mathers, *The Book of the Sacred Magic of Abramelin the Mage* (Dover Publications, 1975), 26.

sets that are being cultivated through the traditional months of buildup toward the successful HGA evocation.

Meeting up with your HGA in a lucid dream has immense benefit over knowing them through physical evocation only. The reason is that in the lucid dream state you don't need to conduct an elaborate ritual, get into a trance state, and then communicate telepathically with a being who is only present in a loosely formed energy body. You will be able to converse with them with full verbal clarity, see every detail of their appearance and take the interactions in as if you were physically conversing face-to-face. These interactions will then serve to enhance your confidence and skill in communicating with them in waking daily life.

You can see that it would therefore be highly advantageous for any magician wishing to undergo the work of communing with the HGA to also develop a sharp lucid dreaming practice and to build the prioritization of associated lucid dream plans into the process of the daily regimen and crescendo toward the evocation. Not only would the work involved in becoming adept at lucid dreaming add to the needed qualities and skills you need to pull off the evocation, but then you'd also have the ability to front-load your summoning process with knowledge and familiarity.

There is no one exercise that I could ever prescribe that would seem as a sufficient preparation for the summoning of the HGA, so I would not deign to do that here. If this is something you aspire to, I recommend you work through as many of the other exercises in this book as possible. If you have worked to cultivate a robust and experienced practice of magick involving relationships with other diverse spirits, personal introspection, and the working of waking magick to come, you may be well on your way to feeling the work of the HGA is the next step. When that happens, consider implementing a lucid dream plan for the summoning of the HGA so that you can discover their identity and ask their advice for how to proceed with the physical plane evocation ritual.

Waking Methods of Exploring Spirit Contacts and Finding Personal Lucid Guides

Maybe you don't yet know what spirits to prioritize summoning in your next lucid dream. Better yet, maybe you are seeking to find and build a spirit relationship with someone who can serve specifically as a lucid dreaming guide for you. Perhaps this could be a well-known deity or spirit, but maybe you seek to explore spirits who are not famous and with whom you can have an even more intimate and unique relationship.

You will likely come to realize that local spirits who are able to have a more directly energetic physical plane relationship, donating more of the wholeness of their attention and presence to you or your causes, are a powerful boon to any magick. It takes confidence in psychic communications to do this but could be much more gratifying overall.

Journey Work

One way to begin the exploration for a personalized lucid dreaming spirit could be through journey work. For help in building safe and responsible skills in this respect, consider studying the works of respected shamanic experts such as Sandra Ingerman and Hank Wesselman.[25] If you are trained and skilled in moving your attention through nonordinary reality, then you can plan a time where you will do just that: begin with your awareness in your established starting place and then see if you can take an upper world journey with the intention of meeting such a colleague.

If you do encounter a spirit who says they are there for this purpose, make sure to ask their name and start to get to know them. It would generally be considered poor magickal hygiene to engage in any meaningful interactions of depth with a spirit whose name you do not know. It is useful to ask the spirit why they are invested in doing this kind of magickal work together with you, and what types of offerings or payments they would expect to receive in exchange for their assistance. If you are not already skilled in traditional journey work and would like to be, you should seek certification and training from a qualified instructor.

Alpha-Style Meditation

Alternatively, you could use an alpha-style meditation induction for a simple psychic questioning to explore which spirits may be available to work

---

25. Sandra Ingerman and Hank Wesselman, *Awakening to the Spirit World: The Shamanic Path of Direct Revelation* (Sounds True, 2010), 29.

with you personally on your lucid dreaming skills. This type of approach was made popular by the modern-day Salem Witch Laurie Cabot and is described in her book *Power of the Witch*.[26] The Cauldron of Wisdom meditation structure in the next exercise is an adaptation of this approach that I first introduced in my book *The Goddess Seals: Sacred Magickal Symbols for Modern Magickal Practitioners*.[27] It is appropriate for this type of approach and appears here for your use.

ARCANUM
Cauldron of Wisdom Meditation

· • ● ○ ● • ·

This is an alpha-state-inducing-style meditation that is ideal for preparing the mind for sittings where you wish to engage in internal psychic divination questioning. It can be used for any exploratory purpose but is particularly useful for engaging with spirits, guides, and deities, learning to ask them questions directly and trust the responses.

It would be great to use this process in advance when considering setting a lucid dream plan that involves a spiritual being, for when you need to ask a guide for advice in creating lucid dream magick, or for when you want permission to call upon them directly for a spell. It creates an opportunity to get the opinion of the being on what dream request would be most beneficial to enact at this time or on what you need to do next to continue to improve your practice.

· • ● ○ ● • ·

Sit comfortably in your chosen position and breathe deeply, beginning to let your body relax. Feel the earthy stability of your bones. Feel the internal fiery warmth and buzz of your energy.

26. Laurie Cabot, *Power of the Witch: The Earth, the Moon, and the Magical Path to Enlightenment* (Delacorte Press, 1989), 183–187.
27. Nikki Wardwell Sleath, *The Goddess Seals: Sacred Magickal Symbols for Modern Magickal Practitioners* (Azoth Press, 2023), 18–19.

Feel the airiness of your breath. Focus on the rhythmic ebb and flow of your inhalations and exhalations, letting the energy of each of your inhalations fill not only your lungs but your whole body completely, and then letting your exhalations help your body to empty and release completely. Begin to imagine this energy that is filling and emptying, filling and emptying, is elemental water energy. Continue to let your body relax, letting go into this watery flow.

Bring your attention to the mind's eye and imagine that you are staring up close upon the surface of a great cauldron of water. Imagine the numbers from thirteen down to one, each appearing for a moment on the surface of that water. Count down slowly, letting each digit appear there briefly before it sinks below the surface and into the cauldron. 13, 12, 11, 10, 9, 8, 7, 6, 5, 4, 3, 2, and 1. When you see that the number one has disappeared, say to yourself three times, "I am one with the cauldron of mysteries, and everything it reveals to me is true wisdom."

After this assertion, you can either address an entity by name and ask any question to which you are seeking an answer or simply ask the question to your own conscious awareness or to the universe in general. Pose the question, then breathe, and clear the mind. You may see images appear on the surface of the water in the mind's eye, you may feel an energetic sensation or emotion in your body, or you may hear or just know the answer. Be sure to simply accept whatever comes, without applying logic. You do not need to know the underlying meanings behind all your received messages or impulses instantly. Ask clarifying questions as needed, using the same attentiveness and acceptance.

When you feel you are done, be sure to say thank you and show respect and honor to any spirits with whom you have interacted. Re-envision the surface of the cauldron of water and imagine the numbers from one up to thirteen each slowly surfacing, counting up with them one at a time as they appear. 1, 2, 3, 4, 5, 6, 7, 8, 9, 10, 11, 12, and 13. When the number thirteen has appeared and then dissipated, bring your attention back away from the cauldron of the mind's eye to the breath circulating in your body. Release the feeling of energetic water and return to watching your normal relaxed breath, then open your eyes, stretch, and acclimate again to your physical surroundings.

· · ● ○ ● · ·

Be sure to journal the results of your efforts so that your findings can be effectively brought to bear upon your lucid dream practice and your magickal planning.

Spirit Networking

Another way to meet specialty spirit allies would be to enter communication with a deity or a primary guide that is already known to you and then ask them to invite a more local spirit who they feel would be a good match for you as a lucid dreaming ally. This way you can use whatever may be your favorite method of deity communication to help get the process started.

In the Society of Witchcraft and Old Magick, for example, our Mage training students are taught to develop a structured Inner Temple technique for developing their skill in communing with primary guides and many of the trusted and recommended local spirits associated with the legions of those guides. In this way, many lesser spirits who are local and able to have a more fully present energy field embodied in the workings with the magicians are introduced and made accessible.

If you are skilled at talking board usage, such as Ouija boards, this is often another great way to do spirit networking. You would conduct your session as usual and start by having a conversation with a spirit you already know and trust. Once they are interacting with you through the board, you can ask them if they are aware of any spiritual colleagues that they might recommend as a lucid dreaming mentor spirit for you.

Spontaneous Visits

Designing a lucid dream plan aimed at meeting a spirit is a wonderful idea, but it should go without saying that you may also encounter lucid dreaming guides in spontaneous non-lucid dreams. This is yet another major reason why it is essential to journal everything that you can recall from your regular dream exploits. Having written records allows you to go back and look for trends or identify dream characters who seem to show up as chauffeurs, teachers, or navigational aids.

Once identified, you could set a dream intention to meet with them more purposefully and discover more about your relationship, or use another system such as scrying, talking board usage, meditative visualization, or journey work to get to know them more deeply. Having a solid and established connection with someone you perceive as a lucid dreaming guide serves to help create a virtuous cycle of perpetuating the ongoing recurrence of lucid dreams.

The Distillation

This chapter has demonstrated the benefits as well as some of the challenges and tips involved in summoning spirits other than deities in lucid dreaming. You have seen ideas for contacting plant spirits, spirits of the dead, familiar spirits, living spirits, and the Holy Guardian Angel. You have been given exercises and ideas for how to shore up connections with some of these spirits that will serve to ease the smoothness and success of your attempts to summon them in lucid dreams. The hope is that the spirit relationships you deepen through your lucid magick exploits will be rewarding and help you fuel the advancement of your magickal practice overall.

DIVINATION

Some classical writers have posited that truly prophetic dreams, or dreams received through higher intelligences or sources beyond our own awareness, are dreams of the lucid variety. In annotating the works of the famed fifteenth-century German occult writer and theologian Heinrich Cornelius Agrippa, modern occultist Donald Tyson describes prophetic dreams as being those that happen in the space of dreaming just on the edges of waking.[28] This would indicate a belief that lucid dreams hold special potential for divinatory magick. Performing any form of divination within the lucid dream is an essential effort for you as a lucid magician to experience. There are several considerations to examine prior to executing a lucid dream plan that contains a personal divination question.

Underlying Principles

In chapter 4, we discussed specific skills necessary for the lucid magician that include the ability to clear the mind for the unhindered receiving of responses to psychic questioning. It is very important to be sure that, after asking a lucid divination question, the magician can clear the mind and remove emotional bias and preconceived expectation to ensure that the dream response is organic and not orchestrated by the mind of the magician

28. Donald Tyson, *Three Books of Occult Philosophy* (Llewellyn Publications, 2007), 625.

alone. This is crucial in order for you to be able to trust the spontaneous nature of the results as psychic information as opposed to your mind controlling the dream to give you what you expected.

Developing lucid divination skills may mean first becoming confident with a technique that works for you that you can use to elicit a quick cleaning of the mental slate or erasing the inner chalkboard. After this, you can then simply watch whatever bubbles up into the no-thought space in response to your question. You will notice that when you function in this way with divination, whether it is a dreaming divination or not, it becomes a more authentic and organic grabbing of a true psychic impulse. This makes the results much easier to trust because you have learned a skill of changing the way the mind functions apart from your normal mode of everyday thinking, which can be kept special and only used for divination.

ARCANUM
Clearing the Mental Slate

· • ● ○ ● • ·

Usually when people are unsure of their divination results, it is because they are in a state where the mind feels as it normally does during routine day-to-day tasks. You can use this exercise for practicing the shift into a purposefully set mind space that is used just for divination.

1. Take one big, deep, purposeful breath in.

2. Upon the exhale, motion your dominant hand, starting over the crown of your head forward, and then coming down to pass your palm in front of your face, then down past your heart.

3. When your hand comes down to reach the level of your stomach, turn your palm to face your hand outward, away from your body in a gesture of clearing by pushing gently forward.

4. This combined pairing of the outward breath and the clearing and pushing hand motion literally feels like wiping the slate clean.

5. Once you have the coordination of the hand and breath down pat, try implementing this breath and gesture combo before every psychic endeavor you undertake while waking.

6. After you have executed it so many times in psychic practices that it becomes a familiar habit, the gesture serves as a nice trigger to automatically help get your mind into the desired open, unthinking place.

The reason for pairing this hand gesture with a deep breath is that you can locate that moment at the top of the inhale but before the exhale begins, which is liminal—that brief glimpse of space that is neither of the inhale nor the exhale, but the quiet space between. The pause between the breaths contains nothing and is a nice way of momentarily experiencing a no-thought state. That glimpse of no-thought paired with the energetic clearing creates a space conducive to noticing the next thing that organically bubbles up in response to the question or intention posed. It's not the easiest skill to develop, as our minds are incredibly complicated, non-stop thinking machines. Certainly, your daily meditation practice also goes a long way in backing up the development of this skill.

Who Are We Talking To?

In addition to preparing oneself to perform a properly unbiased lucid divination, you also need to decide in advance to whom the question will be asked. This is important since there are many sources of wisdom that could theoretically be responding when you perform psychic questioning.

The Dreamscape

One option is simply to yell your question out to the dream scene upon becoming lucid, then clear the mind and wait and see what happens. You might receive a symbolically visual scene, an audible set of words may be spoken to you in response seemingly from out of nowhere, or a dream character might walk up and tell you the answer. Your response could appear in writing, you could just suddenly receive an emotional or telepathic download regarding the answer, or any other number of varied outcomes. In this type of approach, it does not matter how you receive the answer, but rather what your personal philosophy is regarding the nature of the dream itself.

When you communicate directly to a dreamscape, who do you believe is answering? Maybe you believe it is your higher self, or Holy Guardian Angel. You might believe it is your primary deity, the Hermetic All, or the sum of the available intelligences of the universe to whom you are connected. You might believe the dream represents the collective unconscious, or your own stored unconscious wisdom. It really doesn't matter what the specifics of your belief are as long as you have a way to find meaning in their delivery to you. If you haven't decided on your personal philosophies regarding this, that's okay.

Your lucid dream divination experiments may very well be the things that help you develop this specific set of beliefs. Since most of these aspects of dreaming are not yet scientifically provable, it's important to establish personal truths upon which you can build the foundations of your own practice.

Spirit Guides

You may decide to summon a particular guide in a lucid dream and then ask them your question directly. Refer to chapters 10 and 11 on summoning various kinds of spirits for guidance on the details of lucid spirit summoning, as it comes with its own set of challenges. If you are worried that you haven't yet mastered the art of summoning spiritual beings well enough to stay anchored in your dream long enough to summon them, ask your question, and wait for a response, you can simply verbally ask the question of whomever you wish.

For example, upon becoming lucid, you might simply call out, "Great God Zeus, what do I need to know in order to maximize my income next year?" In using this approach, you skip the need to summon the deity directly and are left open for him to respond to you in any way he wishes. It is possible that he still may come forth in a recognizable form and speak to you in an ordinary way, but he may simply cause the answer to be whispered in your ear, delivered telepathically, written on the ground before you, or enacted in a spontaneous change of the dream scenery.

By addressing the specific guide, deity, deceased spirit, or other entity at the beginning of your question, you negate the risk of losing hold of your lucid dream during the time it takes the being to arrive. This method of addressing the entity first makes space for the answer to be sent to you imminently. After confidently and clearly posing your question, practice the mind-clearing technique from the previous exercise. Allow yourself to enter a moment of no-thought so that you aren't expecting the answer to your question to come in a certain form. You may be shocked to find the answer coming in changes to your dream body, changes to the dream scene, or any other number of previously unimagined ways. With practice, you can ask and receive an answer to a lucid divination question swiftly, such that you remain lucid and then can proceed right to your next priority lucid dream plan.

Honing Your Questions

You will notice over time that the wording of your lucid divination questions is very important. There is skill in preparing the question ahead of time very accurately and concisely so that you can keep it memorized and have it roll right off the tongue when you become lucid. A good example of a well-worded query might be, "Great Goddess Hekate, what is the name of the entity currently plaguing my friend Jane Doe?" In contrast to this, if you had asked "Hekate, how do I help my friend Jane Doe?" you leave openings for certain loopholes. You might get another being named Hekate, who is not the famous goddess, giving you the answer. You might receive a message about other ways she needs help that do not have to do with the problem at hand. Practice writing down your lucid dream plan divination questions ahead of time to help develop your skill in wording and memorizing them.

Steering the Dream to Give You an Auditory Response

One approach that can be used in lucid divination to help steer the swift receiving of the answer involves inviting an auditory-only response. After clearly stating your question, take your dominant hand to pull one ear lobe slightly forward and away from your head as in a gesture of listening carefully. Usually, the deity or spirit you are addressing is able to then simply communicate with you in a clearly audible verbal way with the answer to the question. It seems to bypass a lot of the potential laws and restrictions of whichever reality you are in and allows you to make sure that you receive an answer. It's nice when you can do this without having to work hard to remain anchored through other disruptive outcomes or scene changes that can come about as a result of unpredictable responses to the questioning.

Though you may find yourself doubting the accuracy of this right now, you will know with certainty when you've received a valid answer from your specified source. You will be astounded as to how surprising some of these whispered answers can be, with no doubt whatsoever that it came from yourself or an interloper, but rather the surety that it came from the entity you purposefully addressed.

I highly suggest that you attempt this form of clairaudient divination for yourself to see how it feels. Not only will you know when you've received a trustworthy response but you will also find that it allows you to better trust real clairaudient input when it is subsequently experienced in waking life. If you've ever thought you heard a disembodied voice whisper to you in a waking or hypnagogic state, you probably have, but it is much more confidently known once you've felt what that is like in the lucid state.

Effects of Timing

Another consideration for dream divination is timing. If you have a list of lucid dream plans that you desire to conduct, you have the luxury of choosing which acts you will initiate depending on what day it is when you become lucid. It is common in magickal practice to have correspondences of the planetary days of the week as being suited to certain vibrations. For example, in the Wardwell tradition of American Witchcraft, the general daily correspondences are as follows:

Sunday/Sun: new beginnings, friendship, warmth and nurturing, healing, personal growth

Monday/Moon: intuition and psychic matters, dreams and divination, fertility, emotional flow, protection

Tuesday/Mars: strength, courage, victory, success, battle, blood, lust, ambition

Wednesday/Mercury: communication, mental clarity, intellectual matters, study, language, swiftness

Thursday/Jupiter: abundance, wealth, money, good luck, leadership, generosity, finding lost things

Friday/Venus: love, romance, beauty, connection, family matters, compassion

Saturday/Saturn: karmic matters, wisdom, death and ancestors, animal magick, shadow work

Keep in mind either these correspondences or those of your own tradition, when you lie down to cultivate lucid dreaming. You can reiterate which lucid dream plan you have in mind depending on what day of the week it is. If you want to do divination regarding your job ambitions and also about your love life but it is a Friday, it might be better to start with the love divination just because it synchronizes nicely with the energy that is already predominant that day.

You could potentially even take the stance that you prefer to perform lucid dream plans involving divination on Mondays whenever possible, due to the lunar connection to divination in general. This is not absolutely necessary, and just like you can read cards for yourself any day of the week, you can certainly choose to enact your lucid divinations whenever you happen to succeed in becoming lucid. If you cultivate lucidity frequently, though, you may find yourself in the position of being able to make these more specific decisions.

There is an insightful section on dreams written by the classical occult writer Agrippa where he speaks of the mindset one should have for the act of dream divination as well as the astrologically desirable timing.[29] He points to certain times with respect to one's own birth chart, such as when the moon is in the ninth sign from your birth sign, or when the moon is full.

Alternatively, you may wish to perform lucid divination when the moon is in the sign of Cancer, since Cancer is the sign of the zodiac that is ruled by the moon. All of this relates well to the often-accepted idea that the magick of dreams and divination both generally fall under the purview of the moon's rulership, making it an excellent choice of timing when combining lucid dreaming and divination together.

Lunar-based setups are not the only timing options to consider for dream divination projects, however. Agrippa goes on to describe that when the planet Mercury is in a favorable condition, if the magician were to engrave its symbol in silver or write it on parchment that it would "...conduceth to memory, understanding, and divination, and to the understanding of occult things by dreams...."[30]

In addition to the magickal timing of dreamwork, Agrippa has a section on prophetic dreams where he details aspects of diet, lifestyle, and mental state that are needed in order to become skilled in this art.[31] For Mercury to be in a "favorable condition" may mean when Mercury is in Cancer, since this is the sign ruled by the moon. Since the magickal correspondences of Mercury include mental clarity and pursuits related to awareness, it stands to reason that days and hours influenced by Mercury could be good times to help cultivate that special state of clear mind that is associated with lucid dream divination.

ARCANUM
Lucid Divination Prep

· · ● ○ ● · ·

In order to make the best use of your lucid divination attempts, use the following prompts to plan ahead.

---

29. Tyson, *Three Books of Occult Philosophy*, 186–187.
30. Tyson and Freake, *Three Books of Occult Philosophy*, 319.
31. Tyson and Freake, *Three Books of Occult Philosophy*, 633–635.

1. In your dream journal, make a list of divination questions you'd like to ask while lucid.

2. For each question, work on creating clear and concise wording for the question, trying not to leave room for the potential for vague responses.

3. Decide if you are posing each question to the dream in general; to your Higher Self; or to a guide, deity, deceased loved one, or other spirit and make note of this. Adjust the wording of your question accordingly to involve addressing the being.

4. Look at your list of questions and try to discern the primary corresponding magickal vibration of each one, labeling it with a planet and day of the week as best you can.

Working off of this list, you can now state clearly to yourself what your priority lucid dream plan divination question is when you are lying down to cultivate lucidity. You can also change which one is top priority, depending on urgency with what is happening in your life or depending on which day of the week it is and its corresponding feeling of conduciveness to the question's topic area. The more you prepare with exercises such as this, the more you ensure that you will maximize the way in which you spend precious lucid dreamtime.

The Distillation

In this chapter, we discussed important concepts involved in lucid dream divination attempts. It should be clear that there is special importance placed upon the act of clearing the mind to ensure that the response is not dictated by the visualization of expected results in this thought-responsive environment. We also discussed the need to distinguish to whom we are asking our divination questions, as well as the need to work ahead of time to ensure our questions are worded very clearly and concisely to prevent confused responses that waste our valuable lucid time.

We reviewed some considerations for magickal timing that could have a bearing on the strength of the vibrational resonance of a divination.

These include ideas such as: Mondays being suited to divination in general due to the magickal association of the moon to psychic work, choosing a day of the week that the vibe matches the topic matter of the question, classical ideas such as working in the zodiac sign nine months from your birth sign, or considering including timing with Mercury since it relates to the lucid idea of a clear, wakeful mind and vibes of communication.

Throughout all of the chapters of part 2, the Mercury, you have seen examples of some of the profound magick that can be executed in lucid dreams. Hopefully you now have some ideas of what you, personally, hope to accomplish or experiment with in the lucid state. As you begin to feel passionate about what is important to you to cultivate first in your own lucid practice, you will be able to formulate actionable goals that will be fueled by the waking magick coming up next in part 3, the Sulfur.

Part Three

THE SULFUR– CASTING LUCID DREAM SPELLS

Now that you have seen lots of examples of the deep magick that are possible in lucid dreaming, you may be more motivated than ever to work some waking magick at the altar to try to help get lucid dreams to manifest for you. This section is specifically geared toward helping you to skillfully put together and conduct formal customized spells that are thoroughly planned out and cast in a ritual setting. To be clear, this section, the Sulfur, is about the transformative physical actions you do in your waking magick to help you become lucid in your dreams.

I will present all the various correspondences and components to consider that would go into a very thoroughly crafted spell and help you to make custom choices about these for yourself. Then I will provide a sample ritual structure with detailed instructions so that you have a method for casting a circle in which to conduct your spell. Keep in mind that while this part of the book sets you up to consider all the aspects of a big, detailed working, you can also use any of the individual magickal components we discuss on their own as smaller acts of lucid dream magick. Let's proceed now to the crafting of your focused and formal waking work of spell crafting to manifest lucid dreams.

SPELL GOALS
AND TIMING

As we shift into the waking sorcery work of this book, remember that we are now talking about a lucid dream spell as an act of ritual manifestation magick that you will plan out and conduct in physical sacred space. The goal of your lucid dream spell may simply be to help you succeed in becoming lucid in your dreams.

If you already cultivate lucidity, your spell goal may be to accomplish a specific lucid dream plan. If you need to improve your dream recall first, you can write a spell to help you manifest this. Whatever your current goal, this is magick that happens in the physical body, while awake and at your altar, and is not to be confused with lucid dream plans carried out while sleeping and dreaming lucidly as discussed heavily in part 2.

In this chapter, we need to set the foundations that underlie your spell. Care must be taken to figure out exactly what it is you are specifically trying to accomplish within your lucid practice, and then to word your goal accurately and clearly. Once you have finessed your phrasing, you will be better able to choose when will be the best time to conduct this spell.

Refining Your Lucid Dreaming Spell Goal

Believe it or not, one of the most difficult aspects of great spellcasting is clarifying what it is that you really want to do and putting that magickal goal effectively into words. Let's proceed to a discussion of the wording of the actual spell goal—the particulars of a potentially great spell that could be used to enhance lucid dreaming specifically. Sometimes we falter when asked what it is we truly want, and beyond that, we also need to know why we want it. Add to that the fact that it is very important to be clear and meticulous with careful wording in magick, and you have the task of what seems like forming a simple sentence becoming something that requires a practiced skill set.

Let's try to make our aims very clear and straightforward when it comes to lucid dreaming. There is a great chance that you are primarily interested in first crafting a spell for the purposes of enhancing your ability to culti-vate a lucid dream in general. You can work through this part of the book to help you to successfully cast this spell. Once you start succeeding in becoming lucid, you may wish to come back and craft a more specific spell to manifest increased skill or accomplish a certain lucid quest.

If you already have success in becoming lucid, then maybe you would like to cast a spell to increase your ability to anchor the dream body effec-tively within lucid dreams, or any number of other finesse goals related to this topic. Here I will list a bunch of different well-worded spell goal statements that may apply to you depending on what stage of your lucid dream development you are currently working on. You can see that there are also spell goal suggestions for successfully bolstering dream recall or other aspects of a dreaming practice that can help lead up to a lucid prac-tice. Consider the following spell goal statements and consider which may apply to you:

+ I successfully cultivate a fully lucid dream in which I can engage purposefully.
+ I will experience a fully lucid dream in the month of _____ in the year_____.
+ I increase the frequency of my successful lucid dream episodes so that they happen on a monthly (weekly, daily) basis.

✦ I effectively increase the level of stability with which I can maintain solidity and control of my dream body within my lucid dreams.

✦ I successfully increase my dream recall so that I can remember the scene and some details of at least one/two dream(s) per night (week, month, year).

✦ I keep a disciplined practice of daily dream journaling and nightly dream intention statements for the purpose of cultivating a richer lucid dreaming life.

✦ I succeed in cultivating a lucid dream where I can successfully achieve _____.

✦ I successfully implement the habit of carrying out thirty purposeful reality checks per day.

✦ I succeed in lucid dreaming several times per week with high-quality anchoring and engagement for magick and spiritual growth of the best and highest good.

I suggest choosing or adapting one of the listed ideas as the impetus for your spell rather than trying to stack multiple stages and dreaming goals into one spell. It is often more effective to focus on one specific quality or outcome than to try to accomplish too much at once. You will have the satisfaction of seeing how much improvement you make in that one, measurable area, and can then go from there. I liken it to using the hose in the direct stream setting versus turning it to the gentle, spread-out spray. You can spread your focus thinner over more aspects of your dream skills, but it may end up being harder to see exactly where you have progressed and where to focus next.

Timing Your Lucid Dreaming Spell

Now that you have some ideas about what an appropriate goal might be for you that suits the level of lucid dream development in which you find yourself, let's discuss more essential spell crafting details. The next thing to consider would probably be timing—that is, planning exactly when you will perform your spell.

Planning and pinpointing the best possible time not only adds astrological resonance to your work but also allows you to have the advance notice to do a great job in preparing the components and details of your spell as well as possible.

The Day

Generally, any days that fall in the waxing phase of the moon all the way up to and including the full moon are considered prime times for doing works of creation and manifestation, producing something, and drawing forth the results you want. Conversely, any days that fall in the waning moon up to and including the dark moon are good for cleansing, removal, and banishing work.

Workings related to decreasing, such as removing obstacles to dream recall, removing fears related to becoming lucid, removing emotional blocks, or removing poor sleep or lifestyle habits that prevent you from lucid dreaming, would be done in the waning or dark moon and are generally considered stronger when they occur closer to or on the dark moon itself. In contrast, goal statements to induce lucid dreams, create better recall, or otherwise draw to you any new or improved dream experiences would be executed in the waxing moon phase and are generally considered stronger when the timing occurs closer to or on the full moon itself.

Now, every tradition has variations in its set of planetary correspondences, but it is rarely argued, even amongst practitioners of very different traditions, that Monday, the day ruled by the moon itself, is the day of the week that is most associated with the magick of dreaming. Therefore, any spells you do that are for the purpose of cultivating lucid dreams, creating better lucid dreaming frequency or habits, may best be done on the Monday closest to or on a full moon but not after. Your spells for removing obstacles to better lucid dreaming would best be done on the Monday closest to or on a dark moon but not after. You can always refer to a farmer's almanac or other reputable source, such as the lovely smartphone app "Deluxe Moon," to access an accurate calendar of the lunar phases in your time zone so that you can plan for the best day upon which to schedule the working.

In addition to choosing a Monday in the proper lunar phase, you might also want the moon to be in the sign of Cancer, the zodiac sign ruled by the moon itself. This certainly could mean that your ideal date would then be further off into the future than you would like. This becomes a matter of personal preference and priority. Would you rather charge up your efforts sooner or wait a little longer and create a more meticulously planned spell? Neither is right or wrong, but in my circles this discussion would be sure to draw some joke about the Virgos of the crew being such perfectionists that there would be no question of waiting until the most perfectly aligned day and that the impatient Aries of the crew would want the instant gratification of doing it right now!

Planetary Hour

You can certainly go into even further detail with your spell timing and locate the exact best planetary hour for your working on the chosen day. It is often the right move to simply stick wholeheartedly with the vibratory energies of the moon as they relate to dreaming, and to pick one of the hours of the moon that happens on your best day as the time in which to carry out the work. It stands to reason that an hour of the moon that happens at night might create a better resonance than performing the spell in the daytime, simply because dreaming is often a nighttime activity.

This may not apply to your schedule, but there is no need to worry. There are usually four different time slots for the hour of the moon that occur between sunrise on a Monday morning and sunrise the next morning. There will always be an hour of the moon first thing in the morning, another in the afternoon, another in the later evening, and another in the middle of the night, so choose the one that suits you best. This will become clearer as you try an example of the following calculation instructions.

There might also be occasions when you feel you really want to include the vibes of another planet in addition to those of the moon in your spell, and your choice of planetary hour can be a great way in which to do this. For example, if you want to improve your meditation practice and your mental clarity for the purposes of cultivating a richer lucid dreaming life, then this goal might be best reflected by a working done on the day of the

moon but in the hour of Mercury (the planet of sharp mind and intellectual pursuits of clarity and focus), or conversely, on a Wednesday, the day
of Mercury but in the hour of the moon.

Another example might be, say, if your goal was to remove old, ingrained
fears related to the sometimes jarring or disorienting sensations of lucid
dreaming. You could do your spell on the day of the moon but in the hour
of Mars (the planet of courage and victory) and during a waning moon to
best reflect the path to the desired result.

Doing the Calculations

Many occult books contain charts of the planetary hours of the day, but
they may still not be useful to you unless you understand how to calculate
the actual length of a planetary hour for the day in question. The method
by which this is done will be explained here so that you can bring your
magickal timing to an optimal level of accuracy and specificity. To calculate the length of a planetary hour on the day of the spell, do the following:

1. Obtain the times of sunrise and sunset on the day you are planning
   to do your spell. These pieces of information are easily gleaned from
   the Farmer's Almanac.

2. Take these times and figure out the total number of minutes that
   elapses between them. For example, if sunrise is at 6:00 a.m. and
   sunset is at 5:00 p.m., there are eleven hours between them, or
   11x60=660 minutes.

3. Then take that number and divide it by twelve, and that answer will
   be the number of minutes in each planetary hour of the daytime for
   that day. In our example, 660/12=55, which would be the number of
   minutes in a planetary hour on our hypothetical day in question.

4. Each planetary hour of the nighttime will be 120 minus the minute
   length of the daytime hour. In our example, each nighttime hour is
   65 minutes long.

The whole premise here is that a "day," a twenty-four-hour period in
magick, is said to extend from sunrise on the day at hand until sunrise the
next day, not from midnight to midnight in the way that we look at calen-

dar days. The daytime itself is the exact amount of time we have in sunlight, and the nighttime is the exact number of minutes we have in darkness.

It is presumed that there are twenty-four "hours" or planetary categories in the course of this combined period of day and night, but they won't be equally 60 minutes in length like a clock hour unless we happen to be on one of the two days of the year where we actually have an exactly equal number of hours of light and darkness—the equinoxes. On those two days, the length of each planetary hour is actually 60 minutes, with 12 hours between sunrise and sunset, and 12 hours between sunset and sunrise the following day.

Every day in the darker half of the year (fall equinox to spring equinox) is going to have daytime planetary hours shorter in length than 60 minutes and in a complementary manner. The nighttime hours will be longer because we have longer nights than days during that time. The opposite is true during the lighter half of the year, which spans from the spring equinox back to the fall equinox.

Once you have the minute length of your planetary hour, you need to know the order of the sequence of planets through the course of a day. On any given day, the first section of time starting at sunrise is the planetary hour that matches the planet of the day itself. So, as in our example, let's say that we are still in the dark half of the year and have not yet reached spring equinox, and I want to do a dream spell on a Monday in the hour of the moon. I've done my calculation using the sunrise and sunset times and found that a daytime planetary hour on that day is equal to 55 minutes in length. So, from the time of sunrise (for ease let's say that is 6:00 a.m.) until 55 minutes later (6:55 a.m.) is the hour of the moon.

The order of the sequence of the planetary hours throughout the day, called the Chaldean sequence, then proceeds backward chronologically through the planets of the days of the week by skipping one.

Planets of the Days of the Week
Sunday: Sun

Monday: Moon

Tuesday: Mars

Wednesday: Mercury

Thursday: Jupiter

Friday: Venus

Saturday: Saturn

Order of the Planets in the Chaldean Sequence

Sun

Venus

Mercury

Moon

Saturn

Jupiter

Mars

Therefore, in my example, the second planetary hour of that day, from 6:55 a.m. until 7:50 a.m. will be the hour of Saturn. The next 55 minutes will be the hour of Jupiter, and so on. Since the number of classical planets is seven, an odd number, you will always continue to rotate through all of the planets with none being left out. So, the sequence goes Moon, Saturn, Jupiter, Mars, Sun, Venus, Mercury, repeating.

Remember, the sequence is always the same no matter what day it is, but it will start with the planetary hour at sunrise that matches the planet of that day of the week, so the first hour of a Tuesday is the hours of Mars, and so forth. As you count through the planetary hours, when you get to sunset, the start of the hours of the night, the length of the planetary hours in our Monday example would become 65 minutes long.

The sum of a daytime hour length and a nighttime hour length for any given day will always be 120 minutes. Even though the length of the planetary sections changes when you hit sunset, your place in the planetary sequence does not.

ARCANUM
Setting Your Spell Goal Statement and Timing

· • ● ○ ● • ·

It is now time to craft a carefully worded statement that will encompass the goal for your lucid dream spell. While this may seem like a simple and obvious thing at first, it actually takes quite a bit of practice. Your words need to be concise and pointed. They will help you to determine the rest of the spell decisions that come later.

1. Decide now, based on the suggestions and where you are on your own path to lucid dreaming, what you'd like your spell goal to be.

2. Write it in your dream journal as a clear and concise statement.

3. Once you have done this, look at your wording and notice if your statement is one of releasing an obstacle or of creating an experience.

4. Using a moon phase app or almanac, proceed to look forward through the calendar for the next few months and pick out a Monday in the proper lunar phase when you will be available to cast your spell.

5. For additional specificity, use a planetary hour calculation app or the calculation instructions given in this chapter to find which times constitute the hours of the moon for that day.

6. Choose the actual time of that Monday when you will conduct your ritual.

7. Be sure to make a note on your calendar as though you are setting this as an appointment for yourself.

Now that you know when you can cast a spell that is aimed at helping you meet your first lucid magick goal, you will be able to start picking out customized details for the spell in the chapters to follow. You now know when the spell will be so that you can plan ahead to have the components ready to go in time.

The Distillation

Having worked through this chapter, you will have been able to choose and refine the wording of the goal for your upcoming work of formal spell craft to support your lucid dreaming. You also have all of the information you need to wisely choose a time that is aligned with the correspondences of dreaming, and which works for your spell goal as well as your own schedule. You are now ready to proceed forth to the customizing of other important details of this spell as outlined in the coming chapters.

SPIRITUAL GUIDES FOR
LUCID DREAMING SPELLS

Let's proceed with another very crucial aspect of crafting a formal spell, which is deciding which spirit or spirits you wish to call upon for aid in your spell. Many Witches and magicians are very accustomed to working with spirits in their magick and find that the streams of energy that can be created to fuel spell goals when allied spiritual colleagues are involved are often greater than those we can create and project alone.

Spirits that you might consider calling upon during your spell could be deities, angels, goetic spirits, ancestors, animal guides, or any other being you perceive as a spiritual guide. We are generally not using the word *spirit* here to refer to ghosts or other unnamed manifestations of energy. We are referring to named, intelligent beings who inhabit spiritual realms of existence and have the ability to influence our realm.

General Notes on Working with Spirits

Asking for help from powerful benevolent spirits can provide immense benefit to you in your magickal work. Because they are not necessarily localized in a physical body and seem to have more of a broad conscious existence, we can imagine that they may have the ability to influence outcomes by accessing the consciousness of ourselves, our environments, or others involved in our goal.

When it comes to lucid dreaming, it is possible for a deity, an angel, or a guide to create messages or prompts that help you remember to do reality checks for example. Spirits may cause your awareness to travel into certain types of dream realities that lend to your ability to become lucid. Spirits may be able to provide streams of energy that induce greater mental clarity or provide energies that motivate your meditation and other lucid support practices.

It is a common concept to consider that powerful spirits such as deities, angels, and goetic spirits have legions of spirits working for them. This is another huge benefit to enlisting one of these influential beings in your magick. They have the ability to activate someone from among their ranks as a mover and a shaker that aids in your goal on their behalf. Often, the spirit legions of a powerful being include local spirits—spirits who can move around in our earthly plane with an energy body to help get things done. Therefore, calling upon the aid of powerful beings provides you with resources and networking from the realms of spirits.

Deciding Which Spirits Are Right for Your Spell

If you already have contact with powerful spiritual guides such as angels, deities, or goetic spirits with whom you have developed a relationship, they may be more than happy to participate in a dreamworking with you. Even if they are not famous for being a dream deity per se, it would likely behoove them to do so. What I mean is that a spirit that already is venerated by you is receiving energy and attention and possibly offerings, and they would naturally stand to benefit further when positive advancements happen in your personal spiritual growth and practices. Whenever you are in doubt as to whether it is right to include a spirit in your spell, use your preferred method of divination and ask them first.

In some cases, even though you may have some established spiritual guides, you may want to enlist the help of a spirit who is already well-known for having talent or rulership in the area of dreaming. Such beings may be naturally invested in helping people develop dream sorcery skills and may better know how to help than beings who are known for different talents. I am not recommending that you randomly call upon spirits for your spell without checking in, however. As you learn about various spirits of dreaming, if there is one or more whose identity seems to speak to you or especially piques your interest, read a bit more about them. Follow up by attempting to communicate with them using your favorite mode of divination and see what the gut response is. If you get a positive response, you may want to go ahead and call upon them in your spell. You may reap the great benefit of developing a rewarding new relationship as a result of the joint work together.

In addition to considering including your established spirit contacts, consider calling on known specialists in the areas of dreaming. It is okay to call upon multiple beings for the casting of an important spell. Maybe you'd like to call upon a deity with whom you already have a trusted relationship and also a deity who is a dream expert. If you are calling upon beings from multiple pantheons, this is usually still okay, as they can be individual contributors to your cause and are not necessarily working together. If you are in doubt of their willingness to be included together on the project, then certainly ask.

Here is a metaphor that can help in your spirit-calling decision-making process: If your close friend offers to help you put a new roof on your house, that is great, and I'm sure they will do their best. It is still probably a good idea to have someone there who knows what they are doing on a professional level as well. We can use these parallels in our thinking when choosing which spirits to engage magickally. It is not out of the realm of possibility to draw in the participation of a spirit with whom you haven't already engaged if you do it respectfully and provide sufficient offerings in exchange for their help. Offerings for the spirits you involve will be discussed in chapter 15.

Spirits Specializing in Dreaming Are Not Very Common

There aren't as many spirits who are known for working in the areas of dreaming as you might think. Dreaming is a natural human phenomenon and a direct window to all manner of magickal and spiritual experiences, so if you are doing magick for the purpose of working on enhancing dreaming, then you are probably in a decent place in life. You will find many more deities and guides who are known for more urgent and life-sustaining aspects of magick, such as health and healing, fertility and abundance, victory, love, and the like. Because the spirits of dreaming can be fewer and harder to find, I am going to point out some that might be worth considering involving in your future magickal dreaming exploits.

You will find that in popularly circulating information in the modern Pagan world there may be a lot of well-known deities that people have marked as having rulership over dreams, but then that information is often based on the practitioner's own gnosis and not validated through documented mention of dream influence in the actual mythology. Even though you could certainly work with, for example, Cerridwen, Hekate, and other well-known deities for dream magick if it feels right to you (in which case you should), I will focus here on some spirits who have a direct and long-standing association with dreams from some of their oldest source material.

I will attempt to keep this discussion purely to spirits known for dream influence and not foray into the whole host of beings that are associated with night in general, though you could certainly choose to include them in your work. It is understandable that people would associate the spirits and deities of night with dreaming, since many people sleep, and therefore dream, during the night in general. You already know that lucid dreaming, or any dreaming for that matter, does not have to happen solely at night, however. We will stick to a perusal here of spiritual dream specialists.

Deities Associated with Dreaming

When you see reference to deities in this book, we are talking about the well-known gods and goddesses of the many pantheons of the world. These beings are usually known through the mythological literature that has been preserved from their specific cultures. You are probably familiar at the very least with some characters of the Greek, Norse, or Egyptian pantheons, to name some popular examples. Deities from these traditions such as Zeus, Hekate, Odin, Freyja, Isis, and Ra are world famous and have millions of followers and devotees. There are many thousands of known deities from divine pantheons around the world. This list represents some of the most well-known deities from classical mythology from around the world who are known for their engagement specifically with dreams.

Amphiarus

Amphiarus is a being listed in the works of Agrippa as a god of the Boeotians.[32] Boeotia is an ancient region of central Greece that included Thebes. In the noted work, Amphiarus is cited as having been a hero who went on to achieve godhood in the eyes of his people after dying. There are mentions of his temple sites and that he provided healing by way of oracular remedies.

He was considered a god of oracular dreaming, bestowing blessings upon his followers in this way. Since his expertise lies in communicating through dreams, he could be contacted via dream divination for advice on bolstering one's lucid dreaming practice. It would also feel appropriate to call upon him if your spell goal statement involves asking to incubate a dream where you perform successful lucid divination.

Breksta

Breksta is a purported Lithuanian goddess of night and dreams.[33] There is little information to be found on the old gods of Lithuania in general, and the sources we do have were compiled by hearsay and written only by authors from the 1500s onward. In the case of any of these little-known deities, it still stands to reason that when thousands of modern people come to make the same associations around the idea of a being and then reach out to engage and communicate, that a commonality of group consciousness is made. This can theoretically help to find and even form the being that is intentionally being contacted.

In any case, some modern practitioners view Breksta as a protector during dreaming and sleep. This could be useful magickal information if you feel vulnerable to psychic attack when sleeping or if you have frequent "hag attacks" or other unnerving spirit experiences during lucid sleep paralysis. She is also thought to be one who can help you steer the course

---

32. Tyson, *Three Books of Occult Philosophy*, 491–493.
33. Didi Clarke, *Forbidden Wiccan Spells: Dark Goddess Magick* (Didi Clarke, 2019), 11.

of your dreams, and she may show up personally in your dreams with prophetic visions.

As a side note, I summoned Breksta once in a lucid dream and she appeared in the form of a cat. At the time, I did not know the bit about her reputation for providing protection in dreams. There may be an additional bit of synchronicity there, as cats are viewed as protective in some traditions. If you feel drawn to cast a spell to provide you with protection during your dream adventures, then Breksta could be a very specifically aligned choice in terms of assistance.

Caer Ibormeith

It is not really known if Caer Ibormeith is a goddess per se, though she is sometimes listed as a daughter of a member of the Tuatha de Dannan, who are the old gods of Irish mythology. It is postulated by Dr. Green, Celtic Studies Professor at the University of Wales, that she is half human and half deity and that this may be why she alternates between human and swan form.[34] She is described in the passages about the dream of the god Aengus, wherein they loved each other and she would come to him only in dreams, but then every time she showed up in his dreams she would disappear out of reach.[35] She continued appearing to him in dreams this way for a year, and the dreams were so real and the love so intense that Aengus fell sick from not being able to be with her in daily life. She was said to be able to take the form of a human girl, and the form of a swan, alternating between these forms each Samhain.[36]

Eventually Aengus found her and was granted the ability to be with her if he could identify her in swan form from among a crowd of other swans. He did so confidently, and they married. Not only had she been able to come and find her true love in dreams consistently, but the idea that they had such a real and lasting impression upon Aengus speaks to their magick,

---

34. Miranda Green, *Celtic Goddesses: Warrior, Virgins, and Mothers* (George Braziller, 1996), 122.

35. Jean Markale, *The Epics of Celtic Ireland: Ancient Tales of Mystery and Magic* (Inner Traditions, 2000), 48–49.

36. Dr. Daithi O'hOgain, *Myth, Legend and Romance: An Encyclopedia of the Irish Folk Tradition* (Prentice Hall Press, 1991), 40.

potency, and potential bent toward lucidity. When the couple married, they both flew off together in bird form, but not before flying around the loch three times and putting all the dwellers of the area to sleep with their singing for three days.

You can see that this is not a traditional situation of a universally accepted goddess ruling over the realm of dreams, but the story of a supernaturally gifted being making her presence and her reality clearly known by way of dreams. She also seems to have the ability to cast a magickal sleep upon others. If you feel drawn to this story, it may be worthwhile to follow this intuitive pull and explore a potential magickal relationship with this being. Especially for those who enjoy working magick with a Celtic style or who have already established strong magickal relationships with other beings of the Irish pantheon of Gods and heroes, Caer could be an excellent lucid dream spell ally.

Evaki

The goddess Evaki is known from the mythos of the Bakairi Indians of Brazil.[37] She is described as a goddess of sleep and dreams, sometimes associated with the form of a bat. Her stories are not easily searchable, but upon reading various descriptions of her as told by modern Pagan writers online, it seems she could send healing or manifestation dreams and influence them as well as interpret them.[38] Evaki could be a good choice for help if your spell goal involves incubating a lucid dream of healing or another specific outcome, asking her to send it to you.

Gestinanna

The goddess Gestinanna is listed in *The Witches' Goddess*, written by Witches Janet and Stewart Farrar, as being a Sumerian keeper of the records of both heaven and the underworld, even spending half of the year in each.[39] She is

---

37. http://www.native-languages.org/evaki.htm

38. Susan Morgaine, "She Who Is All; The Goddess of Ten Thousand Names," Pagan Pages, September 1, 2016, accessed October 29, 2024, https://paganpages.org /emagazine/2016/09/01/she-who-is-all-the-goddess-of-ten-thousand-names-19/.

39. Janet Farrar and Stewart Farrar, *The Witches' Goddess* (Phoenix Publishing Co., 1995), 223.

also noted as an interpreter of dreams. Maybe it would be a leap to assume that a goddess who has a talent for interpreting dreams is also good at helping you navigate within them, but it may be worth exploring, especially if you feel a pull to the old Sumerian spirits. She would also be an obvious choice to involve if you were doing a spell to increase your own talents of dream interpretation.

Morpheus

According to the *Illustrated Dictionary of Greek and Roman Mythology* by Michael Stapleton, Morpheus was a newer Greek god mentioned by Ovid, and not named specifically in older classical works. He states that Ovid named "…three sons of sleep: Morpheus, who sends dreams of human form; Phobetor, who sends dreams of beasts; and Phantasos, who sends dreams of inanimate things."[40] It is true that not many searches in books of classical Greek mythology reveal mentions of Morpheus, though his name has certainly come to have quite a common modern-day association with dreams.

From my own personal gnosis, I did at one point succeed in having a lucid dream where I was able to call out the intention to meet with Morpheus. What ensued as I stood in the dream scene and waited was that a beautiful, shimmery flock of birds flew down from the night sky. They proceeded to catch me up in their gracefully swirling murmuration, lifting me into the air.

I relaxed and gave myself over to the beautiful feeling of this airy flow, releasing any resistance and succumbing to the unpredictable directions of its movement, and eventually awoke, having gone too far in relinquishing awareness of my surroundings to stay anchored in the dream. Certainly, this was not a "dream of human form," but I think it's a good practice not to be too dogmatic about the statements made about deities in antiquity.

Personally, I believe that gods and elevated spirits can continue to learn, branch out, and experience new things and develop new talents just as we do. Because of that experience, I was left to ponder, at the very least,

---

40. Michael Stapleton, *The Illustrated Dictionary of Greek and Roman Mythology* (Peter Bedrick Books, Inc, 1986), 141.

the idea that the airily transporting energy of Morpheus certainly could lend itself to the magick of being transported through dream realms.

Nanshe

Another ancient Sumerian goddess and sister to Inanna, Nanshe is associated with dream interpretation, oracular prophecy, and a tradition of a priesthood upon which these same skills of dreamwork and prophecy were bestowed.[41] She is also a goddess of fertility, healing, and justice, and she strikes me as someone who has been potentially underappreciated in modern polytheistic and magickal approaches. Many times, goddesses who are not being called upon by large masses of practitioners but are less well known feel more eager and available for help with spellwork.

Njorun

Njorun is the name of a being mentioned briefly in Norse mythology about whom little is known. She has several mentions, though no specific story is attached to her. She is listed as being one of the Asyniur, or goddesses of the Aesir in the Prose Edda.[42] Her name appears again in the same work under a description about the various words for night from the vantage point of different beings, indicating that dwarfs refer to night as "dream-Njorun."[43]

Attempts have been made to guess at her nature based simply on breaking down the possible root words in her name, which has led to theories about her being a potential partner or sister of the god Njord, who is a sea god. Being listed in the Aesir may rule this theory out, however, as Njord is a god of the Vanir, a separate grouping of Norse beings, whereas Njorun is listed as one of the Aesir.

I did succeed in having my own sequence of visionary and lucid dream experiences with Njorun to further divine her nature. She did, indeed, present herself to me as an opener of passageways to other realms and had imagery symbolic of a ship's navigation wheel that she revealed. She used

41. Michael Jordan, *Dictionary of Gods and Goddesses* (Facts on File Inc., 2004), 213.
42. Snorri Sturluson, *Edda* (Everyman, 1987), 157.
43. Sturluson, *Edda*, 144.

water as a portal, and when she appeared as energy only, the colors were pink and gold. This is, again, my own unverifiable personal gnosis, so make of it what you will. You can find specific information on using a ceremonially consecrated seal and suggestions for crafting magickal dream spellworkings with her in my book *The Goddess Seals*.

Angels Associated with Dreaming

Angels are usually presumed to be beings who act as agents of God in the more monotheistic sense. Famous angel names are known not only from Christian literature but also from Hebrew and Islamic literature, to name a few examples. Angels are not necessarily the fluffy, winged beings modern media has promoted. Instead, they are powerful nonhuman spirits enlisted among the ranks of the God of their tradition. The famous seals in *The Key of Solomon the King* are symbols used to call specifically upon angelic spirits.[44] There are lots of known fallen angels as well. For information on the details of hundreds of known angels, consult Gustav Davidson's excellent compilation on the subject, *A Dictionary of Angels*.[45]

There are said to be angels that rule over all kinds of various aspects of life and angels of all different planetary vibrations as well. The following list represents the angels who are known to have direct ties to dreaming.

Duma(h)

Duma is listed in *A Dictionary of Angels* as being an angel over dreams.[46] Similar to Jeremiel, noted further in the list, there is no other detail given as to the nature of his story or specific nature. Duma may be an interesting angel to consider as an ally in your lucid dream spell if you feel drawn to working with angels and to striking up relationships with lesser-known spirits.

44. S. Liddell MacGregor Mathers (trans.), *The Key of Solomon the King* (Weiser Books, 2000), 67–79.

45. Gustav Davidson, *A Dictionary of Angels: Including the Fallen Angels* (The Free Press, 1967), 1.

46. Davidson, *A Dictionary of Angels*, 27.

Gabriel

Gabriel is the well-known archangel often called in the direction of the west in some modern traditions of ceremonial magick. You may recognize the name from chapter 6 and our outlining of the Lesser Banishing Ritual of the Pentagram. It makes sense that this spirit would align with the magick of dreaming since the magick of the west is frequently associated with water, which usually corresponds to vibrations that include psychic functions, divination, dreams, and the idea of the "dream sea."

If you are fond of working with angelic beings or are simply in the habit of doing so due to Solomonic influences in your ritual or magickal practice, then involving Gabriel in your lucid dream spell could be quite effective. Again, a benefit of enlisting such a well-known angel of high hierarchical standing is that such an archangel is usually said to have many legions of spirits at their disposal. These legions could include beings that are then dispatched to help in your magick at the local level once your request to Gabriel has been received and approved.

Jeremiel

Jeremiel is a lesser-known angel listed as an angel of dreams in *A Dictionary of Angels*.[47] No further extrapolation is given as to the nature of this angel, but as previously noted, there are times when a practitioner may choose to go the route of calling upon less famous spirits in the hopes that greater personal availability or investment could be experienced with such a being.

I recommend using meditation or journey work to explore the possible connection between yourself and any spirit new to you prior to engaging them for your ritual spellwork.

Goetic Spirits

Goetic spirits are beings who are known from classical grimoires, who are powerful magickal spirits with legions at their disposal. They are generally spirits who have been discovered through the work of famous occultists but who are not otherwise recognizable as angelic nor as a deity in the

---

47. Davidson, *A Dictionary of Angels*, 27.

classical mythological sense. Some folks use the word *demons* to describe the ranks of goetic spirits, but this comes with unnecessarily dark connotations. Goetic spirits such as those listed in *The Lesser Key of Solomon the King*, one of the most well-known occult grimoires of non-angelic spirits, are not necessarily baneful and can bring many exciting talents to bear upon your magick.[48]

It seems inconceivable that there are no spirits of the famed seventy-two beings of *The Lesser Key* who are specifically named as having the ability to help the conjurer with dreaming, but on the surface, this appears to be so. It is always advisable to read these older works with an attitude of broadening the definitions of the acts that are described, assuming that the language may be a bit archaic and that the write-ups may be purposefully obtuse to ensure that only the skilled and intuitive magician would understand the potentials hidden within. There are lots of ways of keeping the mysteries "hermetically sealed," after all.

Bathin

The spirit known as Bathin has been spoken about with respect to his ability to enhance astral projection, but on careful inspection of the source material this is not specifically stated. His talent is described as having the ability to "transport men suddenly from one country to another."[49] One can understand how this phrasing, or this idea, could easily be applied to the experience of being consciously able to transport oneself from this reality into another reality entirely.

It is feasible that our more ancient forebears may have described being in one reality and then another as having been in two different countries. In lucid dreaming, you can be in one setting and then give the dreamtime instructions to transport you to another setting instantly, so this could be a way in which the talents of the spirit Bathin were perceived. Since Bathin is also listed as knowing the qualities of precious stones, it could be a great

---

48. S. Liddell MacGregor Mathers, *The Goetia: The Lesser Key of Solomon the King* (Weiser Books, 1995), 27–79.

49. Mathers, *The Goetia*, 36.

idea to bless a special dream crystal in his honor and use it when asking
Bathin to help you enter dream lucidity.

Furfur

Furfur is also noted as being able to give "true answers both of things secret
and divine, if commanded."[50] One could then look to him as a potential
spirit teacher with respect to the art of lucid dreaming, especially lucid divination. It does seem that he requires more compelling than the average
spirit and that there is the risk of receiving untruth from him if operations
undertaken to communicate are not performed well or confidently. However, he does take the form of a great deer and does come with an additional list of magickal talents, and these specific qualities may create a dis-
position for a relationship with certain practitioners.

Gaap

Similarly, Gaap is said to be able to carry the magician from one kingdom to another at will.[51] Again, with the need to give careful analysis as
to the possible intent behind older usages of language, this could easily be
interpreted beyond the literal. Gaap is a spirit, after all, and it would make
sense that his ability to transport the magician could mean from one spiritual reality to another, or one plane of being to another.

Other possible perks with respect to Gaap include that he can help make
the magician more knowing. He can also apparently give true answers about
the past, the present, and the future. In this vein, if you are also planning on
conducting lucid dream divination, he could be an ally worth knowing, as
your efforts in relationship building could yield assistance in multiple areas.

Klepoth

In another classical occult grimoire called the *Grimorium Verum*, a spirit
named Klepoth is mentioned who is known for causing you to "see all sorts
of dreams and visions."[52] This is certainly directly in line with the desire to

---

50. Mathers, *The Goetia*, 45.

51. Mathers, *The Goetia*, 44.

52. Phil Legard, *Grimorium Verum* (PDF Version, 1999), 7.

manifest particular sorts of dreams, and dreams of the lucid variety. Interestingly, Klepoth is also said to be able to "cause the sound of a whispered voice to manifest in a person's ear" which, as previously stated, is a specific means of divining that I have used within lucid dreaming many times.[53]

I have successfully asked the Morrigan many questions in lucid dreaming and she has responded audibly directly into my ear, and apparently this is something that Klepoth can also do. He could be a great ally for help in generating lucid dreams where clairaudient divinations are conducted.

Osé

The spirit Osé (or Oso or Voso) is said to give answers and teachings on "divine and secret things."[54] Considering how elusive and mysterious the lucid realm of consciousness can be, it stands to reason that lucid dreaming and lucid magick would fall into these categories. In this way, Osé could serve as a good spirit to call upon for a spell where your goal is to become more masterful with respect to lucid dreaming in general. Certainly, having an ally who can give you teachings on the matter would help here.

A unique bonus with respect to Osé is that he is also cited as being able to help the magician change his or her form, so if you seek to cultivate a lucid dream where you get to experience shape-shifting, he might be a particularly appropriate guide.

Paimon

Paimon, a popular spirit in both media and practice, is said to be able to "…discover unto Thee…what Mind is, and where it is; or any other thing thou mayest desire to know."[55] Being able to know what and where "Mind" is certainly seems like something the lucid magician would endeavor to know in order to gain greater mastery over the clarity of awareness needed for this practice. Lucid dreaming is, after all, the practice of waking up to the nature of conscious awareness from one reality to the next.

53. Michelle Belanger, *Names of the Damned: The Dictionary of Demons* (Llewellyn Publications, 2017), 176.

54. Mathers, *The Goetia*, 36, 45.

55. Mathers, *The Goetia*, 32.

Paimon is described as also having a list of other skills and services that he offers besides those related to the mind, which could make him a very versatile ally for the right practitioner. He is also described as being "obedient unto Lucifer," so if you are not open to engaging that type of spirit then you should, perhaps, explore other options.[56]

The Seven Sleepers

In occult author Claude LeCouteux's The Book of Grimoires there is mention of a group of spirit names known as the "Seven Sleepers."[57] There is a magickal formula that includes the names of seven saints followed by the names of the sleepers to help induce sleep. It is said that "…he who cannot sleep bear these names upon his person: Eugenius, Stephanus, Prochasius, Caudiscius, Dionisius, Chericius, eQuiracius, Malcus, Maximianus, Martinus, Dionisius, Constantinus, Johannes, Seraphion." Obviously, this is not pertinent directly to dream magick, but if you are working firstly on developing the habits of getting enough deep sleep that you routinely achieve REM sleep, which could very well be a viable spell goal, this may be helpful.

Often, when a practitioner settles in to do a purposeful "wake-back-to-bed" lucid dreaming attempt, it is foiled by not being able to fall back to sleep at the desired time, thereby losing the opportunity to tap into that touted REM-loading period that is known to predispose one to lucidity. Perhaps the invocation of the Seven Sleepers could magickally help to avoid this pitfall.

Uncategorized Spirits

Sometimes you may end up meeting a spirit yourself, or through other magicians, who is not famous and has not been cited in mythology or published grimoires. This does not mean that such a spirit is not just as real and potentially as powerful as other spirits. Sometimes you meet an otherwise unknown being who ends up being an incredible ally because they are particularly drawn to you and others like you. It is always advisable to

---

56. Mathers, The Goetia, 31.

57. Claude LeCouteux, The Book of Grimoires (Inner Traditions, 2002), 73–74.

do your due diligence and explore the relationship of any new being for a while before you go ahead and involve them in your spells. The following spirit description represents an example of an uncategorized spirit who is specifically oriented to the magick of lucid dreaming.

Ulcha

Ulcha (pronounced OOL-ka) is a spirit that I have encountered personally who has made herself known specifically as a spirit of lucid dreaming. This information comes from my own psychic endeavors and is not yet known to be anything that can be corroborated in any other published sources, though I did recently go on a radio show with prolific dream author Robert Moss where he reported seeing me in a dream.[58] His description of the dream was exactly like the place where I journey to meet with Ulcha in non-ordinary reality, so this was quite validating.

Normally when I meet spirits who are new to me, I am relatively private about it, and I simply go about exploring the relationship with them as it pertains to my own practice and spiritual development. In the case of Ulcha, she specifically identified herself as a spirit about whom I should teach to other lucid dreamers.

Ulcha presents as a pale, willowy female figure with indigo eyes. Her silvery flowing hair seems to move gracefully about on its own, as if suspended in gently moving water. She is an owl shifter and can take either the form of an owl or a woman, and sometimes a winged woman. I met Ulcha in a celestial-feeling reality in which the skies had tree branches that were home to thousands of owls of every imaginable variety. These spirit birds were the legions and messengers of Ulcha.

Most owls are nocturnal and therefore literally awake at night. This trait creates a direct parallel to the magician who is working to *wake up* within the nighttime activity of dreaming. It needs to be done with wisdom, alertness, poise, and stealth, all traits that the owl has also long represented.

58. Nikki Sleath, "Tales of a Dream Sorcerer," interview by Robert Moss, *Way of the Dreamer*, HealthyLife.net, December 10, 2024. https://www.healthylife.net/RadioShow /archiveWD.htm

I have channeled and created a seal for the spirit Ulcha, which you may use for help in contacting her yourself, or to engage her in a lucid dream spell. Details of the seal and its usage are included in chapter 16.

Ancestral Spirits

Many practitioners of magick enjoy calling upon spirits of the dearly departed in their workings. While the spirits of deceased humans may not be famous or have legions of spirits at their own disposal, there can be immense benefit in engaging allies that you know without a doubt are highly invested in you and have your back. There is also the fact that, in many cases, you don't have to work to develop the relationship, if you are calling upon someone that you knew well while they were alive.

On the other hand, you can also call upon spirits of the deceased that you did not know in this life. Sometimes distant ancestors show up and you feel they would be a natural ally. You might also wish to call upon the spirit of deceased occultists or Witches who are not related to you. As with all of the examples given, if you are feeling drawn to engage a spirit you don't know, explore the connection with divination prior to calling them in your spell ritual to be sure that it is okay with them, and that the connection still feels good to you.

ARCANUM
Choosing Spirits for Your Spell

· · ● ○ ● · ·

You've already chosen a time to cast a spell to enhance your ability to have a lucid dream, so choosing which spirit allies to involve in this important work is the next step. Having read this chapter on dream spirits, scan back through and try to intuit which spirit or spirits might be most appropriate for your spell.

1. Anchor a pendulum in one hand so that it is nice and still.

2. If you don't already have a working relationship with this pendulum, start by asking, "What will be the response for yes?" and watching to see which subtle directional movement the pendulum makes. Still the pendulum and

ask, "What will be the response for no?" Again, wait and watch and make note of which movement answers this question.

3. Next, using the question "Is this being a good ally to enlist in my upcoming dream spell?," look at each of the spirit names in the chapter slowly, one by one.

4. Each time you peruse another name, still the pendulum and ask the question.

5. You may end up with a list of more than one being to include. Write down the names of the beings for whom you received a "yes" response.

6. You may choose to call upon any or all of these during your spell.

7. You can continue to ask clarifying questions and use your pendulum to help you narrow things down.

You could also do additional journey work or use a divinatory meditation technique such as the Cauldron of Wisdom meditation from chapter 11 to help you explore these potential spirit relationships prior to casting your spell.

The Distillation

In this chapter, we have discussed the benefit of calling in spiritual help for successful spellwork. We have talked about various types of spirits that you may gain access to in order to help you begin to think about who feels like a lucid dream spell ally to you. You have been given summaries of an array of known deities, angels, and goetic spirits for comparison, as well as an introduction to Ulcha, an unknown but enthusiastic spirit of lucid dreaming. Finally, you have been given a suggestion for intuitively working through the process of narrowing down which spirits may be right for your upcoming spell. Knowing which spirits you will call in will be important as you do the work of choosing lucid dream spell symbols.

OFFERINGS

One of the things that many people overlook in spell planning and execution is the concept of offerings. We've been talking about engaging various kinds of spirit allies for help in our lucid dreaming spellwork, and it is therefore necessary to consider what the full reciprocity is that will take place.

It is important to think deeply about how we relate to spirits and why they may be willing to be involved in our magick. It is possible that to a certain extent the deity involved, and their legions, may simply want to help you out of kindness or mutual vested interest. You can think of this like you might think of your own willingness to help a friend with a task. Maybe you don't expect anything in return, but if that is the case, it is probably because it is a friendship that you appreciate, which also probably means that it isn't one-sided. You might be helping your friend right now, but in a good relationship it is also probable that they would be willing to help you in turn.

Another scenario may be that you are opting to call in a spirit or spirits that you don't yet know very well. It is important to look at situations like this as being similar to when you might hire an expert for a job. You want to be sure that the price is something you can afford. The idea behind offerings is that everything in the universe is part of some exchange of energy. "You always get what you pay for, kids," my dad would say. It was cliché, but he was completely right.

With magickal workings involving spirits, we want to make sure that we are proposing the price we are willing to pay and the way in which we are willing to pay it. We don't want to call in spirits to help us manifest something and then find out later that there is a steep and painful price being paid that we did not negotiate from the start. Whether you are dealing with familiar spirits that are dear to you or new spirits that you are working with for the first time, it is important to make suitable offerings to them in exchange for their assistance.

What Should I Offer?

In the words of your spell and in the suggested template for this wording, which you will find in the chapter on the ritual working in chapter 22, you will see a place to fill in what the system of offerings is that is being given. I say "system" because a formal ritual spell like this is often done for an important cause—one which may not feel equal to a one-time gift like a glass of wine, the burning of incense, or some cookies.

Sometimes it is wise to offer to do or to give something over a prescribed period. This amplifies the amount of energy that is accessible to the spirits through your offerings and helps to keep you mindfully aware of the progression of the manifestation process over a longer period of time. Ongoing offerings, therefore, are a win-win situation, or a virtuous cycle, if you will.

Whenever you are unsure as to what the best choice of offering for a particular spirit will be, you can always use your own favorite divination or spirit communication methods and ask directly. Here are some example ideas of offering systems for you to consider:

+ Offer to perform a ten-minute gratitude meditation in the spirit's honor every Monday for the next nine weeks.

+ Offer to leave nine drops of jasmine oil (or a suitable substitute of your choice) on the altar (at the crossroads, by a favorite tree, in a special dish—you name the place) for the spirit every Monday for the next nine weeks.

✦ Pledge to chant the spirit's name 100 times each Monday evening for the next nine weeks and to freely donate the energetic output of your efforts to the spirit to do with as they wish.

✦ Offer to procure/plant a lemon balm (or other appropriate) plant and tend to it in the spirit's honor.

✦ Offer to write a poem for the spirit each week for the next nine weeks and then share this poetry with your magickal friends/ community in their honor.

✦ Offer to provide a glass of whiskey and the burning of incense for the spirit every Monday for the next nine weeks.

As you can see, I have used the idea of a nine-week period centering around Mondays, and this is simply because nine is the traditional number and Monday is the traditional day of the week associated with the moon. This takes the assumption that lunar vibrations are the primary planetary resonance being used for your spell, but if you are centering it around another planet, then adapt the day and numerological associations accordingly.

You can also see that the proposed gifts can be anything from repeatedly giving items to artistic acts or even acts of service. Be creative and try to come up with offering ideas that you intuitively think will be pleasing to the specific spirits involved. If you are having trouble coming up with a suitable idea, you can use divination or a direct meditative communication method to ask the spirits themselves. The Cauldron of Wisdom meditation in chapter 11 is one method that would be entirely appropriate for this.

How Do I Dispose of Offerings?

Many people have questions about what to do with physical offering items that have been set out. How long do I leave them? How do I dispose of them? It is a common assumption that when you leave physical offerings, such as food or libations, that the spirits are given access and then take the raw essence of the offerings as they wish. You won't see the cookies on your altar disappear overnight, for example, but you can presume that the energy inherent in them is being used at the discretion of the spirits to whom they were gifted.

There are no universally accepted rules regarding what is right as far as the length of time offerings should sit out. If it is food and drink, I normally remove them after a few days, saying aloud something like, "I will now clean and dispose of these properly. I hope they were to your liking, and that you are pleased and fulfilled." If I have offered art or writing, I may incorporate it as part of a devotional altar to the spirit and leave it as a permanent installation there. It's really all about respect, balance, and reciprocation within the spirit relationship. What is most important is that you are clear about what you plan to give for a spell, that you put finite timing parameters around how often or how many times you will give it, and that you remember to do what you said you would do.

ARCANUM
Choosing Offerings for Your Spell

· · ● ○ ● · ·

Take time to think deeply about the spirits you are calling upon for your lucid dream spell. Do any further research about these beings to determine whether there are already traditional offerings associated with them or not. Consider going into a meditative or journey work state to specifically ask them what they would like in exchange for helping you with your magickal lucid dream goal. Do you get the feeling they like physical offerings? Do you think the offering should be primarily active or energetic on your part? Are you feeling pulled toward an act of service? Trust your intuition and always document what you are sensing when you ask these types of internal questions.

If you are having trouble organically getting these insights to happen, consider writing down the following writing prompts:

+ A spirit I am calling upon in my spell is <insert spirit name>. I would describe them as…

+ I get the feeling that <insert spirit name> is motivated by…

+ If I were a guest visiting the home of <insert spirit name>, I would bring…

1. Try to relax and write a few sentences that complete each of these statements.

2. Allow yourself to write in an automatic manner, cultivating a stream-of-consciousness feeling to the flow of the words rather than thinking about them in a focused or planned manner. You will be surprised what may arise upon the page.

3. Be sure to then journal logical offering ideas that may correlate to the ideas you've written, adding them to your spell-planning list.

Trust yourself and remember that there are no real rules of what is right and wrong to offer in exchange for magickal assistance. If you have come up with your choice thoughtfully and respectfully, chances are very good that it will be appreciated.

The Distillation

This chapter should leave you feeling more confident with concepts of offerings in exchange for magickal assistance. Ideas have been presented that will help you to be creative as well as appropriate when proposing what to offer in exchange for an important spell. Keep these offering ideas in mind for formal lucid dream spell planning while also remembering that smaller offerings can absolutely be given for smaller acts of magick.

SEALS, SYMBOLS, AND SIGILS

In addition to calling on the right spirits for your lucid dream magick, you will need to decide what seals or symbols could serve as powerful adjuncts to the work. Seals are specific images that are meant for calling appropriate spirits forth to fuel a particular type of magick. Seals have often been channeled and then created by a magician who is in contact with a spirit who agrees with the proposed system of communication. Once the magician draws the seal that they have divined to connect to the magick of a particular spirit, it is normally consecrated for use with formal ritual magick. Once created, the seal is accessible for use by anyone who activates it properly.

In contrast to seals, sigils are symbols created by the individual magician for the purpose of embedding a magickal energy signature in their own aura and subconscious so that they attract the result imbued in the construction of the design. Sigils usually work based on theories of energetic and psychological models of magick (except for things such as the classical planetary and angelic sigils), unlike seals, which specifically function within the spirit-calling model of magick.

In addition to seals and sigils, there are also lots of other astrological and alphabetic symbols associated with dreaming. Examples of all of these will be discussed here, with some distinctions for different types of usage in lucid dream spells.

Seals

There are many seals published in various occult grimoires that are available for you to use in your magick. The following is a list of seals that would be particularly suited for inclusion in lucid dream spells. As you read about the various seals described, notice if you feel drawn to any of them in particular for your spell.

Dream Magick Seals

Some well-known seals for assisting dream magick include two dream seals mentioned in *Icelandic Magic* by Stephen Flowers, both of which are supposedly originally found in an older northern grimoire.[59] One is for lucid dreaming, and the other is for sending dreams to a targeted recipient. (See Figure 9.) The latter seal certainly crosses some ethical boundaries unless the dreams being sent are part of a mutually agreed upon magickal project between you and the recipient.

The lucid dreaming symbol can be drawn on a spell parchment or, since the book *Icelandic Magic* mentions that it should be carved in fir, you could carve it into a small piece of wood and place it beneath the pillow. One year at the end of the winter holiday season, I sawed off a disk of wood from the base of our Yule tree, which had been a balsam fir, prior to composting it. It was a thin, flat round about four inches in diameter. The wood was relatively easy to carve into with a jack knife, and then for effect I took pens in pink and silver and gave color to the carved lines. Pink and silver are alternative color correspondences for the moon in some traditions, and the usual white would not have shown up well.

59. Stephen E. Flowers, PhD, *Icelandic Magic: Practical Secrets of the Northern Grimoires* (Inner Traditions, 2016), 104.

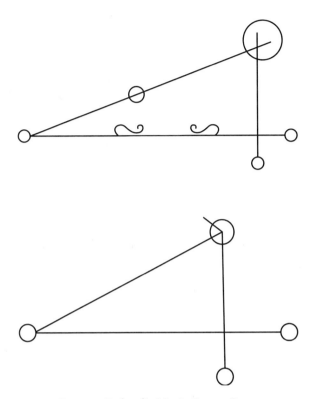

Figure 9: Icelandic Magic Dream Staves

There is also a seal depicted in the Museum of Icelandic Sorcery and Witchcraft that is located in Hólmavík, in the Westfjords region of Iceland. This is purportedly for the purpose of cultivating a dream of your choosing.[60] (See Figure 10.) There is nothing that says the desired dream can't be a lucid dream, so it may be worth a try to include it in your spell.

60. Claude LeCouteux, *Dictionary of Ancient Magic Words and Spells: From Abraxas to Zoar* (Inner Traditions, 2014), 368.

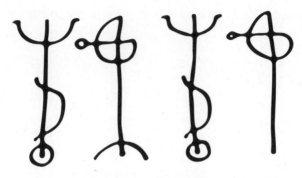

Figure 10: Dream Seals

There is a dream magick seal listed in *The 6th and 7th Books of Moses*.[61] Entitled the "sixth mystery seal," its description reads, "If a man wears this Seal in bed, he will learn what he desires to know through dreams and visions." (See Figure 11.)

Figure 11: Sixth Mystery Seal

In this same volume, it is written "The Ninth Table of the Spirits of Venus makes one beloved in all respects and makes known secrets through dreams."[62] (See Figure 12.)

---

61. Paul Tice, *The 6th and 7th Books of Moses* (The Book Tree, 1999), 10.
62. Tice, *The 6th and 7th Books of Moses*, 19.

Figure 12: Ninth Table of the Spirits of Venus

These seals are quite specifically suited to the magick of cultivating prophetic or precognitive dreams as opposed to lucid dreams specifically, but with the abstract nature of dreams and the fact that our forebears may not have referred to awake dreams as lucid dreams, we need to keep an open mind. It is wholly possible that one could use this magick specific to acquiring revelation "through dreams and visions" in a lucid dream, and not just a spontaneous nonlucid dream.

Seals of the Moon

It would also be totally appropriate to use any of the generic seals relating to the vibration of the moon to empower magickal workings meant to enhance lucid dream skills and experiences. In this vein, you could consider the pentacle of the moon from *Raphael's Ancient Manuscript of Talismanic Magic* as well as the seal for having familiar spirits of the moon at your command, the seal of the spirit of the moon, or the magickal square of the moon, which are all from the same work.[63] (See Figures 13 and 14.)

---

63. L. W. De Laurence, *Raphael's Ancient Manuscript of Talismanic Magic* (Kessinger Publishing, 1916), 43–45.

Figure 13: Pentacle of the Moon

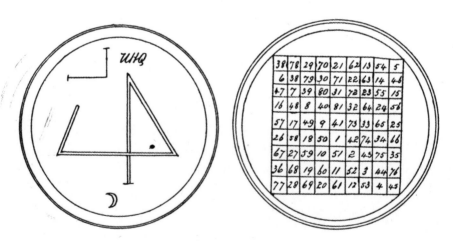

Figure 14: Seal of the Spirit of the Moon

Similarly appropriate in a broad way would be the first pentacle of the moon from *The Key of Solomon the King*, which recruits spirits of the moon in a general manner.[64] (See Figure 15.)

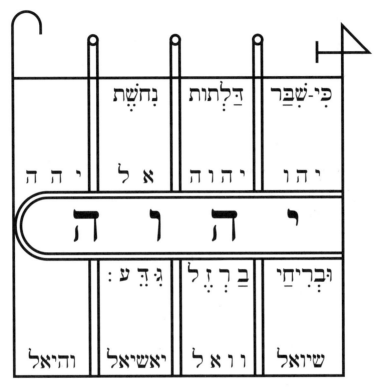

Figure 15: First Pentacle of the Moon, **Key of Solomon**

Also from the *Key of Solomon* is the fifth pentacle of the moon, which may be more specifically aligned to magickal goals of prophetic dreaming, or cultivating a lucid dream where you intend to carry out a divinatory lucid dream plan. The description of this seal states "It serveth to have answers in sleep."[65] (See Figure 16.)

---

64. Mathers, *The Key of Solomon the King*, 76.
65. Mathers, *The Key of Solomon the King*, 77.

Figure 16: Fifth Pentacle of the Moon, **Key of Solomon**

The fifth pentacle does have associations with creating destruction for your enemies and calling upon souls of the dead as well, though, so if you were to choose this seal for your own dream spellworkings, I caution you to have a discussion with the specific angels involved first to make sure that the goal of the work is very clear and agreed upon by all. In the descriptions of the seals throughout the work, there are translations of the angelic names inscribed on the seals. In this case, the names are Iachadiel and Azarel, for example.

Plant Magick Seals for Dreaming

In Raven Grimassi's *Grimoire of the Thorn-Blooded Witch,* the author presents a seal that calls upon the spirit of the oversoul of the nightshade plant for the purpose of "reveal(ing) through drawing lunar light."[66] It includes

---

66. Raven Grimassi, *Grimoire of the Thorn-Blooded Witch: Mastering the Five Arts of Old World Witchery* (Weiser Books, 2014), 76–77.

NIGHTSHADE

Figure 17: Seal of Nightshade

a lovely incantation to use with the seal that calls upon her as a "Dream-gifter Queen."[67] (See Figure 17.)

Usage of this seal could pair extremely nicely with the use of some homeopathic belladonna taken internally or as part of a preparatory potion for your spellwork. Do keep in mind that nightshades are often toxic, and for this reason the homeopathic version, which is energetic in nature and contains almost no actual active plant material, is suggested here.

Goddess Seals

The seal of Njorun is an example of a seal consecrated to work under the purview of a particular goddess. To connect your dream magick to the Norse dream goddess Njorun, you may wish to activate the seal consecrated and listed for her in my prior work *The Goddess Seals*.[68] (See Figure 18.)

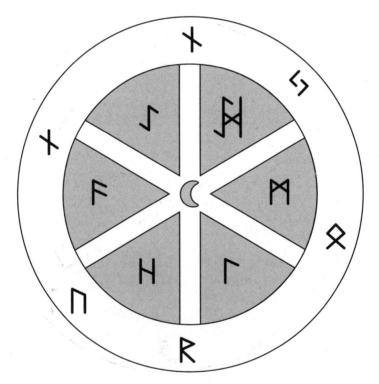

Figure 18: Seal of Njorun

67. Grimassi, *Grimoire of the Thorn-Blooded Witch*, 76–77.
68. Sleath, *The Goddess Seals*.

For more in-depth ideas on how to use a seal such as this one, or for deeper learning on the topic of seals in general, refer also to *The Goddess Seals*. You may find that you have a relationship with one or more of the goddesses described in that book, and if that is the case, then the corresponding seal and its instructions could also become components of magick that you could use to increase your lucid dream talents, as guided by your personal communications with those goddesses.

The Seal of Ulcha

Figure 19 depicts the seal for Ulcha, the owl-shifter spirit of lucid dreaming described in chapter 14. The seal contains her name, a close-up of the face of an owl with indigo eyes and a crescent moon on the third eye, and her name encoded again in Ogham script. It is meant to be drawn in hues of silver and activated using the auditory sigil "Magespral Chundito" (pronounced MAH-jis-prahl Chen-DEE-tow).

Figure 19: Seal of Ulcha

The embedded cue behind this activation is the statement "The spirit Ulcha leads the magician dreamer into lucid dreaming." It can be used to help tip lucid dreaming efforts toward success and can also simply help to facilitate direct communications with Ulcha herself. This seal, when used in a formal spellworking, will be further empowered by adding the burning of a silver candle and anointing it and yourself with jasmine oil. These items were used in the original consecration and would therefore connect the magician very strongly to its original energy.

Your Own Seal

With a bit of confidence, it is possible for you to create your own seals. This would involve intuitively drawing imagery for the seal that you feel is appropriate for the purpose as well as the spirits you intend for the seal to engage. Normally, you would enter into communication with the desired spirits and receive permission to bless the seal for the agreed-upon purpose. This is magick for the practitioner who already has some developed spirit relationships and a good foundation of skill level in communicating with them.

In the works of Agrippa, there are detailed descriptions about the use of an image for the purpose of cultivating true and prophetic dreams.[69] The magician is instructed to create an image of a man sleeping in the bosom of an angel, and then place it under the head of the dreamer while they sleep. It goes on to disclose very specific astrological timing recommendations for the use of this magickal image as well. Using this method would be more akin to creating your own seal instead of simply activating one that has already been consecrated for use by a previous magician's actions, since the art would be your own.

Astrological and Alphabetical Symbols

It is necessary to note the ways in which astrological and alphabetic symbols are different from seals so that you see how they could inherently serve different roles within a spell. Seals are usually more complex images

---

69. Donald Tyson, ed., and Robert Turner, trans., *The Fourth Book of Occult Philosophy: The Companion to Three Books of Occult Philosophy* (Llewellyn Publications, 2009), 180–183.

that work well drawn onto a parchment paper or grimoire page and serve as a central point on the altar during a spell, helping to call the appropriate spirits. Symbols from astrology and magickal alphabets, on the other hand, tend to be simpler and smaller and therefore are easily carved into candle wax, anointed onto the body with oil, or used around the edges of a spell parchment. They serve as meaningful decoration and tools for your mental focus, and they add another layer of sympathy to the spell.

Astrological

In looking at astrological symbols that would be appropriate for including in spells to induce lucid dreaming, there is of course the iconic astrological symbol for the moon, which is simply a crescent shape. (See Figure 20.)

Figure 20: Moon Glyph

The zodiac sign of Cancer is ruled by the moon, so this is another symbol that is said to directly carry dreamy lunar qualities. (See Figure 21.)

Figure 21: Cancer Glyph

Many people associate the zodiac sign of Pisces with dreaminess, and with its modern-day Neptune rulership, the oceanic flows of the hidden realms are an appropriate correlation. Therefore, the Pisces glyph or the planetary symbol for Neptune could be included in your lucid dreaming spell. (See Figures 22 and 23.)

Figure 22: Pisces Glyph

Figure 23: Neptune Glyph

In the Wardwell tradition of American Witchcraft, we also acknowledge what is known as the four-fold moon, a symbol that encompasses the phases of waxing, full, waning, and dark as shown here. (See Figure 24.)

Figure 24: Four-Fold Moon Symbol

Alphabets

Magickal alphabets contain letters that can be used on their own as symbols in spellwork. In terms of the symbology of the classical Elder Futhark runes, the "L" rune, laguz, is associated with water and the mysteries of the depths of the sea, which can be equated to the proverbial "dream sea." (See Figure 25.)

Figure 25: Laguz

There is also the "I" rune, isa, which is an icy rune of stillness and has been found by myself and many others to be a great aid to meditation. (See Figure 26.) Always remember that your meditation skills are a key component in determining your relative predisposition for lucid dreaming, so a well-planned spell may call into account this type of stilled mental focus.

Figure 26: Isa

I am also a fan of including the "M" rune, mannaz, in any magickal working that involves the evolution of our conscious awareness, which lucid dreaming work inevitably does. (See Figure 27.) The M rune stands for the consciousness of humankind and the nature of our minds.

Figure 27: Mannaz

In the Irish Ogham alphabet, the "S" letter, or fid, known as sail (pronounced SAHL) is a symbol of willow, of flow, and of intuition. (See Figure 28.) The willow tree is often associated with lunar vibrations in many classical occult traditions. I would certainly feel a natural connection of this symbol to dream magick work.

Figure 28: Sail

The Ogham fid edad is also associated with otherworldliness, psychic flow, and visionary states and could be easily incorporated in dream magick as well. (See Figure 29.)

Figure 29: Edad

These are only a few examples of well-known magickal glyphs you might use, but certainly do explore other magickal alphabets and systems for their dream symbols as befit you and the traditions you favor.

Sigils

Many people enjoy utilizing the crafting of visual sigils as an enhancement to their spellwork, and you can use them to augment your lucid dreaming spells as well. This is highly recommended, as the classical use of a sigil is meant to embed the customized symbol's imprint into the energy field and subconscious mind of the magician. In this way, once activated, it is always effective with no need on the part of the magician to focus upon it again. This differs greatly from seal usage, as seals need to be purposefully accessed upon each instance where they are being activated.

Creating a Goal-Based Sigil

In order to create a sigil, take a concise goal statement such as "I frequently become fully lucid in my dreams" and transform it into a glyph. Do this by first crossing out any repeat letters in the sentence so that you are just left with the list of each single letter that appears. In the case of this sample sentence, you would have I, F, R, E, Q, U, N, T, L, Y, B, C, O, M, D, A, and S. Then you creatively make a design that has at least one type of line segment that would be needed to re-create each of these letters. To be clear, you would need at least one vertical line, one horizontal line, one of each diagonal line, and at least one of each of the curved segments present to allow the imagining of drawing the rounded letters.

With sigil creation, it is better to keep the image simple rather than too complicated, as you need to stare at it and impress it in your mind during the activation process. Activation is considered by some to be most effective when conducted using solitary, masturbatory sex magick. You stare at the image while becoming aroused and all the way through orgasm, keeping your vision trained upon it and your mind upon the goal. After completion, you put the image away and put your mind directly to something else, to distract from the work, allowing the assumption that the energetic embedding process has successfully taken place.

Technically, after the activation process, you don't need to do any further work with the image for it to be effective, but it can be worthwhile to document it in your grimoire so that you have a record of the lucid dreaming magick you have done to date at any given time. There is also nothing that says you can't carve the sigil on your spell candle to link what is now in your bodily energy to the energetic flow of the spell. For more detailed and accessible descriptions of sigil work in the style of sigil classicist Austin Osman Spare, refer to the excellent work *Practical Sigil Magic* by Frater U∴D∴.[70]

---

70. Frater U∴D∴, *Practical Sigil Magic: Creating Personal Symbols for Success* (Llewellyn Publications, 2015), 7.

Creating Planetary Sigils

One lovely and effective way to combine elements from the energetic and spirit models of magick in your workings to promote lucid dreaming would be to create a planetary sigil for a deity to whom you feel most connected. In this way, you can work with a most trusted or revered spirit for this purpose for support and inspiration even if they have no renown in the realm of dreaming. You would be effectively calling in the lunar aspect of a favored guide, and at the same time creating an energetic connection to that aspect of the spirit's talent into your own magick, aura, and subconscious mind.

Creating a planetary sigil relies upon using the magickal square of the planetary number as a template. A magickal square, or kamea, is a grid of numbers arranged in a specific way that has numerological significance for a particular planet. For a lunar planetary deity sigil, you figure out the numeric values of the letters in your deity's name, and then graph them using the square of the moon. (See Figure 30.)

37	78	29	70	21	62	13	54	5
6	38	79	30	71	22	63	14	46
47	7	39	80	31	72	23	55	15
16	48	8	40	81	32	64	24	56
57	17	49	9	41	73	33	65	25
26	58	18	50	1	42	74	34	66
67	27	59	10	51	2	43	75	35
36	68	19	60	11	52	3	44	76
77	28	69	20	61	12	53	4	45

Figure 30: Magickal Square of the Moon

ARCANUM
Creating a Lunar Sigil for a Spirit Guide

· · ● ○ ● · ·

For this exercise, you will need a printout of the numeric square in Figure 30, another lightweight sheet of paper, and a writing implement.

1. Place your printed square of the moon underneath your lightweight piece of paper so that you can faintly make out the square beneath.

2. Refer to Figure 31 so that you know the number values of the letters in your spirit guide's name.

1	2	3	4	5	6	7	8	9
A	B	C	D	E	F	G	H	I
J	K	L	M	N	O	P	Q	R
S	T	U	V	W	X	Y	Z	

Figure 31: Chart of Numeric Letter Values

3. Mark a solid dot over the number corresponding to the first letter.

4. Next, draw a line from this dot to the next number in the name, then the next, making a line that turns and travels to each number of the name. You do not make a dot or any special mark at each letter, only the first one.

5. When you get to the last number symbol of the name, mark a little vertical line at the end of the path to signify the word's ending.

6. An example of how a planetary sigil might look is shown here in Figure 32, which is a drawing of a lunar sigil for the name Hathor.

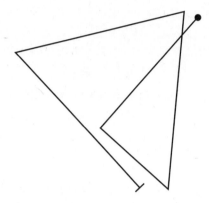

Figure 32: Example of a Lunar Sigil for Hathor

You can think of the resulting glyph as being a representation of the lunar aspects, or knowledge, of this being. It can then be added to the parchment for a dream spell in which you call upon this trusted being for aid. For imagery and further detailed instruction on this process, again refer to *Practical Sigil Magic* by Frater U∴D∴.[71]

Choosing Appropriate Symbols for Your Spell

It's time to do the work of deciding which symbols will best augment your upcoming spell. First, if you have already decided on any spirits through your work in the previous chapters, you will want to see if there is a pre-existing seal that corresponds to any of these beings and strongly consider incorporating it. Having a seal that helps serve as a calling card to a powerful dream spirit can be used as an energetic connector in your spell. You will literally have it pictured on your spell parchment and touch it to channel its energy into the candle magick you will ignite. More detail will be given on this in chapter 22 in the instructions on conducting the ritual itself.

Additionally, you should decide which letter, planetary symbols, or astrological symbols feel best for you to include. You may want them drawn on your parchment as decoration and additional tools of focus, or you may want to carve them into your candle. In both cases, they add valuable energies of sympathy to the work.

71. Frater U∴D∴, *Practical Sigil Magic*, 107–125.

ARCANUM
Psychometric Symbol Sensing

· · ● ○ ● · ·

As you decide which symbols to include in your spell, use the following technique to help you sense the energetic relationship you have with the various symbols presented here. This technique will also help improve your skill in channeling the energy of the symbol during the spell itself.

1. Go back and peruse again some of the symbols discussed in the previous pages. One at a time, take your nondominant hand and touch it to a pictured symbol.

2. Relax, breathe, and imagine that a flow of energy can travel from the symbol into your hand, up your arm, and then pour down into your center.

3. Notice what your energy body feels like as you do this. What sensations stand out? Do you feel any subtle tingling or shifting of warmth or coolness?

4. Keep your mind calm and quiet during this so that you can also notice thoughts and emotions that naturally bubble up as you connect to a symbol.

5. Be sure to jot down your organic responses in connecting to it and repeat this process for any symbol you feel intuitively drawn to.

Once you've noted the symbols that elicit the most powerful-feeling responses in you, you can decide what role they are best suited for in your spell. If you were drawn to simple astrological or alphabetical symbols, you might plan to carve those onto a spell candle. If you were drawn to a seal or two, then consider drawing or printing these out onto the spell parchment or paper that will contain the rest of the wording for your spell. Don't worry, there will be more instruction to come on the thorough organizing and wording of the components of the spell parchment.

The Distillation

Symbols are important in magickal workings because they provide an anchoring of preexisting flows of energy from the universe into your ritual. We have discussed seals, which bring the attention of specific spirits associated with the image. We discussed universally known symbols such as astrological, alphabetical, and planetary symbols that bring added layers of correspondence and specific focal wisdom from the collective consciousness. We also covered sigils as an alternative type of symbology, which allows you to embed the desired magickal vibrations into your own energy field, causing you to be a more effective conduit for conducting the spell and attracting the outcome. Hopefully you now have some ideas forming for which symbols you feel drawn to using, as we proceed to make decisions about incantations and words of power.

WORDS OF POWER

A well-constructed spell often includes what could be considered words of power, or words that help to ignite and/or add to the flow of the energy of your magickal intentions. Words are inherently incredibly powerful, and I like to think this is one of the reasons why works of magick are called "spells." Our thoughts alone have energetic emissions that can be finessed and aimed at our goals, and words help us to do that with greater elegance by adding specifically engineered layers of sound to the mental output.

Repeating words of power for a purposefully chosen amount of time or for a specific number of repetitions as a mantra is an effective way of raising energy to help fuel your magick. Chanted words of power can include incantations that you write, the magickal call words associated with seals and spells from new and old grimoires, words you simply channel and consecrate for a chosen purpose, or words you put together in a foreign language. Auditory sigils, which will be discussed later in this chapter, can also be chanted as words of power in a spell.

Words of Power Already in Existence

The following list represents a sampling of words of power for dream magick that are found in various magickal books and grimoires. There can be a benefit in using words that have already proven to be effective for others, in that you are tapping into a stream of energetic association between the words and the outcomes that is already somewhat established. Also, you will notice that some of these words seem nonsensical in that they don't necessarily spell anything in an earthly language we know. This idea has benefits as well, as the words then are only used for this purpose and have no emotional attachments for us, which could distract us from our focused task of confidently raising magickal energy.

ALLAS, GALLI YNOMINAM

Allas, Galli Ynominam are magickal words that French medieval historian and Sorbonne professor Claude LeCouteux cites from an old Norse book of spells. They allegedly are to be written on one's right hand in order to speak to a particular person in a dream.[72] This would certainly be helpful during times when your top priority lucid dream plan involves summoning a particular being, or if you are doing a spell to manifest a dream where you get to speak with a certain ancestor, for example.

AROX AXAX APORTAXA

Arox Axax Aportaxa are listed as words that ensure a good sleep when written on parchment and placed under the pillow.[73] You could use them simply as such or include them as an incantation in a spell to regulate your sleep schedule for the purposes of lucid dreaming.

EXMAEL EXMAEL

Exmael Exmael are also listed as words to ensure a good sleep when written and placed on the head of the sleeper.[74] The entry in LeCouteux's *Dictionary of Ancient Magic Words and Spells* does not indicate further specificity of instruction. Personally, I would go with writing the words on a slip of paper and placing them under my pillow.

---

72. LeCouteux, *Dictionary of Ancient Magic Words and Spells*, 38.
73. LeCouteux, *Dictionary of Ancient Magic Words and Spells*, 55.
74. LeCouteux, *Dictionary of Ancient Magic Words and Spells*, 128.

STOEXHOR ABALAY

Stoexhor Abalay are words to say before going to bed for the purpose of having angelic visions.[75] Certainly if you have a lucid dream plan that involves summoning an angel, which would be a stellar use of your lucid time, you could chant this before sleep and consider memorizing it to chant during the actual lucid dream to enhance the quality of the summoning. It would also be an appropriate incantation during a spell whose goal is to cultivate communication with angels in a lucid dream divination.

Nikki's Lucid Dreaming Words of Power

The following words of power all come from workings of my own creation and have been found to be effective so far.

I remember my dreams, a night journey I make—I engage the dream realms fully clear and awake.

You can use these words at bedtime while setting your intentions for recall and lucidity. Their rhythmic and rhyming nature also makes these words well suited for use as a repeated incantation in dream spells that are aimed at enhancing recall or inducing lucidity. For example, I have chanted this to raise energy that is then added to the fuel stream created by my lucid dream spell candle magick. It seems to greatly enhance the total energy produced.

Every time I see a tree, checking reality I will be!

Chanting this catchy rhyming intention to yourself in the morning as part of your day-opening practice can be very helpful. We take the existence of trees for granted since they are so common and tend to blend into our surroundings. Intending to notice them more mindfully and have that noticing result in a reality check is beneficial on many levels. This could also be used as a repeated incantation while raising energy in a spell aimed at solidifying a reality check practice.

---

75. LeCouteux, *Dictionary of Ancient Magic Words and Spells*, 307.

Aisling soleir, ser anois

Aisling soleir, ser anois (pronounced ASH-ling so-LARE, SARE ah-NISH) is modern Irish for "dream clear, see now," which I have used frequently for dream magick. These words could serve as a powerful spell incantation for anyone who looks to members of the Irish pantheon for guidance in their own lucid dream magick.

Vard Mog Jenk

Vard Mog Jenk (pronounced VARD MOAG YENK) are the magickal call words associated with the seal of Njorun, mentioned previously in the spirits of dreaming section in chapter 14. The repetition of these words can be used during attempts to communicate or connect with this goddess, or for use augmenting any spellworkings specific to dream magick. These are spontaneously channeled words that do not mean anything in any particular language as far as I know. Though this phrase was channeled for the purpose of enhancing the activation of the seal of Njorun, it can also be whispered or chanted without the seal in spontaneous moments where you are asking for her help in focusing on your lucid dream cultivation.

Magespral Chundito

Magespral Chundito (pronounced MAH-jess-prell chun-DEE-tow) are the magickal call words associated with the seal of Ulcha, mentioned in the spell crafting section for choosing spirits in chapter 14. These channeled words are not words in any known language of which I am aware. These words of activation could also be used on their own, outside of the normal usage of the seal, to facilitate a link with Ulcha for lucid dreamwork enhancement, or during moments of reality checking to forge a connection between Ulcha's talents and your next bout of sleep. These words of power can also be used as an incantation during a lucid dream spell where it is hoped that Ulcha or her legions will help you achieve your lucid goals.

Incantations to Bring In and Honor Your Guides

While not all the gods listed in the following incantation are classically associated with dreaming, they are all powerful spirits with whom I have communicated regarding dreaming at one time or another. There is something special about taking the lunar number nine and creating a call to nine special guides in your life for the purpose of helping you support your lucid practice. I thought the sharing of this incantatory prayer could be powerful for others as well, or at least inspire the creation of similar but more personalized pieces:

> Morrigan, my Queen, my Kin,
> Odin's wisdom deep within,
> Sedna's watery, mysterious flow,
> Valkyrja merging above and below.
> Skuld with sisterly, protective love,
> With Hekate's magick I rise above.
> Freyja, my shaman through time and space,
> Circe keeps me in nature's embrace.
> Morpheus, with you, dreaming I'll be,
> As I navigate with clear lucidity.
> Nine gods with whom my dreams I share,
> I'm with you now, awake and aware.

Auditory Sigils as Words of Power

It is well worth recommending the potential use of an auditory sigil to enhance your work in lucid dream magick. An auditory sigil is a set of nonsensical words that have been purposefully put together to stand for the underlying energy signature of a goal statement. It is like the creation of a classical visual sigil in the sense that you are deconstructing the goal statement down to its individual letter building blocks and then crafting the sigil from those. One major difference between an auditory sigil and a visual sigil is that unlike the visual sigil, the auditory sigil needs no specific means of activation. It is said to be automatically activated every time you utter it.

Why don't we just reiterate the actual goal statement in plain language, you might ask? You certainly can, but part of the premise of sigilry is that the power takes root in the subconscious, not the conscious mind. If you say the outright goal statement, it gets you thinking about it. This can be good sometimes, but not always. Some magicians will do better by not thinking too directly about the goal to prevent skepticism, misaligned emotional states, or their habitual monkey-mind habits from affecting it.

If we take the same statement that we used in the symbol chapter, chapter 16, when talking about visual sigil creation, our goal would be to create a set of nonsensical words from that list of remaining single letters. The words are meant to purposely not be reminiscent of any words we know in languages that we speak so that they are completely free from preexisting emotional associations. The words become words of activation and empowerment of the goal statement, as this is our intent in creating them.

With our letter list, then, you might end up with the words "QUINDYL FRESCAMBO" as your magickal call words. These can then be chanted to raise energy during the igniting portion of the candle magick phase of a spell or repeated to yourself nine times at bedtime, to name a couple of examples. The usage for quick magick at bedtime is particularly appropriate and adds convenience over seal usage in that moment because you can utter the words with your eyes closed, without the need to look at anything visually. This can be part of an effective bedtime ritual leading into the night's dreaming and predisposing you for dream magick, better recall and lucidity.

ARCANUM
Creating an Auditory Sigil for Lucid Dreaming

· • ● ○ ● • ·

These instructions are meant to help you learn firsthand how to create an auditory sigil of your own.

1. Create a concise goal statement that is pertinent to your own specific lucid dreaming practice. For example, it could be something like "When I am dreaming, I become lucid," or "I succeed in having a lucid dream at least once per month," or "I recall at least one dream every day."

2. Write your sentence down all in capital letters for ease of use in viewing the full scope of letters the sentence includes.

3. Look at the first letter of the sentence, then scan along, and anywhere that letter appears again, cross it out. Do this for each letter in turn.

4. You should be left with a list of just the singular letters that were needed to make up this goal sentence. Write them out neatly in a row so they are separate from all the crossed-out letters and easy to see.

5. Now begin to put the letters together in different orders so that you create a few nonsense words out of this specific list of letters. The words should be such that you can pronounce them, but also such that they are not actual words you know that have any preexisting meaning. It can take some creativity and experimenting before you come up with your new nonsense phrase. It needs to include all of the letters from your boiled-down list. It is okay if you need to use a vowel more than once in order to make your phrase pronounceable.

6. Once you have your phrase, this is your auditory sigil. Try repeating it aloud a few times. It contains the energetic building blocks of your goal statement but concealed within these creatively formed words of power.

Now that you have an auditory sigil that reflects a specific dream goal of your own, try to remember to say it frequently. Repeat it to yourself before you go to bed, right after you write in your dream journal, or actually any time at all that you remember to do so. The more you use it, the more effective it will be. You may wish to use this auditory sigil as a chanted incantation to help you raise energy within the ritual space of your lucid dream spell as well, if the goal statement behind it is applicable.

ARCANUM
Deciding on Words of Power for Your Spell

· • ● ○ ● • ·

Use the following prompts to help you decide more definitively on words of power for your spell.

1. Go back through any spell components you have decided upon already. Did you choose spirits or seals? If so, the call words for the seal may be the best incantatory lines to use in raising power for your work.

2. If there are no natural phrases already attached to your spell components so far, do you feel drawn to any of the words of power listed in this chapter? If so, consider asking your spirit allies in a meditative state if those words or phrases would be effective for your work.

3. Finally, if none of this seems to be applying, consider creating your own simple rhyming incantation to use for your words of power.

Be creative, and when you have decided on words that fit your spell that you can use to raise energy, be sure to document them with the rest of the spell specifics you've chosen so far.

The Distillation

In this chapter, you have been given the impetus to create or choose words of power for your lucid dreaming spell. You now know that there are words from existing grimoires, incantatory rhymes and poems, auditory sigils, and seal activation words among some of the many options for spell words of power that are available to you. Your choice in this matter will, of course, depend upon the goal statement you have formed and which spirits and approaches you are choosing to include in your magickal working. Let us continue along to make further choices for other detailed aspects of the upcoming spell.

HERBAL CONSIDERATIONS
FOR LUCID DREAMING SPELLS

In this chapter, I will present a list of some favorite herbs for inclusion in spellwork related to dreaming. This is meant for you to take into consideration when planning which herbal components you might like to include in lucid dream spells of your own.

Herbal components, whether used singly or in combinations, can be burned as incense, used to dress candles and decorate spell parchment setups, or given as offerings. You will be guided through some specific suggestions in chapter 22 regarding the actual casting of the spell. Herbs can also be used in the creation of teas and potions that have an effect on you as a conduit for the spell, though more will be discussed specifically on this aspect in chapter 19.

Cautions and Disclaimers Regarding Herb Usage

Before proceeding, it is necessary to assert that you must never work with any herbs without being 100 percent sure that it is safe for you to do so. The best way to learn about safe herb usage would be through a professional herbalist. There are lots of herbs with varying levels of toxicity, and you must be certain not only that you know what plant you are dealing with but also that you are using it safely. Some plants can cause contact dermatitis, or various types of skin irritation, just from touching them, and, of course, many plants are not safe to consider for any form of ingestion.

Even if you confidently know that a plant is considered safe for ingestion, you may not know what effect it might have on you personally. For this reason, it is wise to consult a doctor or a professional herbalist prior to using any new plant in an ingested or applied way.

It is important to proceed with caution not just with dried and fresh plant materials, but also with essential oils or other plant preparations, such as tinctures or extracts. Do not allow direct contact of essential oils to your skin unless you have verified through a qualified professional that it is safe to do so. Many oils can cause severe reactions. Even an oil that is not known for causing reactions can do so due to sensitivities in certain individuals.

Tinctures and extracts are preparations made by treating or steeping the plant, usually in an alcohol or glycerin base. Do not ingest these unless you have verified with a professional that it is safe for you to do so.

Neither I nor the publishers of this book can be held responsible for any circumstances you incur from your usage of plants in any way, nor for any of your magickal decisions and actions, for that matter. It is crucial for you to take it upon yourself to make wise decisions that align with your own health and safety when it comes to herbs. If you don't have access to trustworthy professionals or herbal teaching resources, then stick to the usage of food-based plants and herbal spices that you already know. There are lots of great herbal components already waiting for you in your own kitchen cabinets.

In reading through the list of lucid dreaming plants described in this chapter, some warnings will be relayed if they are known and obvious. That said, it would be impossible in a work such as this one to relay every potential warning that every individual reader may need to consider when it comes to exploring new plants, so please proceed with caution and due diligence as needed.

How Many Herbal Ingredients Should Be in Your Spell?

In choosing herbs for spells, let us consider that the number nine is the classical Qabalistic numeric association with Yesod, the sphere of the moon, in the Tree of Life. It makes sense then, to add the vibration of nine to a lucid dreaming spell by using nine herbal ingredients in either your potion or your candle magick. The more layers of sympathy the better, and the number adds another layer! For example, one might take a combination of three dried herbs, three oils, and three resins, making nine ingredients in total that all correlate to dreaming or the moon and combine them using a mortar and pestle.

You can use this herbal mixture in one of the simple candle-dressing methods mentioned in chapter 20 on candle magick, as part of your lucid dream spell. The remainder of the herbal mixture can be burned as incense as part of the spell, sprinkled in patterns on top of the actual spell parchment while it's on the altar, or gifted as part of your offerings to any helping spirits involved.

The Herbs
Here are some herbs to choose from that are touted for use in dream magick:

Chamomile (Anthemis nobilis)

Planetary Ruler: Sun

Folk Magick Usage: In addition to its famous association with assisting sleep, chamomile is also associated with drawing money, probably because of its connection to the growth energies of the sun.

Spell Usage: The dried flowers can be used in incense and candle-dressing blends, the essential oil for anointing yourself and your candles, and the tea as a dream potion ingredient.

Personal Observations: Chamomile is one of the most accessible teas to have on hand. Because of its mild flavor, it serves as a great base for the addition of other magickal dream herbs in formulating potions. It can, of course, be used on its own as a tea prior to bedtime, but dream magick potions are also wonderful when imbibed during spellcasting, helping you serve as a better catalyst for the magick by vibrating with the spell's sympathetic qualities from within the body itself.

Clary Sage (Salvia sclarea)

Planetary Ruler: Moon

Folk Magick Usage: In *Culpeper*, clary sage is listed as being under the rulership of the moon, and its description is focused upon clarifying functions related to visual issues.[76]

Spell Usage: The dried herb can be used in incense and candle-dressing blends, and the essential oil can be used for anointing yourself and your candles.

Personal Observations: As a straight anointing oil, I find clary sage essential oil to be a bit more sleep friendly than mugwort, and therefore fitting as part of a dream magick bedtime routine. There are cautions against using clary sage during pregnancy and breast-feeding. Noting the association with vision would cause me to consider this oil for usage when attempting to execute a lucid dream plan that involves divination.

Jasmine (Jasminum grandiflorum)

Planetary Ruler: Moon

Folk Magick Usage: According to popular Wiccan author Scott Cunningham, jasmine flowers can be burned to induce prophetic dreams or the aroma inhaled to help facilitate sleep.[77]

Spell Usage: The dried flowers can be burned or included in incense and candle-dressing blends, and the essential oil used for anointing yourself and your candles. Jasmine tea is a nice base for dream potion recipes.

Personal Observations: I like applying salves that contain jasmine prior to bed, as the scent is incredibly relaxing but also divinely magickal and dreamy at the same time. Since jasmine is an expensive essential oil, a salve is a cost-effective use of this herb, allowing it to go

---

76. Christopher Hedley, foreword. *Culpeper's Complete Herbal and English Physician* (Parkgate Books, 1997), 35.

77. Scott Cunningham, *Cunningham's Encyclopedia of Magical Herbs* (Llewellyn Publications, 2000), 147.

a long way. The scent stays with you nicely and is readily inhaled through the process of falling asleep if applied to the philtrum. This is one of my favorite herbs for dream spells.

Lavender (Lavendula officinalis)

Planetary Ruler: Mercury

Folk Magick Usage: Lavender has many magickal associations including love and peace, but is well known for its energies of relaxation, stress management, and inducing sleep.

Spell Usage: Dried lavender flowers can be used in incense and candle-dressing blends, the essential oil is lovely for anointing yourself and your candles, and the tea can be used as an ingredient in dream potion recipes.

Personal Observations: Lavender is extremely popular due to its beloved scent, which is so often inhaled and followed by a deep sigh of relaxation. I like to mix dried lavender and dried mugwort in the sachet and put it beneath my pillow, bringing a balance with the pleasant and calming beauty of lavender to the more brisk, visionary aspects of mugwort. Lavender is also widely used because it is known to be gentle and nontoxic in its many applications.

Lemon Balm (Melissa officinalis)

Planetary Ruler: Jupiter or Moon

Folk Magick Usage: In the classical plant compilation known as *Culpeper's Complete Herbal and English Physician*, it is stated that lemon balm is ruled by Jupiter but also the sign of Cancer.[78] Since Cancer is ruled by the moon, both of these vibrations can be considered strong in this plant. There is also mention of lemon balm supporting happiness and the heart.

Spell Usage: The dried leaves can be used in incense or candle-dressing blends, the fresh or dried leaves can be made into

---

78. Hedley (foreword), *Culpeper's Complete Herbal and English Physician*, 14.

tea for use in potions, and the essential oil is great for anointing yourself and your candles.

Personal Observations: I have come across a lot of modern usage of lemon balm with respect to dream support. It is an interesting plant in that its essential oil is very expensive, yet it is a plant that grows easily and wildly in my area here in New England. Similar to plants like mint, it will take over your whole garden if you aren't careful. I was thrilled to come across it spontaneously growing along trail edges on my property. The scent is, in fact, very lemony and lovely and the plant serves well for tea in its dried or fresh forms. It has come to be one of my favorite herbal additions to dream magick because of its great wild availability and the relationship that has developed between us while it grows on my land.

Lotus (Nelumbo nucifera, Nelumbium nelumbo, Nymphaea nelumbo, Nymphaea lotus)

Planetary Ruler: Moon

Folk Magick Usage: The sacred lotus plant has longstanding Eastern associations with spirituality and life everlasting. Cunningham lists protection and lock opening as additional folk magick traits of lotus.[79]

Spell Usage: The dried flowers can be used for incense and candle-dressing blends, and the essential oil can be used for anointing yourself and your candles.

Personal Observations: I have often used white lotus essential oil for anointing myself and my petition candles for dream magick. The scent is light, feminine, and relaxing and does seem to lend to the enhancement of visionary states.

Mugwort (Artemisia vulgaris)

Planetary Ruler: Venus

Folk Magick Usage: The dried leaves and flowers of mugwort can be placed inside your pillow or in a sachet under the pillow for

---

79. Cunningham, *Cunningham's Encyclopedia of Magical Herbs*, 162.

increasing the vividness of dreams as well as for increasing the chances of having prophetic dreams.

Spell Usage: The dried leaves, stalks, and/or flowers can be used in incense and candle-dressing blends, the essential oil for anointing yourself and your candles, and a mugwort tincture as a dream potion ingredient.

Personal Observations: My favorite usage of mugwort with respect to dream magick is to place eight to ten drops of mugwort tincture in a cup of chamomile tea and drink it prior to bed. A lot of folks I know like to use mugwort essential oil at bedtime, but personally I find the oil slightly too enlivening, such that it can make it difficult for me to fall asleep when used in that form. I do, however, love to anoint with the essential oil for the enhancement of card readings and other forms of waking divination. The use of mugwort is contraindicated during pregnancy.

Myrrh (resin from Commiphora myrrha or other gum trees of the Burseraceae family)

Planetary Ruler: Moon

Folk Magick Usage: Myrrh is well known as an incense resin for burning and is generally associated with ancient Egyptian sacred usages as well as being a sacred gift given upon the birth of Jesus in the Bible. Cunningham states that it "increases the power of any incense to which it is added."[80]

Spell Usage: Myrrh resin can be used as a base for incense blends, and the essential oil can be used for anointing yourself or your candles.

Personal Observations: I've never been attracted to the scent of myrrh, but it does enhance the burn of homemade incense blends whenever a good resin is included. Of the resins that are widely available to the magickal practitioner, myrrh is the only one I've found that has a lunar rulership.

---

80. Cunningham, *Cunningham's Encyclopedia of Magical Herbs*, 181.

Passionflower (Passiflora incarnata)

Planetary Ruler: Venus

Folk Magick Usage: This plant is most well known for enhancing sleep and creating peace and relaxation.

Spell Usage: The dried plant can be used in incense and candle-dressing blends, and the tea or extract can be used as dream potion ingredients.

Personal Observations: This is another plant that is great as tea or as an extract added to tea, for help in inducing sleep. Because of this, it is a great potion ingredient. The cut, dried herb also works well in herbal mixtures for incense or for dressing candles for your dream magick.

Tansy (Tanacetum vulgare)

Planetary Ruler: Venus

Folk Magick Usage: Tansy is associated with longevity and was used in colonial funereal preparations. Culpeper notes clearing of the eyes as one of the known remedies of tansy.[81]

Spell Usage: The dried flowers can be used in incense and candle-dressing blends, and the essential oil is nice for anointing yourself and your candles.

Personal Observations: I notice a common theme of plants that have medicinal value in clearing the eyes as coming to have associations with inner vision as well. Tansy is beloved among my peers for aiding in divination and journey work, and I have seen blue tansy included in sleep formulae.

Valerian (Valeriana officinalis)

Planetary Ruler: This is listed as Venus, according to Cunningham.[82] It is listed as being ruled by Mercury according to Culpeper.[83]

---

81. Hedley, *Culpeper's Complete Herbal and English Physician*, 176.
82. Cunningham, *Cunningham's Encyclopedia of Magical Herbs*, 250.
83. Hedley, *Culpeper's Complete Herbal and English Physician*, 188.

This Mercury assertion is backed up by British Witch and herbalist Nigel G. Pearson in his work *Wortcunning: A Folk Medicine Herbal.*[84]

Folk Magick Usage: Among its traditional usages, valerian is known as an aid in falling asleep. It may have been placed beneath the pillow, but certainly was and is still used for sleep taken internally as a tea or extract.

Spell Usage: The dried plant can be used in incense or candle-dressing blends, and the tea or extract of the root can be used as ingredients in dream potion recipes.

Personal Observations: Valerian root tea or a teaspoon of valerian root extract taken in another base tea such as chamomile is a wonderful sleep aid. Because of this, either of these options also serves as a great base for a custom dream potion. Note that as with many other ingestible plants, if you use this too often you might build up somewhat of a resistance against its sleep-inducing properties. For lucid dreaming specifically, I am intrigued by plants associated with sleep who also have a mercurial rulership, as this speaks to the mental clarity aspect considered to be key for waking up to full alertness within the dream.

White Sandalwood (Santalum album)

Planetary Ruler: Moon

Folk Magick Usage: Cunningham mentions white sandalwood in association with the magick of protection, wishes, healing, exorcism, and spirituality in general.[85]

Spell Usage: The dried, shaved, or powdered wood can be used in incense and candle-dressing blends, and the essential oil can be used for anointing yourself and your candles.

Personal Observations: I have not used this plant as a central focus in my dream magick, but it seems to be well loved and does have its

---

84. Nigel G. Pearson, *Wortcunning: A Folk Medicine Herbal* (Troy Books, 2019), 111.

85. Cunningham, *Cunningham's Encyclopedia of Magical Herbs*, 225.

lunar rulership. Since the bark or wood has a substantial feel to it, it could serve as a lovely base, providing good, solid substance and structure to herbal blends.

Wild Lettuce (Lactuca virosa)

Planetary Ruler: Moon

Folk Magick Usage: Wild lettuce seems to be popular as a divination and dream herb today. Culpeper is responsible for its written association with the moon and for the description of its feminine cooling and moistening properties.[86]

Spell Usage: The dried leaves can be used for incense and candle-dressing blends, and the plant extract can be added to potion recipes.

Personal Observations: While known for aiding sleep and helping to manage pain, it is likely that the modern association of wild lettuce with dreams and visions is mostly a result of both Culpeper and Cunningham classifying all lettuces under the rulership of the moon.

Wintergreen (Gaultheria procumbens)

Planetary Ruler: Moon

Folk Magick Usage: Cunningham does not list wintergreen for dream magick but describes it as having been placed in children's pillows for protection.[87]

Spell Usage: The dried leaves can be used in incense and candle-dressing blends, and the essential oil for anointing yourself and your candles.

Personal Observations: I have used dried wintergreen in candle-dressing blends for many lucid dream spells with great success. The essential oil, when used in these blends, adds a scent that is both relaxing and mentally clarifying. The folk magick implication of protection

---

86. Hedley, *Culpeper's Complete Herbal and English Physician*, 84.
87. Cunningham, *Cunningham's Encyclopedia of Magical Herbs*, 258.

during sleep paired with its lunar rulership makes this an excellent choice for a dream spell ingredient, in my opinion.

ARCANUM
Muscle Testing to Choose Herbs for Your Spell

· · ● ○ ● · ·

If you are having a hard time deciding which herbal components to incorporate in your spell, here is a muscle testing method that can help. Muscle testing comprises a variety of methods of checking on your personal energetic relationship to a substance or concept in a cause-and-effect way. Normally in muscle testing you expose yourself to an energy by holding it or even just thinking about it, and then see if your muscles seem subtly strengthened or weakened by its introduction. There are various ways to muscle test yourself or others, but a simple way is suggested in this exercise.

Remember that plants are vibrant, living things that each have their own extremely unique energies. Using muscle testing is not only a way to answer yes or no questions using the subtle energetic responses of your own auric field, but in this case, it can help to highlight the relative strength of connection between your energy and a plant spirit's energy.

1. Look at the plant names listed in this chapter and choose one to look up on the internet.

2. Find an image of the plant and leave that image open before you where you can see it.

3. Now make an "O" shape by touching the tip of your left index finger to the tip of your left thumb.

4. With your right hand, make the same type of "O" but have the index and thumb tips connected in the space of the left hand's "O" so that the two "O's" are interlocking.

5. Now, gaze at the image of the plant and say "Is *<insert name of plant>* a good ingredient for the lucid dream spell I'm currently planning?"

6. Immediately after asking this, gently pull your two interlocking finger rings apart from one another.

7. If your finger lock breaks apart with relative ease, the answer is no, and if the interlock feels strong and sturdy without the tendency to fail, then the answer is yes.

The idea with such a technique is that a positive energetic relationship to the component in question will cause a natural strength in your own energy, making the finger links naturally harder to break. It is, of course, important to try to keep a clear mind and put preconceived expectations aside so the results can be natural and spontaneous. You may want to practice this technique first with some questions that you already know the answers to so that you can begin to feel the difference between yes and no responses in your finger holds.

Journal the responses to various plant names that you test until you have a yes response for the number of ingredients you wish to have in your spell. Keep in mind that a no response does not mean that you don't have a good relationship with the plant in question, just that it may not be perfect for this specific spell.

The Distillation

Here you have seen a variety of interesting plants that have differing ways of being considered appropriate components in lucid dreaming spells. This information is meant to be introductory, and to spark ideas for ways in which you, personally, may want to use herbs in your formally crafted spell. Since potions and teas were mentioned as a possible means of bringing plant magick into your work, some ideas and recipes for these will be explored in more detail in chapter 19.

DREAM POTION
AND TEA RECIPES

Potions and teas are unique in magick in that their purpose is to cause an effect in the person who drinks them. This is different from the ideas presented in chapter 18 regarding using herbs to anoint and dress spell candles and parchments, for example. Potion usage is often forgotten or underappreciated, possibly since it is often thought of as an adjunct to a magickal working as opposed to being part of the work itself. While this may be true in some instances, potions may have more of a role to play in the magick of lucid dreaming.

As a lucid magician, you are constantly working to finesse the alertness and clarity of your mind and energy body so that you are primed for lucidity. Ingesting well-prepared potions or teas for this purpose is useful both in preparing yourself to cast waking spells as well as in preparing to lie down hoping to become lucid in dreams.

Reassertion of Herbal Cautions

Do keep in mind the prior warnings about handling and ingesting herbs as discussed in chapter 18. It is exceedingly important to operate with a full knowledge of the relative safety and toxicity levels of any plants you consider including in an ingestible form. Plant preparations have an effect upon you, but you want desired effects, not unpleasant or dangerous ones. Do not experiment with potions or put plants together for ingestion without having consulted with a doctor or professional herbalist. If you don't have enough knowledge to prepare potions safely yourself, you might consider buying teas or potions from an herbal shop where you could consult with the herbalist in person.

Usages for Lucid Dreaming Potions and Teas

There are more applications for lucid dreaming potions than you may think. It seems obvious that such a potion could be taken directly at bedtime with the hopes that it will help to energetically predispose you to lucidity. Better yet, it could be used at a time when you purposefully wake up in the middle of the night to enact the wake-back-to-bed lucid dreaming technique mentioned in chapter 3 of this book. This is when you purposefully work to create a REM stage rebound effect by getting up for a while in the wee hours of the morning and interrupting your sleep cycle before returning to bed. Drinking a relaxing tea or potion that is magickally aligned with lucid dreaming is a perfect activity to do during this waking period.

As an important note in spell planning, a potion can be taken just at or prior to the start of casting your lucid dreaming spell. As the preparation flows through you, it can help your body and energy field prepare to serve as the best possible conduit for this magickal and energetic work. You would literally be causing yourself to vibrate sympathetically with that which you are trying to attract.

You are, after all, the most important ingredient in any magick you undertake. A good lucid dream potion, then, can serve you over the course of multiple actions in a period of time. If you make a large batch of something that you find effective, you could take some when you initially cast the spell, and then use the rest of it for supporting further ongoing individual lucid dreaming efforts.

Potion Effectiveness Varies with Each Individual

It is important to remember that what one magician attests as a favored potion will not necessarily work well for everyone. We all have different constitutions, and just as medications have varying effects on different people, so do plant oils, extracts, and other popular herbal potion ingredients. Everything from your metabolism to sensitivities to your actual relationship with various plant spirits may affect how well a potion works to enhance a given act of magick or the quality of your dreaming.

I will include some favorite dream recipes here for your perusal. Any of these may be used on its own just prior to lying down to sleep and dream as a direct dreaming enhancer. They could also be used to augment your ability to cast your spell, as part of the spell itself, or as offerings to the spirits helping to support a lucid dream spell.

Dreaming Potions Aren't Just for Sleep and Spells

One additional thing that many magicians overlook is the potential usage of lucid dreaming potions during waking hours. If the concoction in question is not intended to cause overt sleepiness specifically, such blends may serve quite well to aid in the quest of waking up to the nature of reality in this waking dream. This rule applies to salves and oils as well.

Drinking a potion or anointing with a creation that has been specifically made and consecrated for the purpose of facilitating lucid dreaming need not be applied only at night. Waking life is a form of dreaming as well, after all, and if we practice awakening to this daytime dream and its true nature then we, in turn, increase the chances that we will inspect our sleeping dream exploits in the same way, predisposing ourselves to lucidity.

The Recipes

The following selection represents a sampling of recipe ideas that I have tried and enjoyed. I include an anointing oil blend that is not a potable potion. You may wish to try some of these, but they are also meant as inspirational ideas. Take dream ingredients that you personally like and see what recipe ideas you can come up with. Whenever creatively concocting, be sure to write down exactly how much of each ingredient you used as well as any specific means of preparation involved. If the recipe turns out to be effective, you will certainly want to be able to re-create it.

Chamomile Tea with Wormwood Extract

Wormwood, or *Artemesia absinthium*, is famous for its use in the controversial beverage absinthe. It does contain a compound that can be toxic, especially if used regularly and in an unadulterated form. The extract of wormwood is available as an herbal supplement and is a convenient way to use this visionary plant as an ingredient in creative dream potions you may concoct.

1. Place either a premade chamomile teabag or 1 tablespoon of looseleaf chamomile in a tea strainer into your cup.

2. Boil 2 cups of water and pour it in the cup.

3. Allow this to steep for 5 to 10 minutes.

4. Add 1 teaspoon of wormwood extract and stir to blend.

This is recommended prior to sleep or evening magickal work as it can cause sleepiness.

Lucid Dream Spellcasting Potion

You will need: 1 jasmine green tea teabag (or white tea for less caffeine), $\frac{1}{8}$ cup Peachtree Schnapps, 1 teaspoon mugwort tincture, 3 drops mugwort essential oil, 3 drops eucalyptus essential oil, 4 drops wintergreen essential oil, 3 drops artemisia annua essential oil, 3 teaspoons white peony extract, 1 sprig fresh lemon balm

1. Boil 2 cups of water and pour in a mug over your jasmine green tea teabag.

2. Allow this to steep for 10 minutes.

3. Remove the teabag and allow the tea to cool.

4. Pour the cooled tea into a large mason jar and add all the other ingredients to the tea, stirring them in.

5. Measure out ¼ cup of this potion to serve as a dose.

6. Store the unused portion in the refrigerator for up to two weeks, drinking a dose at a time on subsequent days to inspire your lucid dream magick.

Consider drinking this powerful brew just prior to casting your lucid dream spell. The remainder can be used as offerings for the spell or on successive nights a couple of hours prior to sleep, as it does not lend directly to sleepiness. This potion, because it does not induce sleep on its own, has also worked very well as a general psychic enhancement potion when taken prior to divinatory readings and channeling sessions.

If you are using this specifically for dreaming and you are someone who has a hard time falling asleep but wish to try this combination of herbs for increasing your chances of lucidity, consider substituting the jasmine green tea with a chamomile or "sleepytime" tea of your choice as the base. Another reason to make the full batch and store it is that it may be more effective for you to set an alarm for 3:30 or 4:00 a.m. and get up and take a serving then than it would be to drink it at your normal bedtime. Your chances of inducing lucidity will tend to increase in the morning beyond what they may be earlier on in the night.

Mugwort Tea

The most popular Witchcraft uses for mugwort certainly seem to be of a lunar nature, these being dream magick and all manner of psychic and intuitive enhancements, so it is a bit odd that Venus is its listed ruler. Even its formal name, *Artemesia vulgaris*, evokes images of Artemis, Greek goddess of the hunt, the wilderness, chastity, and the moon. This is not to say that a spirit of Venus can't be the purveyor of the skills of inner seeing, for they certainly can.

1. To make a basic tea, place 1 tablespoon of fresh or dried mugwort in a tea ball or strainer and add to a cup.

2. Pour in 2 cups of boiling water.

3. Steep for 5 to 10 minutes, then drink the tea if it is cool enough.

This is a nice option for enhancing yourself as a conduit prior to performing dream spellwork, as it does not lead to excessive sleepiness on its own.

Nikki's Sleeping Potion

You will need: 1 chamomile teabag, 1 drop fine lavender essential oil, 1 drop geranium essential oil, 1 teaspoon mugwort tincture, 1 teaspoon valerian extract, 1 teaspoon California poppy extract, 1 sprig fresh lemon balm, 1 lemon wedge, 1 sprig fresh mint

1. Boil 2 cups of water and pour it in a mug over the chamomile teabag.

2. Steep this for 10 minutes, then remove the teabag and allow it to cool.

3. Pour the cooled tea into a large mason jar and then stir in all of the other ingredients.

4. Measure out ¼ cup of the potion as a dose.

5. Drink one dose and then go to bed.

6. Store the unused portion in the refrigerator for up to 2 weeks for use on other nights.

This potion should significantly enhance one's ability to fall asleep as well as the length and restfulness of the night's sleep in general. Remember that it is crucial to have regular sleep patterns to increase the chances of being able to cultivate lucid dreams. While a sleeping potion such as this one can certainly help to facilitate a good night's rest, it is not intended for ongoing daily use. Plants such as valerian and California poppy are very effective, but you can build up a resistance to their efficacy if they are taken too often. Do, however, consider such a potion if you have failed to get a good night's rest recently and want assistance in resetting this, to support your dreamwork.

Wild Lettuce Tea

Wild lettuce can be used fresh or dried to make a simple tea.

1. Use a modest amount, maybe a teaspoon or so in a tea ball or loose-leaf strainer.

2. Place your tea ball in a mug and pour 2 cups of boiling water over it.

3. Allow it to steep for 5 to 10 minutes.

4. Remove the tea strainer from the liquid.

5. Once it has cooled a bit, drink prior to sleep or an evening spell-working, as it can cause some sleepiness.

Wild lettuce can be mildly toxic, so it is not recommended to use it often.

ARCANUM
Nikki's Dream Oil Blend

· · ● ○ ● · ·

You can use the following oil blend to anoint yourself as well as any candles or tools used in workings of dream magick. Note that this blend purposefully includes nine potent dream-related oils, adding the numerological layer of lunar magick.

You will need: dram bottle (or other appropriately sized vial); jojoba oil or other carrier oil of your choice; essential oils: mugwort, lavender, chamomile, spikenard, jasmine, sandalwood, wintergreen, white lotus, clary sage; coffee stirrer (optional)

1. Fill a dram bottle three-quarters full of jojoba oil or your chosen carrier oil.

2. Add 3 drops each of the pure essential oils.

3. Use a coffee stirrer to gently mix, or cap and swirl the bottle gently to combine.

It is also a wonderful idea to anoint the forehead, or third eye area, with such a blend at bedtime prior to saying dream intentions and incantations and moving into sleep.

ARCANUM
Dream Potion Testing

· · ● ○ ● · ·

Before you decide whether to include a specific dream potion or tea into your lucid dream spellwork, test it out to see what the energetic effect of the concoction is upon you personally.

1. Use your intuition to either pick one of the recipes discussed in this chapter or devise a recipe of your own that you might like to try.

2. Take the time to procure the ingredients, and once you have them all, make the brew.

3. Make enough so that you can dose yourself with it a few times over separate occasions as trials.

4. Document in your dream journal that you are trying this potion and under what conditions, such as before going to sleep, before meditating, or before working on reality checking.

5. Take the recommended dose, or in the case of an experimental potion, a very small dose.

6. When you wake, or a couple of hours after taking the potion, journal anything you noticed. This includes not only dreams that were recalled but also whether it was harder or easier to fall asleep, whether you felt any emotions or difference in mental clarity, whether the nature of your recall was different—anything that stands out to you.

These practices will allow you to keep track of what type of influence you can expect to be adding to a spell if you were to prepare your energy field for the casting of it by using this brew.

The Distillation

Here you have seen some examples of teas and potions that can be used as ways to enhance your effectiveness as a conduit for lucid dream spellwork or used directly to enhance your actual lucid dreaming attempts, or both. You should have a decent understanding of some creative ways of brewing and combining ingredients while maintaining respect for the caution that is needed when working with ingestible plants. It is not mandatory that you include potions or teas in your upcoming lucid dream spell, but it can be an effective enhancement to your work, especially if you are fond of plant-based magick.

LUCID DREAMING
CANDLE MAGICK

It is rare to see formal works of magick carried out without a candle, and this is for good reason. All magick requires energy, and in most cases, the energy of our thoughts is not enough. Our minds have lots to do in the course of any given day and are easily distracted. If our minds were the only energy source watering the lawn of our spell, the drops would spritz in dribs and drabs, leaving the grass rather parched and unable to grow. A candle is literal fuel for a flame.

As a candle burns, that fuel source, given by you to your magickal cause, transforms and is released into the atmosphere. Lighting the candle is a metaphor for igniting the process of the spell, and the energetic runoff of the burning candle creates a literal stream of energy flowing out into the world.

When you get to the point of conducting your spell in ritual space, the candle you have prepared for the working will be a central focal point. It will symbolize the energy that you hope to ignite and set forth into the currents of the atmosphere, altering your own conditions as well as getting the attention of the intelligent spirits who may be helping your cause. It is the beginning of the energy exchange, which is crucial in all of magick, if you wish to receive results back. Candle magick helps us do all of this while also helping to remind us that our work is sacred. There is something about a candle flame that quiets the mind and brings us back to the core of our being, and this is the place from which the inspiration for our magick comes.

Lucid Dreaming Candle Correspondences

There are a lot of choices when it comes to the candles that are available to you for use in your magick. There are colors to decide upon as well as size and type, freestanding or contained in glass. Part of the benefit of planning out all the details of a spell ahead of time is that you can really customize it optimally, rather than just making do with what you have available at the last moment. Let us consider some various options when it comes to your spell candle.

Candle Colors

As previously mentioned, lunar vibrations are usually associated with the magick of dreams, so white or silver candles are the most frequently used choices. This is because white and silver are the color correspondences that are most associated with magick ruled by the moon, at least within traditions of American Witchcraft.

White reminds us of the large glowing disc we see in the sky that fills us with awe when the moon is full. Silver and gold are often used as a pairing of colors that represent the female and male divine energies as a complementary pair, with the golden sun representing the yang, bright, hot energy of the god and the silvery moon representing the yin, cool, shadowy and mysterious energy of the goddess.

The moon is the most common planetary energy chosen for dream spells, but if you are going with another vibration, here are the colors commonly associated with each of the seven planetary energies of the days of the week in American Witchcraft:

Sunday: yellow, gold, or orange

Monday: white, silver, or pink

Tuesday: red

Wednesday: purple

Thursday: green

Friday: blue

Saturday: black or brown

Candle Styles

If you like the idea of carving symbols on your spell candles, then a large white or silver pillar or taper will do well so that you have access to the outer wax surface on which to physically carve your chosen dream symbols. Carving symbols into candle wax in the midst of casting a spell is another great way to have more of your energy and focus embedded in the candle, which then creates that powerful fuel stream. It can be gratifying to monitor the burning of a spell candle and see your carved symbols being slowly consumed and transformed as they melt into the flame's heat.

If you prefer the idea of stuffing the candle with herbs, then a glass-encased or seven-day candle could be ideal. Keep in mind though, that even with a typical glass-encased candle, you can still draw (as an alternative to carving) runes, symbols, and sigils on the outside surface of the glass with markers or paints or even glue and glitter. This way you still get to utilize symbology and have the advantage of being able to create some holes in the top wax surface for stuffing in your herbal mixture as well.

In terms of size, there are candle options from a tiny birthday cake-sized candle all the way up to large pillars or "seven-day" candles. The longer the candle takes to burn, the more potential energy is being added to your magickal fuel stream over a period of time. You have to decide if you want one small candle to burn all the way down in the space of the ritual, or whether you are willing to do the work of safely monitoring the burning down of a larger candle over a prolonged time. A tealight or chime candle will generally burn down in about an hour and a half, whereas the tall, glass-encased candles you find in the religious section of the grocery store are said to burn for about seven days if left to burn continuously and unimpeded. Personally, I prefer using a plain seven-day candle as the base for my candle magick for a big spell, as it feels like the tending and burning starts the work off with a good amount of attention and energy.

Dressing Your Candle

There are lots of creative ways to "dress" or prepare your spell candle in a customized way. Let's look at a couple of examples of candle dressing that vary depending on which style of candle you have chosen for the focal point of your spell.

Dressing the Glass-Encased Candle

In the case of stuffing a glass-encased candle with herbs, I enjoy the fact that the spell's herbs are being burned down right along with the candle. Glass-encased candles also tend to be safer, which is an important consideration since you are going to need to burn your spell candle all the way down at some point.

Candles that are poured in glass containers tend to be made with softer wax than candles that are poured into molds and then taken out to be freestanding. Because of this, you can easily take the end of a knife and poke some holes in the top surface of the wax. You can then stuff little pinches of your chosen herb and oil mixtures into these holes. To try an example of this kind of candle dressing, refer to the following exercise.

ARCANUM
Preparing a Stuffed Candle for Lucid Dream Magick

·   ·   ●   ○   ●   ·   ·

For this exercise, you will need: a white glass-encased seven-day candle, 1 teaspoon of dried mugwort, 1 pinch of myrrh resin, and 9 drops of jasmine oil. You may substitute other ingredients, but this is a combination that I find very dreamy.

1. In a mortar and pestle or in a small mixing bowl, combine the mugwort, the myrrh, and the essential oil.

2. Crush and mix together until you have combined the ingredients relatively evenly.

3. Take a common kitchen steak knife or a working knife of your choice and poke three little holes in the top surface of the wax of your candle. Usually if you poke the knife

straight down about an inch and then spin it around a bit, a hole will form with the excess wax being drilled out.

4. Place a pinch of the herbal mixture into each little hole.

5. Take the wax shavings that came out of the carved holes and tamp them back over the holes with the herb mixture as though you are burying the herbs within the candle. It is okay if you can still see herbs sticking out in places, and the surface of the candle will no longer look smooth, of course.

6. Take a drop of jasmine oil in your palm. With your other hand, get some of the oil on your finger and then anoint the candle by dabbing your oiled finger for a moment upon each of the spots where you buried the herbs in the wax.

Your candle is now ready to be lit and used as magickal fuel to enhance the likelihood that you will become lucid in your dreams. Remember that when you stuff a candle in this way, it could either speed up or slow down the usual burn time of the candle. Always monitor how a candle is burning to be sure the flame isn't getting out of hand, and that it remains in a safe place while burning. Never leave your burning candle unattended.

Dressing the Pillar or Taper Candle

Pillar and taper candles present the advantage of not being surrounded by glass, but by standing either on a fire-safe plate or a candle holder base. The wax outer surface is exposed such that you can carve into it. Between the grooves created in carving and the oils you may choose to anoint upon the wax, you can often get some magickal herbs to adhere to the candle. This can have a lovely look to it, but they can also burn much more unpredictably and need much closer monitoring for safety after the spell has been cast and the igniting has gotten underway. To try an example of this kind of candle dressing, try the following example.

ARCANUM
Preparing a Pillar Candle for Lucid Dream Magick

· · ● ○ ● · ·

For this exercise you will need: a metal plate, a white pillar candle, 1 teaspoon of dried mugwort, 1 pinch of myrrh resin, and 9 drops of jasmine essential oil. This is the same herbal combination as in the previous exercise to show how you can use some of the same favored ingredients in a different way. You will also need a knife you can use to safely carve into the wax, or a special magickal tool for this purpose sometimes known as a candle scribe.

1. In a mortar and pestle or in a small mixing bowl, combine the mugwort, the myrrh, and the essential oil.

2. Crush and mix these together until you have combined the ingredients relatively evenly.

3. For a starter dream magick carving idea, take your knife or scribe and try carving little moon symbols in a vertical row down the candle. I like to do three crescent shapes facing one way, three full circles, and then three crescent shapes facing the other way since this gives nine little images in total, and nine is the number of the moon.

4. Put the 9 drops of essential oil into the palm of your nondominant hand.

5. With your other hand, take the carved candle and roll it around in your oiled palm, trying to get a good coating of oil over the entire surface of the wax.

6. Sprinkle the herbal mixture onto the metal plate.

7. Roll the oiled candle around in the herbs, trying to get some of the herbs to stick to the candle. It is okay if only a light amount of the herbs stick, and it is okay if the herbal coating is uneven.

Your candle is now dressed and ready to be lit as an augmentation to the likelihood of becoming lucid in your dreams. Because of the exposed herbs and unpredictable nature of wax dripping without glass encasement, this type of candle burning needs even closer continual monitoring than in the previous example. Never leave your burning candle unattended.

Other Considerations

If you choose an essential oil for your spell that you already know is skin-safe and not irritating for you, you can connect yourself more intimately to your candle magick. Anointing yourself and then the candle with oil is an excellent way to add more specifically appointed energy to the fuel. With a taper, pillar, or chime candle where the wax is exposed, you can anoint your own heart center with a skin-safe oil, and then rub some of the same oil on the candle. For your lucid dream spell, consider anointing yourself and the candle each in the shape of a crescent moon prior to lighting the candle.

There are numerous creative combinations of herbs and oils you could use for dressing candles for your lucid dream spell. It is important to choose things you have or can afford but are also appropriate energetically. For more help in choosing which oils and herbs you want to use for your candle magick, refer to the section on herbal considerations and correspondences in chapter 18.

Candle and Fire Safety

No matter which type of candle you prefer for your spell, always take every possible precaution against the dangers of fire. Never leave an open flame unattended. The main way I have been able to work around this is by taking my spell candle and putting it into the fireplace to continue burning down after the spell ritual is done. If I couldn't do this, I would extinguish my candle and only continue its burning during times when I could be directly there to monitor it.

Candles can spark or fall over, and even the glass of some glass-encased candles has been known to crack apart from the heat, allowing wax and flame to spread unpredictably. I always keep a small sprayable fire extinguisher in the room where I do my ritual magick, just in case. Please ensure that your candle magick is executed safely and accept that this is part of your responsibility as a magician.

ARCANUM
Choosing Your Spell Candle

· • ● ○ ● • ·

In order to decide what type of candle you would like to be the primary focus for igniting the work of your spell, consider the following questions.

1. Do you think you would enjoy carving on candle wax and/or did you feel drawn to some of the smaller dream symbols? If so, and you are willing to have a potentially shorter total burn time for your candle, then consider choosing a white pillar or a taper candle as the focal point for your spell. This would, of course, apply if your primary planetary ruler for the spell is the moon. If you are choosing another planetary ruler, then choose the spell color accordingly.

2. If you would like a longer burn time, then consider choosing a seven-day glass-encased candle. The candle would need to be tended for a longer period, but this extra effort and longer lasting fuel stream can have the benefit of adding extra oomph to the spell.

3. Once you have decided on the color and style of the candle for your upcoming spell, be sure to add to your notes which kind of candle you will need to have on hand so you can procure it prior to the date of the spell.

The Distillation

We have now covered the essential points to consider for planning out the candle magick portion of a lucid dreaming spell. You can now decide if you want to prioritize carving or have the added safety of a glass-encased candle. You should be able to procure the kind of candle you desire in the color that you feel is best for your spell, and also have a plan for burning it down safely. Keep in mind that while we have been talking about the candle magick component of a thorough spell, you can also use candle magick on its own as a smaller or less formal working when that feels appropriate. Let us continue on now to build the rest of the details needed for your ritual spellwork.

LUCID DREAM
CRYSTALS

Many Witches and magicians enjoy the gratifying experience of using crystals as conduits for the magickal energies they wish to attract or project. In researching which crystals are best suited for various types of magick, you are likely to find a wide variety of answers, many of which conflict with one another.

Scott Cunningham's correspondence lists have proven effective and reliable in my practice over time, so I refer to his *Cunningham's Encyclopedia of Crystal, Gem, and Metal Magic* often when choosing stones to match up with specific vibrations.[88] Another great resource for researching established vibrations of crystals is *Love Is in the Earth: A Kaleidoscope of Crystals* by Melody.[89]

Magickal Usage of Dream Crystals

There are many creative ways that you can incorporate crystals into your lucid dream magick. You can sleep with them plainly under your pillow or

88. Scott Cunningham, *Cunningham's Encyclopedia of Crystal, Gem, and Metal Magic* (Llewellyn Publications, 2007), 212–227.

89. Melody, *Love Is in the Earth: A Kaleidoscope of Crystals* (Earth-Love Publishing House, 1991), 26.

include them in sachets or dream charm bags that go under your pillow or on the nightstand. In this way, the energies they conduct are right near you while you try to sleep and dream. You can wear them as jewelry in both sleeping and waking, to help in attracting their associated vibration. Crystals can be placed on the body or held in your hand while performing wakeful meditating so their energy can help you with the cultivation of mental clarity. A purposefully chosen stone can be carried in the pocket to serve as a token that reminds you to carry out the act of reality checking.

In addition to these ongoing daily and nightly functions, we especially want to consider ways in which crystals may enhance the conducting of our lucid dream spellwork. They can be placed on the altar or right on the spell parchment during spellcasting to lend their energy to the work. Small stone chips can be pressed into candle wax in order to be included in the candle magick component of your spellwork. Crystals can also be given as offerings to dream spirits or other allies you may be calling upon in your magick. I'm sure you can think of more applications, but these are some ideas that you can start with.

Stone Correspondences

It is useful to understand how crystals have come to be classified in the occult world so that you can make educated decisions on purchases. The following list contains examples of stones which have some known usage for dream magick, yet they are not all necessarily considered stones of the moon. Sometimes a stone is associated with a zodiac sign that tells you something of its vibration. In order to help you make clearer connections between the zodiac signs and the more well-known planetary energies, here is a list of the planetary rulers of the zodiac signs themselves:

Aries: ruled by Mars

Taurus: ruled by Venus

Gemini: ruled by Mercury

Cancer: ruled by the moon

Leo: ruled by the sun

Virgo: ruled by Mercury

Libra: ruled by Venus

Scorpio: ruled by Mars in antiquity, but ruled by Pluto since the discovery of the outer planets

Sagittarius: ruled by Jupiter

Capricorn: ruled by Saturn

Aquarius: ruled by Saturn in antiquity, but ruled by Uranus since the discovery of the outer planets

Pisces: ruled by Jupiter in antiquity, but ruled by Neptune since the discovery of the outer planets

Amethyst

The popular amethyst is normally seen in sparkling crystal points of purple, although it is available in other colors as well. It has a regal energy of feminine royalty as well as a natural draw toward the exploration of psychism. It has its primary planetary category often listed as being Jupiterian, but Cunningham notes that it also falls under Neptune.[90] This makes sense, as both Jupiter and Neptune happen to be planetary rulers for the zodiac sign of Pisces. This oceanic energy resonates highly with the mysterious concept of the dream sea.

Amethyst does seem to be popular among my peers for all kinds of psychic and visionary work in general. I can verify that I have successfully used delicate pieces of amethyst in dream pillows and felt them to be effective in adding to the vividness and mental wakefulness of my dreams.

Azurite

Azurite, with its deep yet vibrant blue hues is certainly reminiscent of the idea of the dream sea. I have used azurite for years to enhance the energy at the table where I sit to do card readings and can vouch that it certainly does seem to enhance psychism. It is a brittle and more expensive stone, so I have not yet procured another piece that is sturdy enough to have my pillow and head laid upon it. It is, however, lovely to place this upon the altar when casting lucid dream spells.

---

90. Cunningham, *Cunningham's Encyclopedia of Crystal, Gem, and Metal Magick*, 83.

Bustamite

Bustamite is a lesser-known mineral that is usually seen in the form of polished stones in earthy yet feminine hues of peach and salmon with brownish undertones. Popular crystal author Melody, in her work *Love Is in the Earth*, lists Bustamite as being conducive to dreamwork and says that it "… stimulates the state of awareness during dreamtime." This sounds extremely suited to being an energetic support for lucid dream magick. She lists this stone as corresponding to the sign of Libra, which would insinuate that it has inherently Venusian properties.[91]

Celestite

Celestite looks like heaven, so it is easy to imagine where it got its celestial-sounding name. It is usually seen in clusters of icy blue crystal points that reflect light readily. Melody lists this stone as being "an excellent assistant for dream recall" and corresponds it with the zodiac sign of Gemini.[92] It is worth noting, however, that this crystal has developed a reputation for being an unethical purchase in some respects. It is associated with some mining practices in Madagascar that are harmful to the environment as well as the workers. If you do your research, you can find celestite that is sourced more locally. Since you want a stone for its positive energetic attributes, it would be wise to source them as ethically as possible.

Chinese Writing Rock

Chinese writing rock is a unique-looking stone that is normally sold in polished form. The stone is smooth and black with patterned white line markings upon it that look like scratches or tallies. If you don't look too closely, the white marks often look like Chinese lettering.

This stone is said to be an effective aid to dreaming, both in helping attain dreaming as well as in "directing one's [sic] dreams toward the subject that one has pre-determined."[93] The fact that this stone is also associated with the dreamy Neptune makes it a potentially alluring choice,

---

91. Melody, *Love Is in the Earth*, 95–96.

92. Melody, *Love Is in the Earth*, 106.

93. Melody, *Love Is in the Earth*, 114.

especially for spells or lucidity attempts with a specific lucid dream plan in mind. Its smooth worry stone feel makes it a pleasant pocket stone that could be carried as a reminder to do reality checks.

Gaudefroyite

Specimens of gaudefroyite show clusters of small black crystals forming in matrices with the crystal shoots pointing every which way. It almost looks like an enlarged version of what iron filings resemble when they spontaneously adhere magnetically to a lodestone. I have no personal experience with gaudefroyite, but Melody lists it as stimulating in terms of vividness in dreams. She also mentions it with respect to clairaudience in the same listing, and touts that it "…enables one to contact the other worlds while remaining totally conscious of the self."[94] This sounds quite apropos in terms of the very nature of lucid dreaming, though it is a rarer stone and seems to be quite pricey, even for small pieces.

Given its association with both dream vividness and clairaudience, consider putting this on the nightstand or on the altar when working to cultivate a lucid dream specifically for carrying out a lucid auditory spirit divination.

Jade

Jade is a very popular stone that is most commonly seen in polished forms in hues of creamy green that vary from seafoam to mossy. It has an almost liquid smoothness to its energy. Melody speaks of jade with respect to a variety of dream support functions. She mentions improvement of actual recall as well as the facilitation of emotional healing during dreams as some of the perks of this stone.[95] This is not that surprising since many folks associate the green color of jade with the corresponding green of the heart chakra. Jade is associated here with the signs of Aries, Gemini, Taurus, and Libra.

If you are concocting a spell to successfully conduct healing within a lucid dream, jade seems like a great crystal to include. You could have the

94. Melody, *Love Is in the Earth*, 178.
95. Melody, *Love Is in the Earth*, 215.

stone upon your spell parchment during the ritual or hold it in your hand to conduct its energy through you while you project energy into the candle magick portion of the spell. If you were to include a particular piece of jade in such a spell, you could then continue to carry and use the piece for ongoing healing work after the lucid dream plan with the healing command has been successfully carried out.

Kyanite

Kyanite comes in various colors but is most commonly seen in its blue form, its rough bars and lines of blue formations upon white stone having a relatively ordered alignment. It is at once watery and earthy in the energy it gives, with its coloration oceanic and its texture quite brittle. This stone is listed as improving dream recall as well as "…dream-solving, providing for access to solutions during the dream state."[96] Combined with other meditative and astral plane supports, this seems like a good contender for inclusion in a dream recall spell or a lucid dream spell.

Given the inclination of kyanite to have bits of itself flake off, it can be useful and fun to save these little shards instead of getting rid of them. When casting a lucid dream spell, the sharp little kyanite bits can be easily embedded into the wax of your spell candle, adding another lovely layer of energy to the magick. The listed astrological associations include Taurus, Libra, and Aries.

Manganosite

Manganosite is a rare mineral that forms glowing emerald green crystals among its deposits. This is another mineral that is listed as being useful for supporting the remembering of dreams.[97] It is also described as helping one to be present in the moment and has an association with the sign of Sagittarius.

I have yet to procure a sample of this mineral, and maybe I never will due to its rarity, but it is worth knowing about just in case a piece ever becomes available. Since Sagittarius is ruled by Jupiter, a kingly planet of

96. Melody, *Love Is in the Earth*, 230.
97. Melody, *Love Is in the Earth*, 257.

wealth, some of the associations of this sign to this green, rare stone make perfect sense.

Moonstone

Moonstone seems to be one of the most popularly worn stones among Witches today. It comes in a variety of different beautiful colors but the glowing white stones with the blue flash seem to be a favorite.

While Cunningham does not correlate moonstone directly to dreaming, he notes the obvious fact that it is connected to the energy of the moon. Since this is the planetary vibration that is most used for dream magick, this is a significant correlation. He lists moonstone and chalcedony as having connections to the Moon card of the tarot.[98] He also talks of wearing any jewelry with silver as the metal to wear to bed to induce psychic dreams.[99]

Since moonstone is very popular in jewelry pieces, you might consider blessing a moonstone ring or pendant as a magickal tool that helps you in your lucid dreaming practice. You could charge it for enhancing dream recall, helping you carry out frequent reality checks, or for bringing the energy of lucid dreams to you in general, to name a few ideas.

Prehnite

Prehnite is a lovely pale green stone that sometimes has little black flecks or inclusions. The energy has an airy lightness to it, and it feels very pleasing to the mind. In *Love Is in the Earth*, Melody describes this as a "...stone for dreaming and remembering."[100] She correlates it to the sign of Libra and describes more details as to its ability to support prophecy as well as communication with entities.

This could be a great stone to support lucid dream plan quests that involve divination or spirit ally contacts. You could also hold this stone in waking meditations aimed at communicating directly with your lucid dreaming guides.

---

98. Cunningham, *Cunningham's Encyclopedia of Crystal, Gem, and Metal Magick*, 60.

99. Cunningham, *Cunningham's Encyclopedia of Crystal, Gem, and Metal Magick*, 203.

100. Melody, *Love Is in the Earth*, 322.

Star Garnet

Star garnet has the primary deep burgundy color you would expect of garnet in general, but what makes it different is the obvious white asterisk star shapes that appear on its surface when polished. Melody lists this specific form of garnet as being useful in aiding dream recall, so it may be a great amplifier for a dream recall increasing spell or simply to have near you while sleeping and while journaling your dreams.[101]

In the same listing, Melody corresponds garnet in general to the signs of Leo, Virgo, Capricorn, and Aquarius, so the vibrations of this stone seem diverse. This tracks with my personal experience of finding that garnet seems to support more than just fiery pursuits. I find garnet to be protective and empowering, and to help enhance the feeling of connection to my guides and deities.

Other Stones

Cunningham's full list of stones that conduct lunar energy includes aquamarine, beryl, chalcedony, quartz crystal, moonstone, mother-of-pearl, pearl, sapphire, and selenite. Even though he does not associate these specifically with known folk magick for dreaming, their connection to the moon is reason enough to explore them as potential lucid magick aids.

From personal experience, I add to this consideration list scolecite, lepidolite, and merlinite as crystals that might be worth your while in testing for dream magick. These stones just seemed to speak to me as psychic enhancers, particularly for dreaming. They may do so for you as well. Don't forget to keep in mind that any stone, whether it is listed here in any way or not, is applicable if it works for you. It will always ultimately be your relationship to a crystal energy that determines how effective it is for you, more than any classically listed correspondence.

---

101. Melody, *Love Is in the Earth*, 177.

ARCANUM
Choosing Stones for Your Spell

· · ● ○ ● · ·

It is always wise to experiment and see what effects are produced for you personally when engaging with a particular stone. Your auric field may respond differently when exposed to the energy of a crystal than someone else's might. Furthermore, one individual piece of amethyst, for example, can have a different effect on you than the next piece in some cases. Try the following time-tested yet simple way to test the qualities that a stone may produce together with you.

1. Before doing anything, it is important to pause and simply notice how you feel at the outset. Check in with your body and your energy. What is your mood? What is the relative tension level and feeling of your body?

2. Now pick up the stone you are testing and sit quietly with it in your nondominant hand for a few minutes. You don't have to try to direct your thoughts in any very specific way; just relax.

3. After a few minutes have gone by, check back in mindfully with your mood, your energy, and your body. Be aware of any changes to the subtle sensations you might notice. Do you feel more or less alert? Do you feel more or less relaxed? Do you feel more or less mentally clear? Do you feel more or less psychically open? Anything you can glean is a clue as to what the best usage of this stone might be for you.

4. Once you find a stone that intuitively seems like it is favorable to inducing visionary states, making you feel more intuitive, or enhancing dreaminess, spend an evening or two with it under your pillow or right next to your bed on the nightstand and document anything of interest that occurred in that night's dreaming.

5. Compare and document the results gained with different stones until you find a favorite dream stone or two, and then keep these in mind for inclusion in the casting of the lucid magick spell you are working toward.

The Distillation

In this chapter, we have looked at a variety of examples of crystals that may serve as effective adjuncts to your lucid dream spell as well as to your lucid practice in general. We have discussed some suggested uses for stones that identify themselves to you as dreaming stones. We have talked about some of the different planetary and zodiac correspondences that are associated with various stones, and lastly you have been encouraged to begin testing your own stones to identify which ones may have a relationship to your dreaming. These are the ones you will then consider including in your spell. Remember that instructions for putting all of the actions of the spell together will be included in chapter 22.

CASTING YOUR SPELL

Now that you have considered the details of the various components of a thorough and formally crafted lucid dream spell, let's outline the instructions for combining all of this magick and casting the spell ritual.

Remember that while you can now use all of this information to craft a formal and detailed working, you can always use any single idea we've discussed as its own smaller act of quick magick. You can do candle magick on its own, drink a potion in a moment where it feels right, or carry a stone as a reality check reminder, to name a few examples. You are also ready now to put it all together.

The following suggested ritual template parallels what might be used in the Society of Witchcraft and Old Magick, simplified and modified to avoid breaking privacy oaths. The following ritual structure is simple but complete and thorough. You will be able to follow the instructions and do an excellent job at creating an effective container of space for a magickal working. If you already have established ritual skills for circle casting, then you can certainly use your own methods for establishing sacred space for your lucid dream spells.

The Materials

You first will need to gather the materials for your ritual. These include:

Crystals: If you have decided to include any crystals in your spell, have these ready.

Herbs and Oils: Collect the herbal and oil components you have decided upon for candle dressing and anointing. If you are still trying to decide, refer to chapter 18 again for ideas. You may just collect the ingredients and plan to dress the candle within the ritual circle.

Incense: You could use stick or cone incense of a lunar variety, or you could use some of the herbal blend you may be using for candle magick as well.

Incense Burner: You need a holder for your stick or cone incense. If you will be burning an herbal blend for your incense, you will need a fire-safe container such as a cast-iron mini cauldron.

Lighter: You will need a lighter on the altar for igniting your incense and candles.

Offerings: Collect anything that you are planning to offer immediately during the casting of the spell. You do not need to ready things that you will pledge to offer ongoing or in the future.

Parchment: I recommend an 8x12 piece of parchment paper, but you can use any type of paper you feel is appropriate or that you have access to. You will be writing all of the words of your spell out on this paper ahead of time.

Quarter Candles: I recommend using glass-encased seven-day altar candles in yellow, red, blue, and green.

Salt: Have a small container or bowl for the altar with enough salt in it to throw a pinch toward each of the four quarters. It can be any kind of salt you like.

Spell Candle: Have the candle you have decided to use as the main candle for your candle magick ready. Refer back to chapter 20 for help with choosing this if you are still uncertain.

Spirit/Center Candle: I recommend using a white glass-encased seven-day altar candle.

Wand or Athame: If you have one of these casting tools, have it ready for your spell. If you don't have such a physical tool, you can use your first two fingers held in benediction pose.

Preparing the Spell Parchment

The spell parchment should be prepared ahead of the time when you plan to cast your spell, as it requires some careful attention. Refer again to chapter 13, Spell Goals and Timing, if you need further assistance in the wording of your goal as you will be writing it out here. Remember that this is separate from your lucid dream plan, which is what you plan to do once you become lucid in a dream.

Your spell goal is worded specifically around what you'd like the next successes in your personal lucid dream practice to look like. The wording on the parchment will also include your appeal to any deities, guides, or other appropriate spirits you wish to involve, associated seals for the spell drawn on the parchment, any special magickal words, words of power or incantations you will use, and a written outline of your proposed system of offerings in exchange for spiritual assistance given toward your goal.

ARCANUM
Writing the Spell Parchment

· · ● ○ ● · ·

You can use the following instructions to help you to customize what should be written on your spell parchment, while also making sure that you are covering all the bases.

1. Starting at the top of the parchment paper, write: "*I,* <insert name or magickal name>, *call upon* <insert deity or guides being addressed> *for the purpose of* <insert spell goal clearly stated>. *In exchange for assistance given toward this end I will* <insert offerings to be given>. *As long as this is in accordance with my true will and my highest good, as*

I will it, so shall it be!" Fill in the blanks with the answers, which are specific to you and your spell.

2. Beneath this paragraph, write any incantations or words of power you may have decided to use for raising energy during the spell.

3. If you are incorporating a seal to call upon spiritual aid, draw the seal at the bottom of the page. Many seals are circular, and using the bottom of one of your seven-day altar candles to trace out the initial circle is an easy and efficient way to get started. Take your time drawing the details of the seal within the circle as well as you can. It does not have to be exactly perfect. The fact that you are copying it by hand allows you to imbue a lot of extra focus and energy into the spell parchment.

4. In any remaining space on the page, or around the borders, you can add any other small symbols that you felt drawn to that you may have wanted to include. By decorating the page with appropriate symbols, you heighten your focus and add the energetic vibrations of the symbols to your work.

Your spell parchment is now ready for use in the ritual. On other pieces of paper, you may wish to either write or print out the words for the actual ritual of circle casting presented further on in this chapter in advance. This may be helpful if you don't already have a different memorized means of conducting your ritual so that you will be able to make it flow smoothly.

The Altar

It would be appropriate to cast your dream spell either at your usual working altar or at a specially erected dream altar. In ideal situations, a general working altar is often set up facing the east, symbolizing the dawn and the magician's ability to usher in new things. A dedicated dream altar could be set up facing west to symbolize access to the element of water, our psychic faculties, and the dream sea. It is not necessary to have your altar facing any particular direction, however, if it is too difficult or inconvenient.

If you don't already have an established dream or working altar, your altar can be set up on a tabletop, dresser, nightstand, shelf, or any other similar surface if it is clean and accessible. You can use a spot you envision as a permanent altar, or you can set one up temporarily just for the sake of casting the spell and then take it down again afterward. The space in the room does not need to be big, just large enough for you to turn around in a small circle, even if that is only a few feet across.

If your chosen altar is very small, it is fine to make appropriate substitutions to your materials list, choosing tealight candles instead of the big glass-encased candles for the quarters, for example. If you prefer, you can also consider putting all of your spell materials in a picnic basket and finding a private outdoor space in which to conduct your spell. A traditional wooden picnic basket with a flat, hinged top makes a nice portable altar!

During the ritual, you will be moving the quarter candles that started on the altar so that they end up around you in the room to your front, back, and on either side, marking the directions of your circle. Again, this doesn't need to be a large space, but if you feel your altar and ritual space is not conducive to this, you have another option. Instead of following the script and placing the candles in their specific quarters after you do the quarter calls, you can just put them back upon the altar. If you don't even have space for the whole quarter candle setup, you can just say the words of the quarter calls without using candles at all. You will still be doing a thorough job of establishing sacred space. Whatever altar and space you can manage is workable, as the end result is a product of your words, ideas, spirit relationships, energy, and actions first and foremost.

Once you have decided upon your altar, set it up with your spell candle and parchment or paper in the center, and the white candle just above that for the divine. Place the yellow, red, blue, and green candles on the corners of the altar to symbolize the cardinal directions of east, south, west, and north, respectively. Since these quarter candles also relate to the four earthly elements of air, fire, water, and earth, you can place all other items that belong on the altar closest to the area for its corresponding element.

For example, the incense and the athame are considered tools of air and would be placed near the yellow candle. The incense burner and wand, if used, are considered tools of fire and would be placed near the red candle. Essential oils or other watery implements would go near the blue candle, and the salt and any herbal ingredients you may be combining during the candle dressing would go near the earthy green candle. Crystals can be placed near the green candle as well, or you can place them around the spell parchment.

If All of This Is Overwhelming

You have been given lots of information to consider for the customization of your lucid dream spell. I would like to give you a fleshed-out example here that gives you an idea of what these choices might look like. You can simply use these choices and plug them into the spellcasting instructions that follow, if you like. You can, of course, proceed in using all of your own custom choices as encouraged in the exercises throughout the chapters of this section of the book. For my basic sample lucid dream spell, here are the details:

Spell Goal: I will succeed in achieving a fully lucid dream within the next nine months.

Timing: The spell will be conducted on the next Monday available to me that falls within the waxing phase of the moon. It will take place during the hour of the moon that falls in the evening before bedtime.

Spirits: I will call upon the Norse dream goddess Njorun for help in this spell.

Offerings: I will offer wine to Njorun during the ritual, and I will also pledge to write a poem in her honor each Monday for the next nine weeks and share it on social media to honor her and spread awareness of her.

Symbols: I will draw the seal of Njorun on the bottom of my spell parchment. I will decorate around the edges of the page with the runes laguz and mannaz and the crescent moon symbol.

Words of Power: To raise energy during the spell, I will intone the call words of the seal of Njorun, "Vard Mog Jenk," nine times.

Herbs and Oils: I will have jasmine oil for anointing my candle. I will have the following for creating an herbal mixture: a pinch of dried mugwort, a pinch of dried lemon balm, a pinch of dried wild lettuce, a pinch of myrrh resin, a pinch of sandalwood powder, a pinch of amber resin, 3 drops white lotus oil, 3 drops jasmine oil, and 3 drops mugwort oil.

Tea: I will drink a cup of mugwort tea just prior to conducting the spell.

Crystal: I will have a piece of prehnite upon the altar during the spell and will then keep it under my pillow after the spell ritual is done.

This list represents a choice made for every component of the full spell-casting. With these or similar choices ready, you will be able to carry out all aspects of the spell ritual that follows.

Conducting the Spell Ritual

This ritual is inspired by the ritual style of the Wardwell tradition of American Witchcraft as well as popular Wiccan circle casting methods. After placing all the tools, parchment, and spell ingredients on the altar, stand at your altar and light your incense.

1. Say, *"I cleanse and purify myself of all negative energies and sources of unnecessary harm."* Holding up the burning incense, take a deep breath in, and then exhale out forcefully through the rising smoke.

2. Raise your arms toward the sky, palms up, and say, *"I call upon and connect myself to the divine as I embark on my magickal work. Energies of Goddess and God, of within and without, of above and below, I honor and call to you. Aligned, guiding intelligences of my spirit, be with me now as I open this sacred space. Blessed Be!"* Lower your arms.

3. Look at your altar and all of the implements that you have laid out as necessary for the spell at hand. Holding your right hand over the altar palm down, say, *"I cleanse this altar and all spell components thereon to be purified."* Pause, and feel the energies of purification

flowing down into you, through you, and then out of your extended hand and into the altar and tools.

4. Then say, *"I charge this altar and all spell components thereon to be blessed as proper agents for my working. As I will it, so shall it be."* Pause and feel the energies of powerful charging and blessing flowing through you and out of your extended hand and into the altar and tools.

5. Turning to walk in a counterclockwise circle around the room in which you are working, state, *"I cleanse this sacred space to be purified of all negative vibrations and unnecessary harm."*

6. Return to the altar, then change directions to walk the room in a clockwise circle and say, *"I charge this sacred space to serve as a proper container for my magickal working today. As I will it, so shall it be."* Return to the altar.

7. Taking a pinch of salt and throwing it toward the east, say, *"Profane beings of the east be banished!"* Repeat this in the south, west, and north, and then return to the altar.

8. Standing in the east, with arms raised, say, *"I call upon my aligned and benevolent guides of the east and of the element of air to grace my circle and support my work. Guides of clarity, inspiration, swiftness, and communication, hail and welcome."* Light the yellow candle and place it in the eastern side of your ritual space, or, if there is inadequate room, on the eastern side of the altar.

9. Turn to face the south, raise your arms, and say, *"I call upon my aligned and benevolent guides of the south and of the element of fire to grace my circle and support my work. Guides of strength, courage, passion, and ambition, hail and welcome."* Light the red candle and place it in the south or on the southern side of the altar.

10. Turn to face the west, raise your arms, and say, *"I call upon my aligned and benevolent guides of the west and of the element of water to grace my circle and support my work. Guides of intuition, emotional flow, divination, and love, hail and welcome."* Light the blue candle and place it in the west or on the western side of the altar.

11. Turn to face the north, raise your arms, and say, *"I call upon my aligned and benevolent guides of the north and of the element of earth to grace my circle and support my work. Guides of stability, loyalty, groundedness, and abundance, hail and welcome."* Light the green candle and place it in the north or on the northern side of the altar.

12. Take your athame, wand, or index and middle fingers and begin to envision energy flowing down through you and then out your arm, pointing the tool toward the eastern quarter of your circle. Walk around your space in a clockwise manner, trailing the energy from the casting tool or fingers in a full circle, envisioning the energetic line of demarcation settling along the walls or far enough away from you that you won't accidentally step over it and disrupt it. As you cast this energetic circle to contain your space, say, *"I cast this circle for the purpose of* <state nature of spellwork>. *I do so with the power and support of my aligned and benevolent guides, goddesses, and gods. As I will it, so shall it be."* When you have fully connected the circle at the point where you began, return the casting tool to the altar.

13. Raise your arms overhead, palms up, and say, *"The circle is cast, the energies flow, time out of time both above and below. With the help of my guides of the earth, sky, and sea, so will the spells in this space come to be."* Light the main white altar candle in honor of the helping spirits.

14. Proceed now to do any combining of oils or herbs, any dressing, carving, or anointing of your spell candle that will be needed for the candle magick component of the work. I find that as long as it isn't something that takes so long that it has to be done ahead of time, that working of the materia within the cast circle amplifies the construction of the spell.

15. Raise your arms overhead again and now read the words you have written out on your spell parchment: *"I,* <insert name or magickal name>, *call upon* <insert deity or guides being addressed> *for the purpose of* <insert spell goal clearly stated>. *In exchange for assistance given toward this end, I will* <insert offerings to be given>. *As long as*

this is in accordance with my true will and my highest good, as I will it, so shall it be!" With this proclamation, light the spell candle.

16. If you are using any seals or magickal symbols to help fuel the spell, touch your nondominant hand to the seal you are using and point your index finger, wand, or athame at the spell candle using your dominant hand. Chant or vibrate the magickal activation words of the seal or an incantation you have chosen for raising energy nine times. While raising energy in this way, envision a stream of energy flowing into your nondominant hand from the seal or symbols on your parchment, moving through your heart center, down along your other arm, and then being projected into the spell candle with your dominant hand. If you have any other incantations or words of power you want to include, add those in at this point as well to continue increasing the stream of energetic output that you are creating for the spell.

17. Proceed to take some time now to sit in front of the altar and meditate upon the vision of your spell goal as the candle burning gets underway. If possible, also try to allow yourself to feel emotionally the way that you would feel if this goal were already accomplished and intend to walk through your world embodying this emotional state from now on.

18. When done meditating, raise your arms skyward and say, *"I give thanks and praise to you, my deities and benevolent guides, for your magickal support and for joining my circle. May all depart, pleased and fulfilled by my offerings to you, and be open to returning again when I call. Blessed Be."*

19. Pick up your casting tool or use your fingers to flow energy through them. Start in the east and peel back your originally cast circle, traveling counterclockwise. When you return to the altar and replace your tool, if used, raise your arms, and say, *"The circle is open, the spellwork is done; my heart, my mind, my spirit are one. With thanks for the powers available to me, as I do say, so shall it be!"*

Be sure to extinguish your white, yellow, red, blue, and green altar candles when you have finished your ritual and return them safely to the altar. These are altar tools that can be used again and again to symbolize spirit and the elements in any other workings you conduct. It is ideal to allow the incense and the actual spell candle to burn to completion, but this should only be done if you remain in the area and are available to monitor for fire safety purposes. If you are going to need to leave the vicinity, extinguish the incense and the spell candle for the time being. You should relight them whenever you have the chance to hang around again in the room with the altar, continuing safely in this manner until you do get them to burn to completion.

After the Spell Ritual

Following the spell, be sure to set reminders so you don't forget to follow up on offerings that were promised as part of the deal and that you spoke aloud from your parchment during the spell. Once the spell candle has been burnt down, burn the parchment all the way down to ash and release it into free-flowing water in the case of a productive or benevolent spell, or bury the ashes for a baneful spell.

Be sure to photograph your lovingly prepared spell parchment before burning though, so you can paste a small printed-out copy into your grimoire if you like, to document a record of your magickal work. You may choose either to recycle or to wash and reuse the glass if your spell candle was glass-encased.

All the Options, Pros and Cons

I have mentioned that you can build the preplanned detailed spellworking as just described, or you can opt not to do this, and instead use smaller individual acts of magick here and there. For example, you might dress and light a candle and simply intend that its energy help you to become lucid. On another occasion, you might say an incantation or prayer to a deity or guide, asking them to help prompt you to become lucid. On yet another occasion, you may be inspired to brew a lucid dreaming potion and try it before bed. These are perfectly valid ways of using magick, especially if you prefer to be spontaneous rather than planning and casting a fancy ritual.

The choice is yours and comes down to personal preference. If you want a big push toward an outcome that may happen faster and be more measurable, then the efforts of the big spell could be well worth it. Remember the concept of energy exchange, and that the likelihood is that the results you see will proportionately reflect the amount of thought, energy, and action put in. Some people like to do little things over time, and some like to line up all their resources and weave them together into a bigger picture. There is no right or wrong, and this is your lucid magickal practice. That said, and in the spirit of dream sorcery and the alchemy of your own lucid evolution, you won't know how powerful or effective a fully formalized working of ritual spellwork could be unless you give it a try.

The Distillation

You have now had the opportunity to truly cast some relatively advanced lucid dream magick. It is important to remember to stop and appreciate that you are promoting your skills as a magickal adept. The actions you put together are the alchemical sulfur—the catalysts of transformation and ultimately manifestation. Not every magician has the ability to successfully cause their desires to be made real in the physical plane. You, on the other hand, are striving to manifest outcomes that quite literally take place in other realms of existence, and this is no small feat. Congratulations for having come this far in your dream sorcery.

DREAM SPELLS FROM
CLASSICAL GRIMOIRES

In this chapter, I will share some references to the magick of sleep and dreams as found in the *Greek Magical Papyri (PGM)* and *Carmina Gadelica Vol. I and II* by Alexander Carmichael as examples of preserved classical magickal works in existence. The reasoning for singling out these two grimoires is simply because I have personal relationships with the goddess Hekate as well as the Morrigan and other members of the Irish pantheon, and I have studied these works in depth. Hearkening back to older sources such as these for dream magick references may help to inspire further specific and more advanced spellworkings in your lucid magickal practice.

The prayers and incantations from the *Carmina Gadelica* are mostly collected from the Scottish Highlands but contain a lot of references to the goddess Brigid as well as other magickal concepts common to Irish culture. The *Carmina* and the *PGM* are by far not the only sources on the topic of dreaming in these cultures, but they happen to both be excellent compilations of spells, prayers, incantations, and words and names of power.

I have found that there is great benefit to be gained from using or adapting spells or components of spells that have existed for a long time. The fact that they have potentially been used by many people helps to increase the energy of the group consciousness surrounding the familiarized words and actions. Sometimes reading these preserved excerpts also serves to provide inspiration for a magician's own creative spell crafting endeavors or simply lends validation to some of the concepts underlying our own work.

The *PGM*

In the *PGM*, there are many spells that are listed involving dream and sleep magick. There are spells to create insomnia in another person, to send dreams to a target person, and to create "evil dreams."[102] I will focus the discussion specifically on the spells that are for the purposes of receiving oracles or revelation from dreams. There are no spells listed that specifically use the word *lucidity*, but that is our modern term for awakening in the dream.

We can't be sure that lucidity may not have been what was meant by "revelation" or being able to be certain of psychic answers received in dreams. For our own purposes, these types of spells could be interesting to consider as powerful divination approaches surrounding important circumstances, whether the result was actual full lucidity or not.

Dream-Producing Charm

PGM IV.3172–3208 outlines the instructions for creating a "dream-producing charm" using certain words of power to do so, which are outlined in the passage.[103] There are instructions then for directions to face and words to say, culminating in the final recitation of "I conjure you by the sleep releaser because I want you to enter into me and to show me concerning the NN matter, IERORIETHEDIEN THROU CHAORA ARPEBO ENDALELA."[104]

The barbarous words of power included here make apparent that the magician is appealing to certain spirits who have the ability to provide answers to the question of the magician. "NN" throughout the work seems to be the notation for "Fill in the blank with words describing your specific desire."

102. Hans Dieter Betz, ed., *The Greek Magical Papyri in Translation: Including the Demotic Spells* (The University of Chicago Press, 1986), 127.

103. Betz, *The Greek Magical Papyri in Translation*, 99.

104. Betz, *The Greek Magical Papyri in Translation*, 100.

Calling Besas

There are a couple of mentions, such as *PGM* VII.222–49, that refer to spells for a "Request for a dream oracle from Besas."[105] Besas may refer to the Egyptian god Bes, who was popularly looked to for presiding over matters of the family, hearth, and home and served apotropaic functions as well. He is not listed as being a god of dreams per se but seems to be a multifaceted spirit who was apparently trusted for divination advice pertaining to important life matters.[106]

The spell referenced here involves creating special ink out of precious substances (the blood of a dove and a crow as well as rainwater, "juice of single-stemmed wormwood," and cinnabar) and writing a formula with it.[107] Following the instructions and then making the proper recitations will apparently cause this god to come to you on the edge of sleeping just before waking. Interestingly, this is also one of the times at which one is most likely to be able to become lucid in dreaming, so it very well may have had an intentional usage as magick to induce lucidity.

A Dream Oracle Request

Not every entry in the *PGM* has such tedious instructions and the requirement of ingredients that are so difficult to come by. *PGM* VII.250–54 may be more accessible to the modern-day magician. It states, "Request for a dream oracle, a request which is always used. Formula to be spoken to the lamp. 'NAIENCHRE NAIENCHRE, mother of fire and water, you are the one who rises before, ARCHENTECHTHA; reveal to me concerning the NN matter. If yes, show me a plant and water, but if not, fire and iron; immediately, immediately, quickly, quickly.'"[108]

I like the concept behind this approach to dream divination. Essentially, the dreamer is asking a yes or no question and delineating in advance that having a dream with certain qualities would indicate a yes and other very different qualities would mean no.

105. Betz, *The Greek Magical Papyri in Translation*, 122.

106. Jordan, *Dictionary of Gods and Goddesses*, 49–50.

107. Betz, *The Greek Magical Papyri in Translation*, 123.

108. Betz, *The Greek Magical Papyri in Translation*, 123.

Dream Oil Lamp

Another spell from this collection that seems manageable is *PGM* VII.359–69, where the magician is to write the prescribed words on a strip of clean linen.[109] It is then rolled up and used as a wick in the oil lamp. There is an incantation listed that is to be repeated seven times while this wick is burning. These words include asking for revelation about the concern at hand. When the incantations are done, the fire is extinguished, and the magician goes to sleep to await the answer. This is another interesting concept in that it feels like the lamp is being used to fuel and ignite the magick of receiving divinatory answers in a dream.

Calling Hermes as a Dream Messenger

PGM XII.144–52 is not quite as simple, as it requires "blood from a quail" in which the magician is to draw an image of an "ibis-faced" Hermes.[110] There are words for the request to be said along with secret names for Hermes. Since the blood is to be used as an ink, and many modern magicians would strive to find ingredients that would not cause harm to animals, it would be reasonable to try this with a substitute. I would consider using regular red ink and mixing into it a bit of egg white to give the ink the airy bird energy that was intended.

An interesting aspect of this entry is the notion of calling upon Hermes for the purpose of bringing dream answers to the magician's questions. Hermes is not normally associated with dreams in the common literature on the gods, but it does stand to reason that as a messenger and deity of communication he could certainly have the talent to provide such a function. Dreams are, after all, in the eyes of many magicians, a form of communication between our own conscious awareness and that of other beings and realities. In this way, as suggested earlier, we may be inspired not only to avoid limiting our dream magick spirit interactions only to known gods of dreaming, but to consider enlisting any spirits of communication to whom we feel connected, as well as possibly any deity with whom our own communication is especially established.

109. Betz, *The Greek Magical Papyri in Translation*, 127.
110. Betz, *The Greek Magical Papyri in Translation*, 158.

The *Carmina Gadelica*

The previously mentioned *Carmina Gadelica* is an anthology of collected prayers, incantations, and lore from Scotland. Many of the pieces of this compilation call upon God, Christ, or Mary for aid in the desired aim, as Christianity has been the overarching religion in Scotland for some time, and certainly during the period when this folklore was collected. I have seen examples of Pagan practitioners using some of the formats from this work, however, and replacing the Christian spirit names with Pagan ones to reflect potential older usages of these seemingly traditional passages.

For example, instead of praying to the Lord Almighty for a given protection, one might appeal to the god who is the Irish father figure of the Tuatha de Dannan, The Dagda. You may see a charm praying to Mary for healing and approach the goddess Brigid instead, if you are so inclined. The idea is that the practices of praying for assistance in these traditional areas of life is universal and older than Christianity. Taking all of this into consideration, it is interesting for the lucid magician to examine the sleep spells that exist in this work.

There is a whole section of prayers in the *Carmina Gadelica* that fall into the category of protection during sleep, sleep consecration, and bed blessings.[111] Most of these call upon God, and some also involve Mary, Bride (another name for Brigid), and the angels as hosts of the protection and blessing of the person's spirit during slumber.

From the collection of pieces there are some interesting things for the magician to note. One is the huge benefit that every prayer or incantation presented is given both in English and Scots Gaelic. There is a great deal of effectiveness to be gained by appealing to guiding spiritual beings in their native language, or language of cultural origin. It shows effort, respect, and seriousness on the part of the occultist, and this goes a long way in building the spirit relationship and bolstering their level of investment in your magick.

Another benefit to speaking magickal invocations and appeals in another language is that it causes the words to have a better chance of breaking free

---

111. Alexander Carmichael, *Carmina Gadelica, Vol. I and II* (Alexander Carmichael, 2019), 33–47.

from the emotional skepticism or bias that sometimes underlies our usual communications. Foreign language words used as magickal incantations often naturally take on the otherworldly feel of barbarous words of power. Whether or not you call upon any Celtic spirits in the magick you craft to enhance your lucid dreaming practice, it is possible that adding some of these blessings or protections in the original language could be an elegant and powerful approach.

Resting Blessing

In the "Resting Blessing" from this collection, the emphasis uniquely appears to be focused more upon the healing powers of sleep than on the usual request for protection.[112] It is valuable from a cultural perspective to consider the level of importance that was being placed upon sleep here.

All the need for protection was possibly not just because people may have perceived themselves as being vulnerable during the state of sleep but also potentially implies the attitude that the process should be guarded so that important personal work could be done. The lucid dreaming magician surely understands this opinion and could consider adding such a blessing to their work. I certainly consider healing to be not only the process of recovering from maladies but the general process underlying personal spiritual learning and evolution. All the adventures and exploits of lucid magick are therefore healing, in my book, and should be safeguarded as such.

Sleep Consecration

In the piece entitled "Sleep Consecration," the appeal is simply to be allowed to be together with the spirits of God, Mary, Jesus, Michael, and Bride.[113] Similar to the lucid occultist who is aspiring to carry out a lucid dream plan of communing with a particular guiding spirit, the space of sleep is being prized as an opportunity for this type of communion. This could be an excellent passage to recite when conducting a spell to induce a lucid dream for communing with your deity of choice.

---

112. Carmichael, *Carmina Gadelica*, 39.
113. Carmichael, *Carmina Gadelica*, 39–40.

The Death-Sleep

There is a passage from a sleep prayer that states "If death be to me in the death-sleep, be it that on Thine own arm O God of Grace, I in peace shall waken."[114] This line hints at the idea that sleeping and/or death are potential sources of waking in and of themselves. The lucid magician never forgets to treasure this philosophy for it lies behind every effort, so this piece also could provide inspiration for words to include in associated lucid dream magick. Exploring the afterlife, exploring oneself as a spirit, or exploring the type of awakening that happens upon death are all things you could consider incorporating into a lucid dream plan or a lucid spell goal.

Soul Shrine

In the prayer called "Soul Shrine," not only is the space of sleep referred to as "my soul-shrine" indicating a sacredness inherent in it, but the passage ends with "Be Thyself the guiding star above me, Illume Thou to me every reef and shoal, Pilot my barque on the crest of the wave, To the restful haven of the waveless sea, Oh the restful haven of the waveless sea."[115]

This lovely metaphor for sleep as a navigation over mysterious waters is very akin to the modern occult take on the dream sea. The lucid magician who has kinship with Celtic spirits or feels pulled by their own Celtic ancestry will appreciate forging the connection of belief to their cultural forebears through such words.

Other Grimoiric Dream Spells

There are lots of other grimoires accessible to you besides the ones mentioned in this book. As a dream sorcerer, it would be beneficial for you to explore the various collections you come across for evidence of documented dreaming magick. You may find powerful spells or words for potential lucid spells in old and new grimoires as well as in compilations of mythology or cultural lore.

114. Carmichael, *Carmina Gadelica*, 42.
115. Carmichael, *Carmina Gadelica*, 45–46.

To Dream of a Future Spouse

In other old grimoiric mentions of magick for dreams and sleep, there is a spell in an old French grimoire by a writer known as "Petit Albert" whose description is relayed in the works of Claude LeCouteux.[116] The spell includes instructions, magick words, and an orison to be recited for the purposes of seeing one's future husband in a dream. If you have a priority lucid dream plan that involves summoning a lover or doing divination regarding love, then this spell may be one to research for potential enhancement to your spellwork in helping to manifest this experience.

To Overcome Insomnia

LeCouteux also mentions an obscure Greek compilation that includes a spell to overcome insomnia.[117] He included the detailed instructions, magickal words, and the spellworks for calling the famed Seven Sleepers that were mentioned previously in chapter 14, the chapter on choosing spirits for lucid dream spells. Sometimes lucid exploits are thwarted by insomnia or sleep patterns that are disturbed, and the magician may need to create an interruption by use of such a spell to restore sleep that is routine and robust enough for the cultivation of lucidity.

Dream Magick from The Picatrix

In the Arabic grimoire known as *The Picatrix*, many of the described "confections for sleep" seem to be created for the purposes of imposing a magical sleep upon another person unbeknownst to them.[118] The implications are that some of these spell concoctions can cause not only enforced sleep but even death. This extreme ethical conundrum provides an example of why it is important to research thoroughly before deciding to include classical grimoiric components in your magick.

On the other end of the spectrum, *The Picatrix* does describe some magick of Hermes whereby he was able to receive answers to questions about

116. LeCouteux, *Dictionary of Ancient Magic Words and Spells*, 66–67.

117. LeCouteux, *Dictionary of Ancient Magic Words and Spells*, 128–129.

118. John Michael Greer and Christopher Warnock, trans., *The Complete Picatrix: The Occult Classic of Astrological Magic—Liber Atratus Edition* (Adocentyn Press, 2010), 207–208, 215–216.

the mysteries in dreams, given by his "Perfect Nature."[119] This may be another term referencing the spirit that occultists commonly call the Holy Guardian Angel, as discussed previously in chapter 11. Studying the approaches in *The Picatrix* could therefore provide some deeper insights into your practice if you are doing HGA work as described in the lucid dream plan discussions of this book. In addition, it may illuminate ideas for including the HGA in lucid divination experiments, or for incorporating the Hermes spell concepts into a spell you create to manifest a lucid experience of your own HGA.

The Distillation

This review of dream spells found in other magickal writings is here, in part, to help inspire you to continue to seek lucid dream spell ideas from diverse traditions. It is also meant to remind you that even after working on all of the magickal bullet points highlighted in this book, that you should continue to study, to find new ideas, and to see how they might influence your own magick. There are so many amazing words, concepts, and experiences that have been compiled by other magickal dreamers out there. It is comforting to know that the spells and grimoires of the magicians and alchemists who came before us can provide us with the unending ability to continue to breathe new life and heightened skill into our magick.

---

119. Greer and Warnock, *The Picatrix*, 150.

LUCID DREAM
TALISMANS

A simple but wonderful piece of magick to do to support your lucid magickal practice is to create a lucidity talisman. This is an enchanted item whose job is to remind you to carry out your frequent checks upon the nature of your reality. Occultist Donald Michael Kraig, in his book *Modern Magick*, gives his proposed definition of talisman as "…any object, sacred or profane, with or without appropriate symbols, which had been charged or consecrated by appropriate means and made to serve a specific end."[120] Essentially, a talisman can be any item of your choosing and can stand for any purpose you like as long as you officially deem it to be so.

Keychain Talisman

There are some nice keychains available online at the Lucid Talisman that are visually pleasing and have a moon on one side with the word *dream* and a sun on the other side with the word *awake*.[121] The idea behind this is that because it is a keychain it is an object that you would frequently have

---

120. Donald Michael Kraig, *Modern Magick: Twelve Lessons in the High Magickal Arts* (Llewellyn Publications, 2022), 253.

121. You can find the keychains and more at LucidTalisman.com.

with you and that would become visible to you frequently in your day-to-day life. Each time you see it, not only does an item like this prompt you to remember to do a reality test to see if you are dreaming or awake but you could literally use it as the visual point of focus for the reality check as well. Instead of staring at your hand and turning it back and forth waiting for your fingers to warp, you can study one side of the keychain talisman, turn it over to look at the other side, and then come back to the first side again to see if it has changed at all as is likely in dreams.

Jewelry as Talismans

Along the same lines as the keychain idea, you could choose to wear a ring or a pendant that serves the purpose of reminding you to do reality checks. A piece of jewelry may be composed of any material or gemstone, giving you many options for built-in energies that would be especially aligned with its cause. It would be important to consecrate the item for its purpose, formally embedding it with the energy of its role.

ARCANUM
Consecrating a Reality Check Talisman

· · ● ○ ● · ·

This exercise gives you a simple way to imbue a piece of jewelry of your choice with the role of reminding you to carry out reality checks, which is a crucial part of your lucid magickal practice. You will need a simple piece of jewelry and some jasmine or other suitable essential oil.

1. Choose a piece of jewelry that you wouldn't mind wearing routinely, on a daily or near daily basis, such as a comfortable ring, pendant, or bracelet.

2. Place the jewelry item on the altar.

3. Anoint your third eye and then the jewelry, each with a drop of jasmine essential oil.

4. Hold your nondominant hand up with your hand overhead and your palm raised toward the sky as if you were holding a tray.

5. Hold your dominant hand over the jewelry item with your palm facing down and your fingers splayed out.

6. State aloud and confidently, "I charge this <*insert type of jewelry*> to serve as an effective lucid dreaming talisman. Its presence shall remind me to perform reality checks at numerous intervals throughout each day. I imbue this <*insert type of jewelry*> with the power to do so. By the realms of land, sky and sea, as I do will, so shall it be!"

7. Stay in the same standing posture and imagine empowering energy flowing into your receptive, upraised hand. Allow the energy to flow from your hand, down through your arm, across your heart center, into your dominant arm and hand, and forth into the talisman. Allow this energy flow to continue pulsing from the atmosphere to you and into the jewelry piece for a couple of minutes.

8. Relax your arms and pick up the talisman. Look at it, inspecting its details closely.

9. Now perform your favorite physical reality check, such as inspecting your hand, breathing through pinched nostrils, or pinching your own arm. As you do your reality test, look at the talisman again to cement the relationship of it to this process.

10. Now put the jewelry on and remind yourself that you will do a reality check every time you notice it.

If you really wanted to make this process of jewelry consecration special and bring more divine energies into it, you could use the suggested template for ritual spellcasting proposed previously in chapter 22.

ARCANUM
Ritual Talisman Consecration

· · ● ○ ● · ·

The following instructions show how you might use your circle casting skills to set sacred space specifically for the blessing of a lucid dream talisman. You will need the same altar tools as in the main ritual format given in chapter 22 as well as a drawn or printed copy of the seal of Ulcha, a white chime candle, and some jasmine or other suitable essential oil.

1. Cast your circle using the same ritual instructions in steps 1 through 13 of the ritual template as outlined in chapter 22.

2. Anoint yourself, your talisman item, and a white chime candle each with jasmine essential oil.

3. Place the talisman upon the seal of Ulcha.

4. Raise your arms and say, "I, <insert magickal name>, call upon the lucid dreaming goddess Ulcha for assistance in the consecration of this reality check talisman. May you assist me in filling it with the energy needed to ensure that it prompts me to do at least ten reality checks per day. In exchange for your blessing upon this act, I offer you these white flowers. May their energy be yours to do with as you wish, leaving you pleased and fulfilled."

5. Light the white chime candle saying, "As I will it, so shall it be!"

6. Take your circle casting tool or your dominant hand and hold it over the talisman.

7. Imagine the intelligent and talented lucid dream energy of the owl shifter goddess Ulcha flowing down through the crown of your head, into your heart, down your arm, and out into the talisman. As you imagine and feel this

energy flow, vibrate the magickal activation words of the seal of Ulcha, "Magespral Chundito," nine times.

8. When finished, put the jewelry piece on and practice looking at it and instantly doing a reality check directly after to help establish the connection between it and its role.

9. Proceed to close out your ritual using steps 18 and 19 from the ritual instructions in chapter 22.

10. Allow the white chime candle to burn all the way down while safely monitoring it and extinguish your other altar candles. Always use excellent fire safety habits as previously discussed in chapter 20.

This exercise is an example, but you can, of course, use this as inspiration to create your own custom consecrations. You could construct your circle per these instructions or per your tradition's usual method. You could write your own words of honoring the spirit or spirits of dreaming with whom you feel connected, followed by words of asking them to help you in imbuing your item with the power to spur your effective reality checks.

You could get more elaborate with the candle magick aspect of the ritual consecration, drawing from some of the ideas in chapter 20 or some of the herbal ideas from chapters 18 and 19. Whatever details you decided on for this ritual, the most important part is to remember to actively charge the item to serve its purpose.

Tattoos as Talismans

Another great idea for a reality check talisman would be a tattoo. A special symbol that is inked upon your skin doesn't have the option of being worn each day or not and, instead, is always with you. That said, it is more effective if the tattoo is in a place where it's easy for you to seek it out visually under varying circumstances. The creative options that comprise the reality check or dream imagery within a tattoo are endless, so design something that you love. Tattoos are not everyone's cup of tea, but if they are something that you enjoy then they can serve as amazing reality check tools.

I have a tattoo on my right wrist that is wrapped all the way around and looks like a warrior's gauntlet or bracer. It has a Valkyrie theme, and on the palmar side of my wrist it includes a runic inscription of *drom*, which is the Norse word for "dream." On the other side of my wrist is a runic inscription of *vaken*, which means "awake." Because of its two-sidedness it also can be slowly turned back and forth while being inspected, like the classically recommended looking-at-the-hands method of reality checking. Not only does the tattoo's very existence remind me to check the nature of my reality, but its familiarity on my body can be used as a test for warps, blurs, or missing parts, which would indicate an incongruency, or the changeable nature of a dream reality.

Other Lucid Talisman Ideas

I have mentioned the keychain, the jewelry talisman ideas, and reality check tattoos, but you can use your creativity to come up with other lucid talisman approaches that suit you. If you don't wear jewelry, you could choose a small pocket stone that is easy to carry on you. Choose a meaningful gemstone, such as moonstone or prehnite, and ensure it is a small enough piece that fits in your wallet. This way you can develop the habit of putting it in your pocket or bra when you get dressed or putting it in your wallet when you prepare to go out. When you get back home again, put it on your nightstand.

Develop a habit of putting it there every night and then having it with you on your travels during the day. Having to move it around to ensure it is with you ensures you'll see it and then actually do the reality checks it is meant to inspire. You can use one of the consecration exercises suggested to charge it if you wish.

In a similar fashion, you could use a drawn or printed seal of a lucid dreaming guide as a talisman. Draw or print it on a small square of cardstock or parchment and keep it on your nightstand. When you prepare to leave the house, put it in your wallet to take with you. When you get to work, take it out and put it on your desk, or place it somewhere where you will see it during the day. Remember to return it to the nightstand before bed to cement the habit.

Substances Suitable for Lucid Talismans

You can refer to chapter 21, the chapter on lucid dream magick crystals, for some ideas of stones that might serve as good lucid talismans. Generally, for something like this that you would be either wearing or carrying around a lot, you want to avoid the more brittle stones such as kyanite or the stones that are very expensive.

Moonstone, prehnite, lepidolite, jade, and amethyst are some examples of gemstones that you may be able to find in jewelry or in small, polished stone pieces readily and at affordable prices. They all have potential preexisting energetic relationships with dreaming and are also durable enough for daily wear.

Silver is the metal most associated with the moon, so simple silver rings or necklaces are great ideas for jewelry items that are very practical for daily use. There are also loads of different silver jewelry pieces with unique designs and symbols. You can easily find silver jewelry that contains imagery of the moon or of runes, for example. Something like this adds extra meaning that can help to remind you to carry out your reality checks. Be creative and have fun looking for something that feels just right for you. There is nothing quite so satisfying as being on a witchy treasure hunt for just the perfect new magickal tool.

The Distillation

As a lucid magician, it is always a good idea to have some sort of talisman in your midst so that you don't become complacent with your reality checking habits. Use the ideas in this chapter for a starting point in implementing this type of magick into your practice and go from there. I have found that it can be a good idea to replace an old lucid talisman with a new one every few years, or to renew the energy of consecration every year or two on an existing one. The lucid talisman helps to remind you that your waking attention is just as important as your sleeping attention when it comes to maintaining the robustness of your lucid dreaming.

CONCLUSION

Who are we to even consider claiming that the events and experiences of dreams are not real? We accept that thoughts are real and that electricity is real, yet our society has the audacity to act as though dream material is less than real—that it is some confabulation of the mind or some blip in the system that does not deserve our attention. Magicians who are both skilled and fortunate enough will be able to prove to themselves through a practice of cultivated dreaming lucidity that this modern cultural approach is deeply flawed or at least incredibly naive.

The occultist has the great privilege of having already developed other interests and belief systems that will lend perfectly to the skill development needed for purposeful lucid dreaming. Within the dreaming-awake state it is then possible to understand that the clarity involved in that state of conscious awareness is, in fact, more real than anything we can experience while physically waking.

The lucid occultist can have evolutionary experiences as a spiritual being instead of only as a physical being, and with all the fears and distractions of physical mortality laid aside. By the Hermetic law of correspondences, since a lucid dream is a conscious learning experience in one plane of awareness, it must have some direct influence, relationship, or connection to our other levels of awareness as well.

Every lucid magick exploration is an experiment in the greatest naturally occurring alchemy lab of the universe. Here we evolve and encounter nuances of the mysteries, which would otherwise be impossible to engage during our mortal lives in this reality. As you have seen through the examples in this book, the revelations, energetic shifts, information downloads, and experiences gained while awake to your ordinary reality and simultaneously engaged in the dreamtime will indelibly change and even elevate you to levels of being previously unimagined. This is indeed part of the Great Work, and an accessible way of transforming our base components toward the elusive gold standard. The work of this book is the gathering up of the philosopher's stone—the missing ingredient needed to hasten the experiment of spiritual evolution in this life to supernatural levels of success.

There are lucid dreamers who are not magicians and there are magicians who are not lucid dreamers, but the magicians who also become lucid dreamers will find themselves understanding things about the nature of life, awareness, and energy that are indescribable to anyone who has not experienced this combination of approaches for themself. While this unique set of roles creates an exceedingly powerful set of skills when cultivated together, striving after these states for the sake of power itself will not yield the results that are possible when the practices are undertaken with humility and with the sheer joy of exploring the mysteries.

Finding oneself in the unique position of engaging both the role of magician and the role of lucid dreamer healthily will feel as though a jackpot of spiritual evolutionary springboard potential has been won in this lifetime. When the occultist gains the ability to become lucid frequently in dreams, they will have acquired what feels like a truly supernatural magickal talent. There are simply not enough occultists who have gained regular access to this unparalleled magickal laboratory, but I hope you can come to number yourself among them.

There are also countless benefits to lucid dreaming that are nonmagickal that we have not spent time on in the course of this book, since there are other books on the subject and our focus here is lucid dream sorcery. Lucid dreaming can be used to reprogram nightmares and stop the scary experiences that sometimes happen during sleep paralysis. It can be used as a space of rehearsal and personal programming in preparation for things you'd like to be better at during waking life, such as sports and public speaking. It can be used for healing and exploring aspects of mental health, and it can be used as a space to spark creativity and receive ideas for inventions, projects, and problem solving.

The common denominator here is that whether you seek to expand your practice of lucid dreaming for exploits that you deem to be sorcerous or not, the end goal is always to improve the quality of your life overall. Lucid dreaming is not separate from waking life but is rather just a more supernatural version of it.

Finally, even if we did put our personal magickal goals aside, let us not forget a very important universal experience of lucid dreaming: the ability to learn how to quickly release fear. When we become lucid, realizing that all functions are happening in a dream body, it becomes possible to confidently exert actions that we would otherwise doubt or fear.

Knowing there are no imminent repercussions for our body allows us to have daring firsthand experiences with unbridled enthusiasm. This mindset, once learned and integrated enough, can carry over to waking life and allow us to act with a similar though appropriate level of fearlessness. This leads to richer living, whether you are talking about taking magickal risks or just being more fearless in day-to-day situations. What good is magick, after all, if it does not enhance our overall human experience? A lucid magick practice can catalyze the benefits described in this book and help them to be interwoven in a rewarding life like no other discipline can.

It is my hope that this book has found its audience in readers like you who seek to weave together the strands of their magick with the strands of waking clarity that are sparked within the dreaming. It is also my hope that there will be some motivated readers who are inspired to truly dive in and create the type of disciplined life that lends to the practice of magickal lucid dreaming. Once you have tasted the rich depths that come from working on your magick in the space of lucid dreaming, I know that you, too, will prize these experiences forever and never stop trying to become lucid. Are you dreaming right now?

Appendix A
RUNIC HAND GESTURES

The following images represent the magickal hand gestures for the letters of the Elder Futhark alphabet of runes in the style of prolific runic academic and author Edred Thorsson.

Fehu

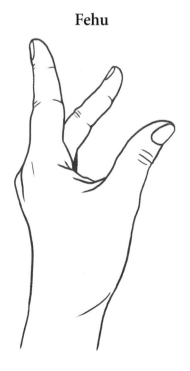

Uruz

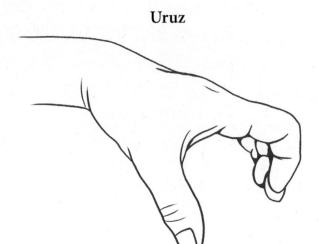

Thurisaz

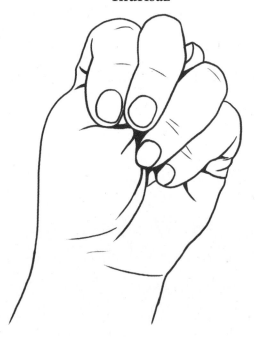

Ansuz

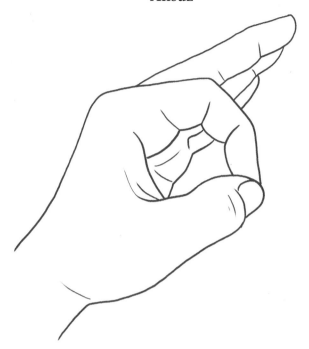

Raidho

Kenaz

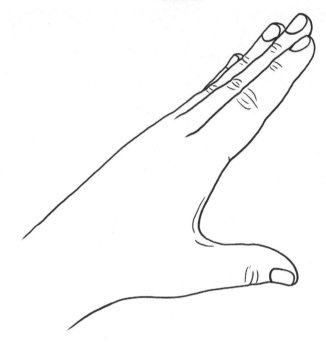

Gebo

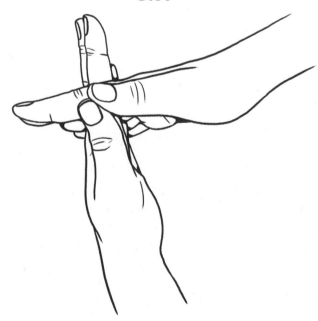

Wunjo

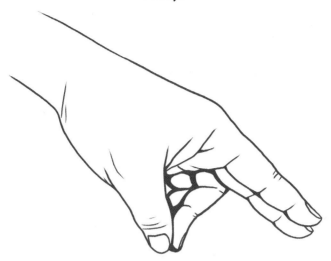

Hagalaz

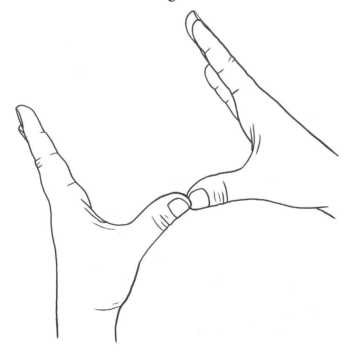

Nauthiz

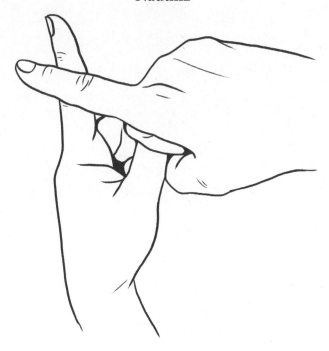

Isa

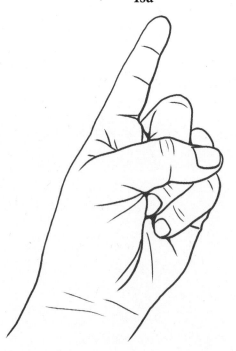

Jera

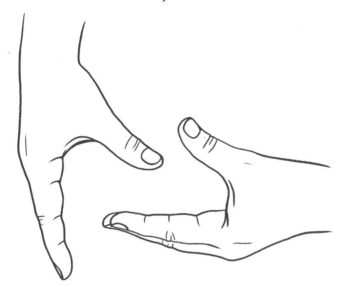

Eihwaz

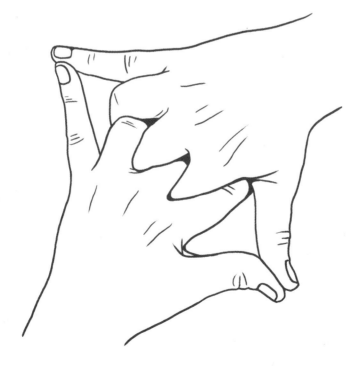

Perthro

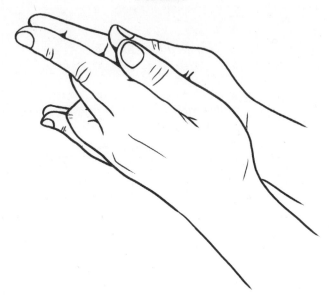

Elhaz

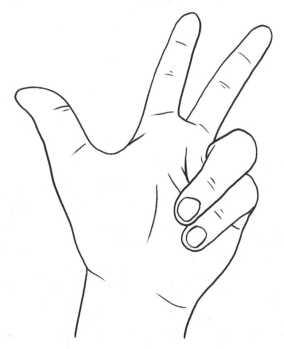

Sowilo

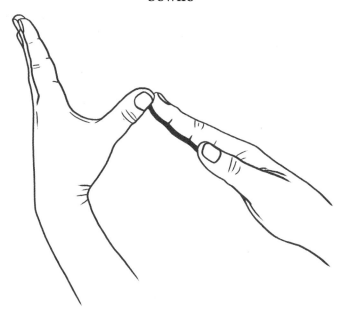

Tiwaz

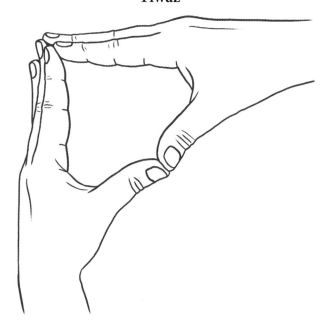

Berkana

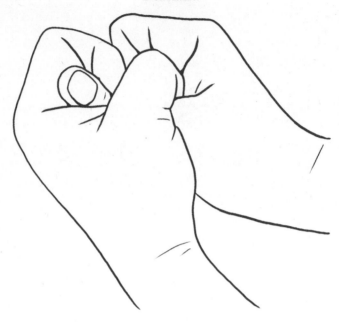

Ehwaz

Mannaz

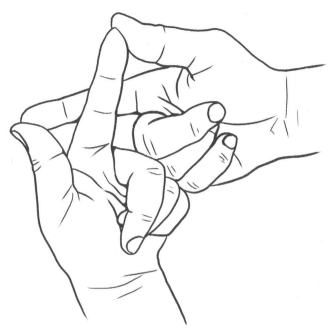

Laguz

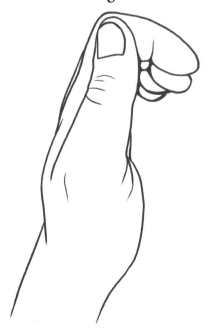

Ingwaz

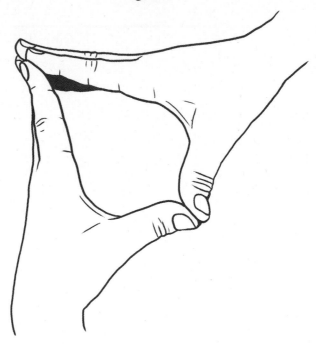

Dagaz

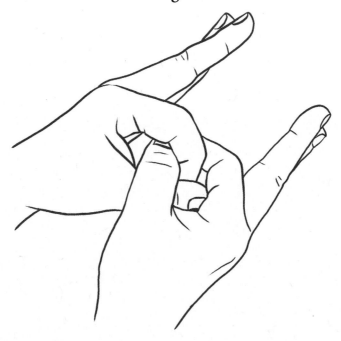

Othala

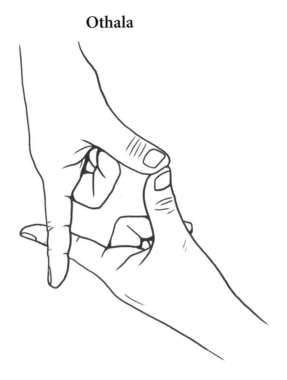

Appendix B
MAGICKAL ALPHABET PRONUNCIATION GUIDE

Elder Futhark Runes

Fehu: FAY-hoo

Uruz: oo-ROOZ

Thurisaz: THOR-eh-sahz

Ansuz: ahn-SOOZ

Raidho: rye-THO

Kenaz: KAY-nahz

Gebo: GAY-bo

Wunjo: WOON-yo

Hagalaz: HAG-ah-lahz

Nauthiz: NOW-theez

Isa: EE-sah

Jera: YEAR-ah

Eiwaz: EYE-wahz

Perthro: PARE-thro

Algiz: AL-geez

Sowilo: SO-wee-lo

Tiwaz: TEE-wahz

Berkana: BARE-cah-no

Ehwaz: EH-wahz

Mannaz: MAH-nahz

Laguz: LAH-gooz

Ingwaz: ING-wahz

Dagaz: DAH-gahz

Othala: o-THAH-lah

Irish Ogham Alphabet

Beith: BAY-uh

Luis: LOOSH

Fern: FAIRN

Sail: SAHL

Nion: NIN

Uath: HOOH-aah

Dair: DAHR

Tinne: TIN-uh

Coll: KULL

Ceirt: KAIRT

Muin: MOO-in

Gort: GORT

Ngetal: NYEH-tal

Straif: STREF

Ruis: ROO-ish

Ailm: AHL-um

Onn: OWN

Ur: OOR

Eadhadh: AY-dahd

Iodhadh : EE-dahd

BIBLIOGRAPHY AND RECOMMENDED READING BY TOPIC

This resource list is the bibliography for this book, representing all of the sources used for its research as well as many sources that have informed the knowledge and beliefs behind the concepts covered. This bibliography is organized by topic rather than simply being presented in one long list. It is hoped that this format will aid you in identifying works that may serve to support further learning in specific areas of magickal practice and philosophy as needed.

Astral Projection

Bruce, Robert. *Astral Dynamics: The Complete Book of Out-of-Body Experiences*. Hampton Roads Publishing Company, 2009.

Denning, Melita, and Osborne Phillips. *The Llewellyn Practical Guide to Astral Projection*. Llewellyn, 1980.

Ophiel. *The Art and Practice of Astral Projection*. Weiser Books, 1974.

Divination

Eason, Cassandra. *Scrying the Secrets of the Future: How to Use Crystal Balls, Fire, Wax, Mirror, Shadow, and Spirit Guides to Reveal Your Destiny.* New Page Books, 2007.

Greer, John Michael. *Earth Divination Earth Magic: A Practical Guide to Geomancy.* Llewellyn, 1999.

Kenner, Corinne. *Tarot and Astrology: Enhance Your Readings with the Wisdom of the Zodiac.* Llewellyn, 2013.

Moss, Robert. *Sidewalk Oracles: Playing with Signs, Symbols, and Synchronicity in Everyday Life.* New World Library, 2015.

Ross, Edward T., and Richard D. Wright. *The Divining Mind: A Guide to Dowsing and Self-Awareness.* Destiny Books, 1990.

Tyson, Donald. *Portable Magic: Tarot Is the Only Tool You Need.* Llewellyn, 2006.

Waring, Philippa. *A Dictionary of Omens and Superstitions: The Best-Selling Guide to the World of Premonitions.* Souvenir Press, 1998.

Dream Resources Not Specific to Lucidity

Belanger, Michelle. *Psychic Dreamwalking: Explorations at the Edge of Self.* Weiser Books, 2006.

Bluestone, Sarvananda, PhD. *The World Dream Book: Use the Wisdom of World Cultures to Uncover Your Dream Power.* Destiny Books, 2002.

Boyer, Corinne. *Dream Divination Plants in the Northern European Tradition.* Three Hands Press, 2020.

Daniel, Sophia. *Dream Healing: A Practical Guide to Unlocking the Healing Power of Your Dreams.* Element Books Limited, 1999.

Dumpert, Jennifer. *Liminal Dreaming: Exploring Consciousness at the Edges of Sleep.* North Atlantic Books, 2019.

Eagle Feather, Ken. *Toltec Dreaming: Don Juan's Teachings on the Energy Body.* Bear and Co., 2007.

Hurd, Ryan. *Sleep Paralysis: A Guide to Hypnagogic Visions and Visitors of the Night.* 2nd Edition. Enlightened Hyena Press, 2020.

King, Serge Kahili, PhD. *Dreaming Techniques: Working with Night Dreams, Daydreams, and Liminal Dreams*. Bear and Co., 2017.

Morley, Charlie. *Dreaming Through Darkness: Shine Light into the Shadow to Live the Life of Your Dreams*. Hay House, 2017.

Moss, Robert. *Active Dreaming: Journeying Beyond Self-Limitation to a Life of Wild Freedom*. New World Library, 2011.

Moss, Robert. *Conscious Dreaming: A Spiritual Path for Everyday Life*. Rivers Press, 1996.

Moss, Robert. *The Dreamer's Book of the Dead: A Soul Traveler's Guide to Death, Dying, and the Other Side*. Destiny Books, 2005.

Moss, Robert. *The Secret History of Dreaming*. New World Library, 2009.

Reed, Henry. "Improved Dream Recall Associated With Meditation." *Journal of Clinical Psychology*, vol. 34 (1) (January 1978).

Rinpoche, Tenzin Wangyal. *The Tibetan Yogas of Dream and Sleep*. Snow Lion Publications, 1998.

Schredl, Michael. "Creativity and Dream Recall." *The Journal of Creative Behavior*, vol. 29 (1) (1995): 16–24.

Schredl, Michael. "Gender Differences in Dream Recall." *Journal of Mental Imagery*, vol. 24 (1–2) (2000): 169–176.

Tonay, Veronica K. "Personality Correlates of Dream Recall: Who Remembers?" *Dreaming*, vol. 3 (1) (March 1993).

Van de Castle, Robert L. *Our Dreaming Mind: A Sweeping Exploration of the Role That Dreams Have Played in Politics, Art, Religion, and Psychology, From Ancient Civilizations to the Present Day*. Ballantine Books, 1994.

Grimoiric Magick

Betz, Hans Dieter, ed. *The Greek Magical Papyri in Translation: Including the Demotic Spells*. The University of Chicago Press, 1986.

Carmichael, Alexander. *Carmina Gadelica Vol. I and II*. Alexander Carmichael, 2019.

De Laurence, L. W. *Raphael's Ancient Manuscript of Talismanic Magic*. de Laurence, Scott and Co., 1916.

Flowers, Stephen E., PhD. *Icelandic Magic: Practical Secrets of the Northern Grimoires*. Inner Traditions, 2016.

Greer, John Michael. *The Celtic Golden Dawn: An Original and Complete Curriculum of Druidical Study*. Llewellyn, 2013.

Greer, John Michael, and Christopher Warnock, trans. *The Complete Picatrix: The Occult Classic of Astrological Magic—Liber Attratus Edition*. Renaissance Astrology and Adocentyn Press, 2011.

Grimassi, Raven. *Grimoire of the Thorn-Blooded Witch: Mastering the Five Arts of Old World Witchery*. Weiser Books, 2014.

LeCouteux, Claude. *The Book of Grimoires: The Secret Grammar of Magic*. Inner Traditions, 2013.

LeCouteux, Claude. *Dictionary of Ancient Magic Words and Spells: From Abraxas to Zoar*. Inner Traditions, 2014.

Leitch, Aaron. *Secrets of the Magickal Grimoires: The Classical Texts of Magick Deciphered*. Llewellyn, 2016.

Mathers, S. L. MacGregor, trans. *The Book of the Sacred Magic of Abramelin the Mage*. Dover Publications, Inc., 1975.

Mathers, S. L. MacGregor, trans. *The Goetia: The Lesser Key of Solomon the King*. Weiser Books, 1995.

Mathers, S. L. MacGregor, trans. *The Key of Solomon the King*. Weiser Books, 2000.

Shah, Idries. *The Secret Lore of Magic: Books of the Sorcerers*. The Citadel Press, 1975.

Tice, Paul. *The 6th and 7th Books of Moses*. The Book Tree, 1999.

Woodfield, Stephanie. *Priestess of the Morrigan: Prayers, Rituals, and Devotional Work to the Great Queen*. Llewellyn, 2021.

Lucid Dreaming

Adams, Lee. *A Visionary Guide to Lucid Dreaming: Methods for Working with the Deep Dream State*. Destiny Books, 2021.

Auchincloss, Douglas. "On Waking Up: An Interview with Joseph Campbell." *Parabola: Myth and the Quest for Meaning—Sleep*, vol. VII, number I (January 1982): 80.

Brown, David Jay. *Dreaming Wide Awake: Lucid Dreaming, Shamanic Healing and Psychedelics*. Park Street Press, 2016.

Castaneda, Carlos. *The Art of Dreaming*. Harper Perennial, 1993.

Godwin, Malcolm. *The Lucid Dreamer: A Waking Guide for the Traveler Between Worlds*. Simon and Schuster, 1994.

Johnson, Clare R., PhD. *Llewellyn's Complete Book of Lucid Dreaming*. Llewellyn, 2021.

Johnson, Clare R., PhD. *Mindful Dreaming: Harness the Power of Lucid Dreaming for Happiness, Health, and Positive Change*. Conari Press, 2018.

Laz, Athena. *The Alchemy of Your Dreams: A Modern Guide to the Ancient Art of Lucid Dreaming and Interpretation*. Tarcher-Perigee, 2021.

McElroy, Mark. *Lucid Dreaming for Beginners: Simple Techniques for Creating Interactive Dreams*. Llewellyn, 2009.

Morley, Charlie. *Dreams of Awakening: Lucid Dreaming and Mindfulness of Dream and Sleep*. Hay House, 2013.

Tucillo, Dylan, Jared Zeizel, and Thomas Peisel. *A Field Guide to Lucid Dreaming: Mastering the Art of Oneironautics*. Workman Publishing, 2013.

Waggoner, Robert. *Lucid Dreaming: Gateway to the Inner Self*. Moment Point Press, 2009.

Magickal Alphabets and Symbols

Laurie, Erynn Rowan. *Ogam: Weaving Word Wisdom*. Megalithica Books, 2007.

McManus, Damian. *A Guide to Ogam*. Maynooth Monographs, 1991.

Thorsson, Edred. *The Big Book of Runes and Rune Magic: How to Interpret Runes, Rune Lore, and the Art of Runecasting.* Weiser Books, 2018.

Thorsson, Edred. *Futhark: A Handbook of Rune Magic.* Weiser Books, 1984.

Thorsson, Edred. *The Nine Doors of Midgard: A Curriculum of Rune-work.* The Rune-Gild, 2016.

Thorsson, Edred. *Northern Magic: Rune Mysteries and Shamanism.* Llewellyn, 2005.

Thorsson, Edred. *Runelore: The Magic, History, and Hidden Codes of the Runes.* Weiser Books, 1987.

U∴D∴, Frater. *Practical Sigil Magic: Creating Personal Symbols for Success.* Llewellyn, 2015.

Magickal Correspondences

Cunningham, Scott. *Cunningham's Encyclopedia of Crystal, Gem, and Metal Magic.* Llewellyn, 2007.

Cunningham, Scott. *Cunningham's Encyclopedia of Magical Herbs.* Llewellyn Publications, 2000.

Hedley, Christopher, foreword. *Culpeper's Complete Herbal and English Physician.* Parkgate Books, 1997.

Melody. *Love Is in the Earth: A Kaleidoscope of Crystals.* Earth-Love Publishing House, 1991.

Pearson, Nigel G. *Wortcunning: A Folk Magic Herbal.* Troy Books Publishing, 2018.

Skinner, Stephen. *The Complete Magician's Tables: The Most Complete Tabular Set of Magic, Kabbalistic, Angelic, Astrologic, Alchemic, Demonic, Geomantic, Grimoire, Gematria, I Ching, Tarot, Pagan Pantheon, Plant, Perfume and Character Correspondences in More Than 777 Tables.* Llewellyn, 2009.

Whitcomb, Bill. *The Magician's Companion: A Practical and Encyclopedic Guide to Magical and Religious Symbolism.* Llewellyn, 2004.

Magickal Philosophy and Teachings

Bonewits, Isaac. *Real Magic*. Weiser Books, 1989.

Cabot, Laurie. *Power of the Witch: The Earth, the Moon, and the Magical Path to Enlightenment*. Delacorte Press, 1989.

Carroll, Peter J. *Liber Null and Psychonaut: An Introduction to Chaos Magic*. Weiser Books, 1987.

Curott, Phyllis. *Book of Shadows: A Modern Woman's Journey into the Wisdom of Witchcraft and the Magic of the Goddess*. Fourth Rune Books, 1998.

Dominguez, Ivo Jr. *The Four Elements of the Wise: Working with the Magickal Powers of Earth, Air, Water, Fire*. Weiser, Books, 2021.

Evola, Julius. *The Hermetic Tradition: Symbols and Teachings of the Royal Art*. Inner Traditions International, 1995.

Frost, Gavin, and Yvonne Frost. *The Witch's Magical Handbook*. Reward Books, 2000.

Hall, Manly P. *The Secret Teachings of All Ages*. Tarcher/Penguin Books, 2003.

Hine, Phil. *Prime Chaos: Adventures in Chaos Magic*. New Falcon Publications, 1993.

Kraig, Donald Michael. *Modern Magick: Twelve Lessons in the High Magickal Arts*. Llewellyn, 2022.

Miller, Jason. *Sex, Sorcery, and Spirit: The Secrets of Erotic Magic*. New Page Books, 2015.

Miller, Jason. *The Sorcerer's Secrets: Strategies in Practical Magick*. New Page Books, 2009.

Sleath, Nikki Wardwell. *You Might Be a Witch*. Wardwell Books, 2017.

Starhawk. *The Earth Path: Grounding Your Spirit in the Rhythms of Nature*. Harper Collins, 2004.

Stavish, Mark. *The Path of Alchemy: Energetic Healing and the World of Natural Magic*. Llewellyn, 2015.

Three Initiates. *The Kybalion*. Tarcher/Penguin Group, 2008.

Tyson, Donald. *Kinesic Magic: Channeling Energy with Postures and Gestures.* Llewellyn, 2020.

Tyson, Donald. *Three Books of Occult Philosophy.* Llewellyn Publications, 2007.

Tyson, Donald, ed., and Robert Turner, trans. *The Fourth Book of Occult Philosophy: The Companion to Three Books of Occult Philosophy.* Llewellyn, 2009.

U∴D∴, Frater. *High Magic.* Llewellyn, 2020.

Psychic Skill Development

Auryn, Mat. *Psychic Witch: A Metaphysical Guide to Meditation, Magick, and Manifestation.* Llewellyn, 2020.

Chestney, Kim. *The Psychic Workshop: A Complete Program for Fulfilling Your Spiritual Potential.* Adams Media, 2004.

Cheung, Theresa. *The Element Encyclopedia of the Psychic World: The Ultimate A-Z of Spirits, Mysteries and the Paranormal.* Harper Element, 2006.

Dispenza, Joe, Dr. *Becoming Supernatural: How Common People are Doing the Uncommon.* Hay House, 2017.

Frazier, Karen. *The Psychic Handbook: A Practical Guide to Developing Your Intuition.* Quarto Publishing Group, 2022.

Graf, Suzy. *The Enlightened Psychic.* Booklocker.com, 2011.

Kierluff, Stephen, PhD, and Stanley Krippner, PhD. *Becoming Psychic: Spiritual Lessons for Focusing Your Hidden Abilities.* New Page Books, 2004.

Klocek, Dennis. *The Seer's Handbook: A Guide to Higher Perception.* Steiner Books, 2005.

Naparstek, Belleruth. *Your Sixth Sense: Activating Your Psychic Potential.* Harper Collins, 1997.

Parkinson, Chanda. *Meditations for Psychic Development: Practical Exercises to Awaken Your Sixth Sense.* Llewellyn, 2021.

Weschcke, Carl Llewellyn, and Joe H. Slate, PhD. *Psychic Empowerment for Everyone: You Have the Power, Learn How to Use It.* Llewellyn, 2012.

Whitaker, Hazel. *Develop Your Psychic Ability: Unlock Your Intuition and Psychic Potential.* Barnes and Noble Books, 1999.

Shamanic Approaches

Andrews, Lynn V. *Teachings Around the Sacred Wheel: Finding the Soul of the Dreamtime.* Harper Collins, 1990.

Andrews, Ted. *Animal Speak: The Spiritual and Magical Powers of Creatures Great and Small.* Llewellyn, 1993.

Ingerman, Sandra, and Hank Wesselman. *Awakening to the Spirit World: The Shamanic Path of Direct Revelation.* Sounds True Inc., 2010.

Matthews, Caitlin. *Singing the Soul Back Home: Shamanic Wisdom for Every Day.* London: Connections Book Publishing Limited, 1995.

Penczak, Christopher. *The Temple of Shamanic Witchcraft: Shadows, Spirits, and the Healing Journey.* Llewellyn, 2010.

Perkins, John. *Shape Shifting: Techniques for Global and Personal Transformation.* Destiny Books, 1997.

Roberts, Llyn. *Shapeshifting Into Higher Consciousness: Heal and Transform Yourself and Our World with Ancient Shamanic and Modern Methods.* O Books, 2011.

Roberts, Llyn, and Robert Levy. *Shamanic Reiki: Expanded Ways of Working with Universal Life Force Energy.* O Books, 2008.

Sams, Jamie, and David Carson. *Medicine Cards.* St. Martin's Press, 1988.

Secunda, Brant, and Mark Allen. *Fit Soul, Fit Body: 9 Keys to a Healthier, Happier You.* Benbella Books, 2010.

Villoldo, Alberto, PhD. *Courageous Dreaming: How Shamans Dream the World into Being.* Hay House, 2008.

Spirits and Deities

Belanger, Michelle. *Names of the Damned: The Dictionary of Demons.* Llewellyn, 2017.

Buckland, Raymond. *Buckland's Book of Spirit Communications.* Llewellyn, 2014.

Clarke, Didi. *Forbidden Wiccan Spells: Dark Goddess Magick.* Didi Clarke, 2018.

Daimler, Morgan. *Pagan Portals: Gods and Goddesses of Ireland—A Guide to Irish Deities.* Moon Books, 2016.

Daimler, Morgan. *Pagan Portals: Irish Paganism—Reconstructing Irish Polytheism.* Moon Books, 2015.

Davidson, Gustav. *A Dictionary of Angels: Including the Fallen Angels.* The Free Press, 1967.

Day, Christian. *The Witches' Book of the Dead.* Weiser Books, 2011.

Dominguez, Ivo. *Spirit Speak: Knowing and Understanding Spirit Guides, Ancestor, Ghosts, Angels, and the Divine.* New Page Books, 2008.

Farrar, Janet, and Stewart Farrar. *The Witches' Goddess.* Phoenix Publishing, 1987.

Green, Miranda. *Celtic Goddesses: Warriors, Virgins, and Mothers.* George Braziller, 1996.

Gregory, Lady. *Irish Myths and Legends.* Running Press, 1998.

Ingerman, Sandra, and Hank Wesselman. *Awakening to the Spirit World: The Shamanic Path of Direct Revelation.* Sounds True, 2010.

Jordan, Michael. *Dictionary of Gods and Goddesses.* Facts on File, 2007.

Karlsdottir, Alice. *Norse Goddess Magic: Trancework, Mythology, and Ritual.* Destiny Books, 2003.

LeCouteux, Claude. *Encyclopedia of Norse and Germanic Folklore, Mythology, and Magic.* Inner Traditions, 2016.

Markale, Jean. *The Epics of Celtic Ireland: Ancient Tales of Mystery and Magic.* Inner Traditions, 2000.

O'hOgain, Daithi, Dr. *Myth, Legend and Romance: An Encyclopedia of the Irish Folk Tradition.* New York: Prentice Hall Press, 1991.

O'hOgain, Daithi, Dr. *The Sacred Isle: Belief and Religion in Pre-Christian Ireland.* The Boydell Press and The Collins Press, 1999.

Perkins, John. *Shape Shifting: Techniques for Global and Personal Transformation.* Destiny Books, 1997.

Sleath, Nikki Wardwell. *The Goddess Seals: Sacred Magickal Symbols for Modern Magickal Practitioners.* Azoth Press, 2023.

Stapleton, Michael. *The Illustrated Dictionary of Greek and Roman Mythology.* Peter Bedrick Books, 1986.

Sturluson, Snorri, trans. Anthony Faulkes. *Edda.* Orion Books, 1987.

Sturluson, Snorri, trans. Carolyne Larrington. *The Poetic Edda.* Oxford University Press, 1996.

http://www.native-languages.org/evaki.htm

https://www.patreon.com/posts/evaki-brazilian-51517080?l=it

INDEX

To Write to the Author

If you wish to contact the author or would like more information about this book, please write to the author in care of Llewellyn Worldwide Ltd. and we will forward your request. Both the author and the publisher appreciate hearing from you and learning of your enjoyment of this book and how it has helped you. Llewellyn Worldwide Ltd. cannot guarantee that every letter written to the author can be answered, but all will be forwarded. Please write to:

Nikki Wardwell Sleath
℅ Llewellyn Worldwide
2143 Wooddale Drive
Woodbury, MN 55125-2989

Please enclose a self-addressed stamped envelope for reply,
or $1.00 to cover costs. If outside the U.S.A., enclose
an international postal reply coupon.

Many of Llewellyn's authors have websites with additional information and resources. For more information, please visit our website at http://www.llewellyn.com.